# Where the Green Jobs Are: Jobs & Careers in DC

*By Dan Triman and Anca Novacovici*

ISBN: 978-0-578-10709-7

Printed in the United States of America

Second Edition: April 2012

Visit our website at www.eco-coach.com.

# Authors and Collaborators

**Dan Triman, CSBA, LEED AP+, EIT**
Sustainability Consultant
dtriman@gmail.com
(410) 300-0360

**Anca Novacovici, LEED AP**
President, Eco-Coach, Inc.
anca@eco-coach.com
(202) 559-0777
www.eco-coach.com

We would like to thank the following individuals for their guidance, support, and letting us use some of their materials for this Guide:

**Vicki Lind, MS, NCC**
Career Counselor & Marketing Coach
vlind@teleport.com
(503) 284-1115
www.vlind.com

**Gail Nicholson, MA, LPC**
Personal & Career Counselor
gailcareer@aol.com
(503) 227-4250
www.gailnicholson.com

**Jim Cassio**
Career Information/Workforce Development Consultant
jim7@cassio.com
(916) 984-9615
www.cassio.com

In addition, the following individuals have also contributed to the Guide:

**Carol McClelland, PhD**
Founder and Executive Director
Green Career Central
greencareers@greencentral.com
(650)322-8661
www.GreenCareerCentral.com

**John Friedman**
Vice Chairman of the Board
Sustainable Business Network of Washington
JohnF@sbnow.org
(202) 370-1333
www.sbnow.org

**Andi Joseph**
Director, Research & Communications
Washington, D.C. Economic Partnership
ajoseph@wdcep.com
(202) 661-8678
www.wdcep.com

**Pauli Ojea**

**Mark Starik, PhD**
Visiting Professor of Management and Sustainability,
College of Business, San Francisco State University and
Professor of Strategic Management and Public Policy
School of Business, George Washington University.
starik@gwu.edu
(202) 994-5621
http://business.gwu.edu/faculty/mark_starik.cfm

Finally, we would like to thank the following individuals for providing research and editing support for the Guide:

Dina Salem
Bill Johnson
Theresa Meehan
Tim Sandusky
Michelle Kim

A special thank you also goes to Omar Gaitan for providing the cover art for the Guide as well as formatting support for the Guide.

# This book is carbon neutral!

In keeping with the spirit of this book, our personal philosophies and lifestyles, and the mission of Eco-Coach, we are offsetting the carbon footprint for the publication of each book that is purchased.

We have calculated that the total carbon emissions generated from the publication of one book is 8.0 pounds. This includes sourcing and production of the raw materials, printing, binding, and shipping. We're working with Carbonfund to offset the emissions.

# Table of Contents

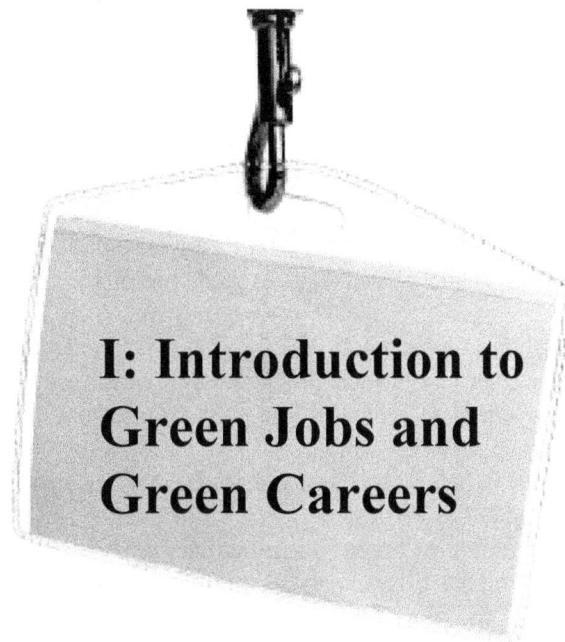

# I: Introduction to Green Jobs and Green Careers

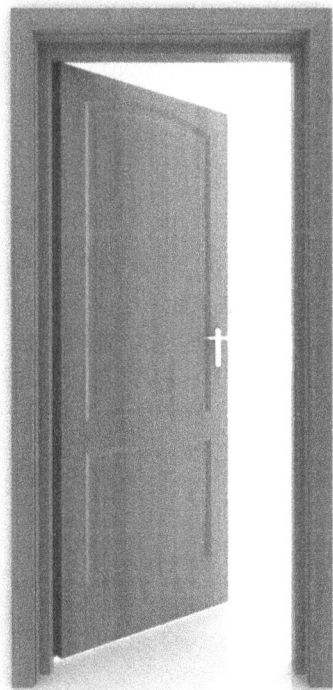

# Introduction

Welcome to the D.C. Metro Area Green Career & Jobs Guide!

Green jobs have become a hot topic in the United States in the last few years. The basic idea behind green jobs is to provide gainful employment for individuals so that their jobs involve activities that promote the sustainability of human lives, the planet, and the economy. The definitions of the terms "green jobs" and "green collar jobs" are still highly debated and are likely to vary based on the organization or individual defining them. Nonetheless, it is generally understood that these types of jobs are extremely important to our nation and will continue to be a vital part of the future of our country for various reasons, including economic stability, national security, and decreasing our contributions to global warming.

The viability and number of green jobs is being discussed and debated in many reports and community boardrooms across the country. In addition, local and federal government as well as the private sector are providing initiatives and competing to develop the best framework for creating and maintaining successful green jobs programs. Washington, D.C., as the nation's capital, is ideally situated to set an example for the rest of the country when it comes to sustainability issues and green job programs.

The federal government's commitment to green job initiatives has kick-started a frenzy of activity in the Washington, D.C. metro area to take advantage of this opportunity to solve several problems that currently face our region. Some of the more immediate issues we need to address include pollution in our rivers and other waterways, roadway congestion, air pollution, high unemployment rates, the use of non-renewable energy sources and the inefficient use of energy, rapid decline of native plants and animal species, and increased health risks resulting from these and other issues.

Well thought-out, and comprehensive green jobs programs and initiatives can be a significant help in combating these key issues. When we are able to provide individuals with the training and skills they need to be a part of the green movement, we empower them to address these problems on a small as well as larger scale. In doing this, we can make the Washington, D.C. metro area a leading example of what can be accomplished when sustainability is at the forefront of everything we do and the decisions we make.

Ideally, everyone who wishes to find a green job, or to gain a skill set which they can use to start on a green career path, should be able to easily find the resources with which to do so. Unfortunately, until now, a comprehensive resource for green jobs in the Washington, D.C. metro area did not exist. While there are many individuals and groups doing great work in the region, the general public is not privy to this information most of the time. This is the reason we created this Guide, to provide you with the resources we think you should be aware of and to save you the time, effort, and frustration of going to various websites and organizations to find out about green careers and green jobs in the D.C. metro area.

This Guide is the product of a collaborative effort between many local and national experts on green jobs. It is unique in that it is specific to the Washington, D.C. metro area, and it may very well be one of the first comprehensive green job guides in the country. While the Guide mainly focuses on Washington, D.C., it is important to realize just how connected Washington, D.C. is with the areas immediately surrounding it in Maryland and Virginia. So we have also included resources for these areas as well. For the purposes of this Guide, the Washington, D.C. metro area includes the following:
* Washington, D.C.
* Montgomery County, Maryland
* Prince George's County, Maryland

- Arlington County, Virginia
- Fairfax County, Virginia

Due to the scale of the green movement that has occurred within the past few years in the Washington, D.C. metro area, this Guide is not meant to be an exhaustive list of all the green job resources that exist; rather, it is meant to provide you with an overview of the key resources we feel will get you started in the right direction during your job seeking and research process. Regardless of where you are in your career path, what your past experience is, what kind of green job you are looking for, or how familiar you already are with the green job scene in the Washington, D.C. metro area, we feel there is something for you in this Guide. With that said, if you feel we have left out any important local or national resources for green jobs, please let us know, so that we can include them in the next version. The more people we can have collaborate on this Guide and get the word out about it, the more successful it will be in the long run. If you would like to help with future versions of this Guide, please let us know as well.

It is our sincere hope that this Guide will save anybody who reads it the vast amount of time and effort that can be spent trying to familiarize oneself with the Washington, D.C. green scene. We know that it can be an exhausting and often frustrating process seeking the right job for you, or even to find a job at all. It is no secret that the economy is struggling at the present time, but fortunately green jobs seem to be one of the few industries which are staying strong, if not creating more jobs than have been available previously. While there is often strong competition for the highly coveted green jobs, a lot of what will set you apart is your preparation, work ethic, and your commitment to being successful.

## Background on the Guide

We want to give you some perspective on how this Guide came to be created because the story is itself an example of how connecting with the right people and expressing your interests in green jobs can lead to amazing things. So here is how it all began:

The idea for this Guide traces back to 2007 in Portland, Oregon where Dan Triman met Gail Nicholson at a sustainability conference and they discussed the need for a Green Jobs Guide for the Portland area. Gail also knew that Vicki Lind had already started working on such a guide. The three of them then worked together and went on to publish the *Portland 2008 Green Guide to Networking and Jobs*. Dan moved back to Washington, D.C. at the end of 2007 after a short stay in Portland, Oregon. After a few months in Washington, D.C., working in the green industry and speaking to others doing the same, he realized that there was a need for a Green Jobs Guide for the Washington, D.C. area similar to the one he had worked on in Portland.

While Dan knew that he was committed to working on this Guide, he knew that he would need to enlist the help of others to make the Guide a true success, because it is quite the undertaking to compile a guide of every green resource in the Washington, D.C. metro area. Dan's work as a Green Building Consultant and Sustainability Consultant in Washington, D.C. included several projects for Eco-Coach, Inc. Eco-Coach's President, Anca Novacovici, had published a guide called *Sustainability 101: A Toolkit for Your Business,* so he knew she would be a good partner in helping to create a Washington, D.C. Green Jobs Guide. Dan and Anca's personal experience and expertise in the green and sustainability community in Washington, D.C. put them in a great position to publish this Guide. Dan and Anca reached out to several local D.C. area green experts to provide articles for the Guide, and many of them were happy to help out.

Dan and Anca also enlisted the help of Gail and Vicki, since part of the content from the Portland, Oregon guide related to career guidance was still pertinent to green job seekers in the Washington, D.C. metro area. Gail and Vicki were kind enough to offer the material from the Portland guide to use in the D.C.

guide. Vicki also connected Dan and Anca with Jim Cassio, who has generously offered some of the material from his *Green Careers Resource Guide* after meeting with Dan and Anca at the Good Jobs, Green Jobs conference in Washington, D.C. in early 2009.

Since the completion of the original guide in 2009, we have been working to update the guide to produce a 2012 version, which you are currently reading. We will continue to update the guide as time goes by to keep the content and information relevant.

## Content of the Guide

This Guide is a compilation of many separate articles that are intended to function as a coherent group. It is not intended to function as a book in chronological order, but rather it is supposed to provide each reader with a clear understanding of the specific topics they are interested in. So feel free to jump around the Guide and don't feel like you have to read it page by page. We hope that you will at least briefly take a look at all the articles in the Guide, but we realize that depending on your specific interests, some articles may be much more relevant than others in your personal journey.

Use this Guide as a workbook; highlight parts that really speak to you, or that you want to remember, take notes in the Guide as you are reading it, or as you are researching green jobs. The more you can keep track of who you have talked to, which websites you have been to, etc. the easier it will be for you to determine what the next steps should be.

The Guide is divided into three sections, each of which provides a different type of insight into green jobs. The first section is the introductory section that is meant to provide the reader with a general understanding of green jobs. It includes basic information, such as the definition of a green job, the importance of green jobs, and current local and national trends. The second section focuses on career guidance and provides tools and resources to use during your job search. If you are unsure as to how to make yourself more marketable when it comes to getting jobs, how to choose which green jobs are right for you, or what to say when you speak to potential employers, then this section will be of assistance to you. The third, and last section, is the heart of this Guide because it provides D.C. metro area specific resources for finding green jobs and identifying the best places to start your green job search. Think of it as your one-stop-shop for green in the Washington, D.C. metro area.

We'd like to thank all of the individuals who helped make this Guide possible, and we look forward to hearing feedback from the community (that means you!) as to how we can make this Guide even better in the future. We would also love to hear from you if this Guide helps you land a green job, as we could use this information to compile a list of success stories for green job seekers.

All the best to you in your green job search.

-Anca Novacovici and Dan Triman

# Defining "Green Jobs" and "Green Collar Jobs"

Even if you picked up this Guide, you still may be wondering exactly what qualifies as a "green job" or a "green collar job", and with good reason, because there still isn't a comprehensive definition of either that has been unanimously accepted. Depending on whom you ask or what the subject matter is you are reading, you will find a wide range of different definitions out there. Many of these definitions just give characteristics of these types of jobs, or list examples of these types of jobs. While we don't want to spend the entire time debating what is and isn't a green job or green collar job, we do feel it is important to set the context for the rest of this Guide around this topic. So below we have provided some examples of definitions that have been provided by others for the terms "green jobs" and "green collar jobs" for you to evaluate. Some people use these two terms interchangeably, while others feel that green collar jobs are just one type of the larger variety of green jobs. There really isn't a specific origin to the term "green jobs". Although it has become much more popular of late, it is a term that has been around for many years. It is generally agreed upon that the term "green collar jobs" was introduced in 1999, when Alan Thein Durning wrote a book called *Green Collar Jobs*.

## Green Jobs Definitions

"Green jobs are either:
>    A. Jobs in businesses that produce goods or provide services that benefit the environment or conserve natural resources.
>    B. Jobs in which workers' duties involve making their establishment's production processes more environmentally friendly or use fewer natural resources."

*The Bureau of Labor Statistics*

"Green jobs are jobs that provide products and services which use renewable energy resources, reduce pollution, conserve energy and natural resources and reconstitute waste."

*The White House Middle Class Task Force*

"Pay decent wages and benefits that can support a family. It has to be part of a real career path, with upward mobility. And it needs to reduce waste and pollution and benefit the environment."

*Phil Angelides, chair of the Apollo Alliance*

"Good local jobs that pay well, strengthen communities, provide pathways out of poverty, and help solve our environmental problems."

*Van Jones, Founder of Green For All*

"Career-track employment opportunities in emerging environmental industries as well as conventional businesses and trades, created by a shift to more sustainable practices, materials, and performance. The definition includes both lower and higher skilled employment opportunities that minimize the carbon footprint of all necessary inputs and directly result in the restoration of the environment, the generation of clean energy and improved energy efficiency, the creation of high performing buildings, and the conservation of natural resources."

*The District of Columbia Government*
*The District uses the terms 'green jobs' and 'green collar jobs' interchangeably*

"We define green jobs as work in agricultural, manufacturing, research and development (R&D), administrative, and service activities that contribute substantially to preserving or restoring environmental quality. Specifically, but not exclusively, this includes jobs that help to protect ecosystems and biodiversity; reduce energy, materials, and water consumption through high-efficiency strategies; de-carbonize the economy; and minimize or altogether avoid generation of all forms of waste and pollution."

*United Nations Environment Programme Report*

"Green jobs are jobs that espouse or reflect green values, either because of the nature and purpose of the job, or the nature and purpose of the employer. And what are those values?
*   Energy efficiency, green building, and sustainable design
*   Environmental protection and preservation
*   Organic and natural products
*   Renewable energy
*   Sustainable business practices, including cleantech"

*Jim Cassio*
*Author of the "Green Careers Resource Guide and Green Careers: Choosing Work for a Sustainable Future"*

"Green-collar jobs, as we define them, are well paid, career track jobs that contribute directly to preserving or enhancing environmental quality"

*Green For All and The Apollo Alliance*
*From their report "Green-Collar Jobs in America's Cities- Building Pathways out of Poverty and Careers in the Clean Energy Economy"*

"Green collar jobs are blue collar jobs in green businesses - that is, manual labor jobs in businesses whose products and services directly improve environmental quality. Green collar jobs are located in large and small for-profit businesses, non-profit organizations, social enterprises, and public sector institutions. What unites these jobs is that all of them are associated with manual labor work that directly improves environmental quality."

*Raquel Rivera Pinderhughes*
*From her report "Green Collar Jobs: An Analysis of the Capacity of Green Businesses to Provide High Quality Jobs for Men and Women with Barriers to Employment"*

# Where are the Green Jobs? What industries?
## By: Jim Cassio

Although green jobs can be found in all industries, the majority of green jobs can be found in certain sectors of the following industries:

## Advertising Services (Green)

## Agriculture
- Sustainable/Organic Farms
- Sustainable/Organic Nurseries/Greenhouses
- Sustainable Aquaculture Farms/Fish Hatcheries

## Alternative Fuel Vehicles
- Advanced Technology Vehicle (ATV) Manufacturers (hybrid and fuel cell technologies)
- Alternative Fuel Vehicle Manufacturers (vehicles designed to run on biodiesel, electricity, ethanol, hydrogen, natural gas and propane)
- Alternative Fuel Producers/Distributors/Retailers
- Alternative Fuel Vehicle Repair/Modification Services (technicians, first–responders)
- Alternative Fuel Vehicle Sales/Service
- Battery Manufacturers & Suppliers (for Alternative Fuel Vehicles)

## Bicycles
- Bicycle Courier & Cargo Services
- Bicycle Manufacturers
- Bicycle Sales & Service

## Biotech/Life Sciences
- Blue Biotechnology (marine and aquatic applications)
- Green Biotechnology (agricultural applications)
- Red Biotechnology (medical applications)
- White Biotechnology (industrial applications)
- Bioeconomy (investments and economic output)

## Clean Tech
While "Clean Tech" is often used to describe a select group of industries, it is actually a reference to the clean technologies and eco-friendly business practices used in various industries in order to dramatically reduce the use of natural resources as well as the output of emissions and wastes.

## Cleaning & Janitorial Services (Green Cleaning)

## Clothing & Accessories (Organic/Recycled Material)
- Design
- Manufacturing
- Wholesale
- Retail

**Ecotourism**

**Engineering Services**
- Chemical
- Civil
- Construction Management Services
- Energy
- Environmental
- Land Planning
- Manufacturing/Production
- Surveying
- Transportation

**Environmental Services**
- Carbon Trading & Offsets
- Emissions Control Services
- Energy Auditing Services
- Environmental Consulting Services
- Environmental Health & Safety Services
- Environmental Monitoring/Compliance Services
- Hazardous Materials (HazMat) Services
- Environmental Engineering Services – see *Engineering Services*

**Food Processing/Manufacturing (Natural/Organic Food Products)**

**Food Services (Natural/Organic Foods Eating Places)**

**Geography & GIS Services (Green)**

**Government Agencies**
- Federal – *e.g. Army Corps of Engineers; Bureau of Land Management (BLM); Centers for Disease Control and Prevention (CDC); Department of Energy; Environmental Protection Agency; Fish and Wildlife Service; Forest Service; Geological Survey (USGS); National Oceanic and Atmospheric Administration (NOAA); National Park Service; Natural Resources Conservation Service (NRCS)*
- State – *e.g. Agriculture and Food Safety; Coastal Zone Management; Community and Economic Development; Emergency Services; Energy; Fisheries and Wildlife Protection; Parks and Recreation; Planning; Pollution Control and Prevention; Public Health; Water Resources*
- Local (cities, towns, counties, special districts) – *e.g. Air Quality Management; Conservation/Park Land Management; Electricity; Green Building; Green Business; Public Transportation; Recycling; Regional Planning; Waste Management; Water and Wastewater Treatment*

**Green Building, Sustainable Design & Energy Efficiency**
- Architectural Services
- Building Maintenance, Repair and Weatherization Services (including Handyman Services)
- Building Materials (Manufacturers, Suppliers and Retailers of Sustainable Building Materials)
- Building Performance Contractors
- Electrical Contractors
- Energy Efficiency Companies
- ESCO (Energy Service Companies)
- Furniture/Cabinet Makers (using environmentally certified/recycled wood)

- General Contractors
- HVAC (Heating, Ventilation and Air Conditioning) Contractors
- Interior Design Services
- LEED/Green Building Planning/Consulting Services
- Lighting Systems Design and Installation Services
- Plumbing Contractors
- Roofing Contractors
- Salvage & Deconstruction Services
- Solar Energy Systems Contractors
- Water/Wastewater Services (private conservation, treatment and collection)
- Other Specialty Contractors (stone, cement)

## Investment Services (Sustainable/Socially Responsible Investing – aka SRI)

## Journalism & Publishing (Green/Sustainable)

## Landscaping & Habitat Restoration Services
- Arborist/Tree Services (certified)
- Gardening/Landscape Maintenance Services
- Habitat Restoration Services
- Landscape Architectural Services
- Landscape Contractors

## Legal Services (Environmental and Land Use Law)

## Natural Sciences Consulting Services
- Atmospheric and Space Scientists
- Biochemists, Biophysicists, and Toxicologists
- Chemists and Forensic Toxicologists
- Environmental Scientists
- Epidemiologists
- Foresters and Forest Pathologists
- Geoscientists, Environmental Geologists, Hydrogeologists, and Marine Geologists
- Hydrologists and Water Resources Managers
- Microbiologists and Environmental Health Microbiologists
- Physicists and Health Physicists
- Soil and Plant Scientists
- Soil and Water Conservationists
- Zoologists, Wildlife Biologists, and Marine Biologists

## Nonprofit Organizations (Green/Environmental)

## Pesticide Services (Natural/Organic)

## Printing (Green/Sustainable)

## Public Relations Services (Green)

**Recycling (Green)**
- Electronics (cell phones, computers)
- Glass
- Metal
- Paper
- Plastics
- Textiles

*Sad Fact: While recycling is one of the basic fundamentals of being green, many recycling companies are not green due to inefficient processes and GHG (greenhouse gas) emissions.*

**Renewable Energy**
- Biomass
- Solar Energy Systems Manufacturing
- Solar Energy Systems Sales, Installation and Service
- Solar Power Plants (Utility Scale)
- Wind Turbines Manufacturing
- Wind Turbines Sales, Installation and Service
- Wind Farms (Utility Scale)
- Also small hydro/marine power and geothermal power

**Utilities (Committed to Clean Energy and Energy Efficiency)**
- Electric Power Generation, Transmission & Distribution
- Natural Gas Distribution
- Water Treatment

**Other – Misc. Retail (Green/Sustainable/Organic Products)**
- Crafts/Artwork Made by Third–World Artisans
- Gardening Supplies
- Recycled, Reclaimed and Earth–Friendly Products
- Outdoor Apparel/Equipment
- Scooters

# What Occupations Can Lead to Green Jobs?
## By: Jim Cassio

The short answer to that question is "Virtually all occupations can lead to green jobs." But with all the jobs in our economy grouped into about 1,000 occupations, which does little to help guide people through the occupational research that is necessary for smart, long-term career planning. On the other hand, short lists such as the *hot green jobs*, or the *top 10 green careers* are useful for getting attention, but they are far too limited in scope to help most career explorers and job seekers identify their best individual choices. So the list of 100 (or so) occupations that follows is intended to give people an idea of the types of occupations that can lead to green jobs and green careers. However, this is not to say that these are *green occupations*. Traditionally, occupations have not been defined on the basis of the greenness of their jobs. So, to one degree or another, virtually all occupations can lead to both green jobs and non-green jobs. Take the occupation of attorney, for example. Most jobs for attorneys are not green. But there are green attorneys. Most of them work in environmental or land use law. There are also attorneys in non-green jobs who are personally green, but that doesn't make their jobs green unless they can apply their green values to their jobs. But what about a corporate attorney who works for an organization that is committed to sustainability? The answer probably depends on the degree to which the organization is sustainable.

Another useful example is the occupation of environmental scientist. Most jobs for this occupation are green jobs – perhaps even the vast majority. But what about the environmental scientist who works for a strip-mining company? Is that a green job? To make that determination, you would have to look at the nature and purpose of that individual job. Just looking at job titles is inadequate at best.

After reviewing this list of occupations, you may be wondering why a certain occupation wasn't on the list. Omission of an occupation from the list doesn't mean that occupation can't lead to a green job. It's just that those jobs are, generally, few and far between.

## Engineering and Mechanical Careers
- Automotive Master Mechanics, Including Alternative Fuel Vehicle Service Technicians
- Chemical Engineers, including Green Chemical Engineers
- Civil Engineering Technicians
- Civil Engineers, including Green Building, Irrigation/Reservoir, and Waste Management Engineers
- Conservation, Biological, and Agricultural Engineers
- Drafters and CAD Technicians
- Electrical and Electronic Engineering Technicians
- Electrical Engineering Technicians, including Photovoltaic, Wind, and Biomass Energy Technicians
- Electrical Engineers, including Recycling, Solar/Photovoltaic, Wind, and Biomass Engineers
- Energy Engineers
- Engineering Managers
- Environmental Engineering and Pollution Control Technicians
- Environmental Engineering Professors
- Environmental Engineers, including Ecological and Air Quality Engineers
- Machinists
- Materials Engineers
- Mechanical Engineering Technicians
- Mechanical Engineers
- Sales Engineers, including HVAC Systems
- Sales Engineers, including Solar/Renewable Energy Systems

- Solar Energy Systems Designers/Engineers
- Team Assemblers

## Environmental Health & Safety Careers
- Environmental Health & Safety Engineers
- Environmental Health & Safety Technicians
- Hazardous Materials (HazMat) and Asbestos Abatement Workers
- Industrial Hygienists and Environmental Health & Safety Analysts/Managers

## Government Regulation & Planning Careers
- Construction and Building Inspectors, including Green Building Inspectors
- Environmental and Regulatory Compliance Inspectors and Specialists
- Urban and Regional Planners, including City/County, Environmental/Land Use, and Transportation Planners
- Urban and Regional Planning Aides, Assistants, and Technicians

## Green Building, Sustainable Design & Energy Efficiency Careers
- Architects, including Green and Natural Building Architects
- Building Materials Specialists/Sales Reps/Salespersons (green/sustainable building materials)
- Drafters and CAD Technicians
- Electricians
- Energy Auditors
- Green Building/Construction Cost Estimators
- Green Building/Construction Managers and Consultants
- Green Building and Energy Efficiency Trades Workers and Supervisors (multiple occupations)
- HVAC Service Technicians & Installers
- Interior Designers
- Maintenance and Repair Workers, General
- Plumbers, Pipefitters, and Steamfitters
- Refuse and Recyclable Material Collectors, including Recycling Technicians
- Roofers
- Solar Energy Systems Service Technicians
- Solar Energy Systems Installers/Technicians
- Solar Energy Systems Installation Supervisors/Project Managers

## Green Business & Enterprising Careers
- Accountants, including Environmental Accountants
- Buyers and Purchasing Agents/Managers
- Financial Analysts, including Sustainability and Sustainable Investment Analysts
- Green Entrepreneurs and Consultants
- Marketing Managers, including Environmental Marketing Specialists
- Sales Representatives, including HVAC Salespersons
- Sales Representatives, including Natural/Organic Products
- Sales Representatives, including Solar/Renewable Energy Systems
- Vehicle Salespersons, including Alternative Fuel Vehicles

## Green Education, Communication & Law Careers
- Customer Service Representatives, including Energy Efficiency Specialists
- Health Educators, including Environmental Health Educators and Sustainability Coordinators
- Health Specialties Instructors, including Environmental Health Education Instructors
- Lawyers, including Environmental and Regulatory Attorneys

- Public Relations Specialists, including Environmental/Sustainability Specialists
- Reporters and Correspondents, including Green Journalists
- Sustainability Coordinators
- Travel Guides, including Ecotourism Guides and Operators

## Landscaping Careers
- Drafters and CAD Technicians
- Landscape Architects, including Habitat Restoration Specialists
- Landscaping and Grounds keeping Workers (Eco–Friendly)

## Natural & Land Resources Management Careers
- Fish and Game Wardens, including Wildlife Officers
- Park Naturalists, including Park Rangers and Interpreters
- Range Managers, including Natural Resource Managers

## Natural Sciences Careers
- Atmospheric and Space Scientists, including Air Analysts, Environmental Meteorologists, and Climatologists
- Biochemists and Biophysicists, including Toxicologists and Ecotoxicologists
- Biological Technicians, including Environmental and Wildlife Technicians
- Chemical Technicians, including Environmental and Green Chemical Techs
- Chemists, including Environmental and Green Chemists and Forensic Toxicologists
- Earth Sciences Professors (multiple occupations)
- Environmental Science Technicians, including Lab Techs and Air Pollution Auditors
- Environmental Scientists, including Environmental Researchers, Analysts, and Investigators
- Epidemiologists, including Environmental Epidemiologists
- Forest and Conservation Technicians, including Soil Conservation and Biomass Technicians
- Forest and Conservation Workers, including Conservation and Reforestation Aides/Workers
- Foresters, including Environmental Protection Foresters and Forest Pathologists
- Geoscientists, including Environmental Geologists, Hydrogeologists, and Marine Geologists
- Hydrologists, including Environmental Hydrologists and Water Resources Managers
- Microbiologists, including Environmental and Public Health Microbiologists
- Physicists, including Health and Atmospheric Physicists
- Soil and Plant Scientists, including Agronomists
- Soil and Water Conservationists, including Ecologists and Erosion Specialists
- Tree Trimmers and Pruners, including Arborists
- Water Treatment Plant Operators
- Zoologists and Wildlife Biologists, including Marine Biologists

## Physical Geography Careers
- Geographers, including Physical and Geographic Information Systems (GIS) Geographers
- Physical Geography Professors, including Geographic Information Systems (GIS) Instructors

## Sustainable Agriculture Careers
- Agricultural Science Professors, including Organic and Sustainable Agriculture Specialists
- Agricultural Technicians, including Organic and Sustainable Ag Techs
- Aqua cultural Managers, including Sustainable Aquaculture Farm and Fish Hatchery Managers
- Farmers and Ranchers, including Organic and Sustainable Farmers and Ranchers
- Farm workers, including Organic and Sustainable Farm and Ranch Workers
- Nursery and Greenhouse Managers, including Organic and Native Plant Specialists

# A Green Wave to Lift All Boats: Green For All and the Green Jobs Movement

## By: Pauli Ojea

Fires, floods and financial collapse are the latest signs that we are caught in twin crises: economic downturn and environmental devastation. These problems exacerbate the already profound inequalities that exist in our country: low-income communities and communities of color are benefiting the least and suffering the most in our pollution-based economy. But, the good news is that the green economy is growing, and that, if done right, it'll help create access and opportunity for all people.

That's where Green For All comes in.

Green For All is dedicated to building an inclusive green economy, strong enough to lift people out of poverty. We believe that efforts to fight pollution and curb global warming can simultaneously create well-paid green-collar jobs, safer streets and healthier communities.

Nationally, we advocate for policies that will spur demand for green-collar jobs. Locally, we help cities 'go green' with aggressive plans to create green-collar jobs and attract green business. At the community level, we connect leaders to help them become as strong, smart and sophisticated as possible and we assist the business sector to ensure that people of color, low-income people and others from disadvantaged backgrounds have access to the opportunities that the new clean energy economy brings.

## Green Jobs and Washington's Role

The passage of the Green Jobs Act (late 2007) and the American Recovery and Reinvestment Act (early 2009) has created the greatest opportunity to create green pathways into prosperity to date. The Green Jobs Act will help prepare workers for jobs in the clean energy economy, with a substantial emphasis placed on providing career pathways out of poverty through green jobs.

The American Recovery and Reinvestment Act includes $48 billion in investments in job training and education, nearly $100 billion in funding for transportation and infrastructure, $20 billion in tax incentives for renewable energy, and more than $41 billion for energy-related programs. The Recovery Act creates an unprecedented opportunity to start repairing the economy and the environment at the same time.

Climate change legislation also has the potential to create thousands of green jobs, especially if a significant portion of the revenues generated by putting a price on pollution are invested in energy efficiency and emerging green technologies.

## Green Jobs Success Stories Around the Country

Policy changes will help move the green economy forward. But it's people power that will get the jobs done. All across the country, people who have been at the tailpipe end of the grey economy are creating green solutions to improve life in their communities and help restore the planet. Below are just a few of the many success stories from the green-collar economy.

**Oakland, California**

Founded in 2008, the Oakland Green Jobs Corps Program (OGJC) is a green-collar job training program that provides the skills necessary for participants to succeed in the ever-expanding green workforce. The program specifically targets low-income 18 to 35 year olds who have previously experienced barriers to employment. OGJC operates on a comprehensive curriculum of training courses that include hard and soft skills, vocational skills, and financial and environmental literacy. Hands-on training activities range from installation of energy efficient technologies to green construction. Program partners work with program graduates to connect them to green employers and facilitate entry into the workforce.

**Newark, New Jersey**

Newark is pioneering a joint effort between the city, Laborers United of North America and Garden State Alliance for a New Economy to create jobs weatherizing and retrofitting homes that need it. The new weatherization program – called Laborers United Local 55 – trains Newark residents in green construction techniques and give them the opportunity to earn accreditation and union pay while weatherizing homes of low-income senior citizens. In March 2010, 200 homes were successfully weatherized through the program. Before the funds expire in 2012, New Jersey aims to weatherize over 13,400 homes.

**Denver, Colorado**

The Mile High Youth Corps in Denver, Colorado gives urban youth a chance to work on a variety of projects including planting trees, building paths and trails, renovating houses, painting, and landscaping. Corps members complete various energy efficiency projects, like weatherizing homes to help low-income people save energy and water — and thus, money on their utility bills. In total, the Mile High Youth Corps has serviced more than 1,100 homes, installing about 15,000 compact fluorescent light bulbs, more than 300 high-efficiency toilets, and completing various other energy efficiency projects. The Corps predicts that these improvements will save residents about $150,000 annually.

These programs are helping ensure that the green economic wave lifts all boats. Green For All is pleased to be a part of this rapidly emerging sustainable and equitable green economy. To learn more about these and other success stories, visit www.greenforall.org.

*When this article was written, Pauli Ojea was a Policy Associate at Green For All, a non-profit organization working to help build an inclusive green economy strong enough to lift people out of poverty. Pauli helped advocate for federal commitments to job creation, job training, and entrepreneurial opportunities in the emerging green economy – especially for people from disadvantaged communities. Stacey Meinzen and Ying-Sun Ho also contributed to this article.*

# Show Us the Money: How Green Is the Stimulus Package?
## By: Carol McClelland, PhD and Dan Triman

How have you been feeling about the green economy lately?

Hopeful? Apprehensive?

Excited? Skeptical?

Curious? Wary?

Motivated? Disillusioned?

There are more and more signs from the Obama Administration that we are moving into a new era where climate change, green jobs, and renewable resources are front and center in discussions, negotiations, and policy. Fortunately, there are many reputable organizations that have developed an expertise around green jobs that are working tirelessly to provide support for the Obama Administration as key decisions are made.

On February 27th, 2009 Vice President Joe Biden convened the first meeting of the Middle Class Task Force in Philadelphia, Pennsylvania, which was titled "Green Jobs: A Pathway to a Strong Middle Class." For a summary of the official White House Staff Report from this meeting and a link to the updated report, please see the 'Recent Publications on Green Jobs and the Green Economy' article on page 31 of this Guide.

The second meeting of the Middle Class Task Force was held on March 19th 2009 in St. Cloud, Minnesota and was titled "Road to Recovery: Building a Strong Middle Class Starting with the Recovery Act."

You can find out more about the Middle Class Task Force by visiting the White House's website at http://www.whitehouse.gov/strongmiddleclass/.

Another step the Obama Administration has taken to show its commitment to green jobs was the hiring of Van Jones in March of 2009 as the Advisor for Green Jobs, Enterprise and Innovation at The White House Council on Environmental Quality (CEQ). Van Jones is the founder of Green For All, an organization focused on creating green jobs in impoverished areas. He is also the co-founder of the Ella Baker Center for Human Rights and Color of Change, and the author of the 2008 New York Times best seller, The Green Collar Economy. After a short stay in his position as Advisor for Green Jobs, Enterprise, and Innovation at the White House, Van Jones left this position, and is now currently a senior fellow at the Center For American Progress. Additionally, he is a senior policy advisor at Green For All.

You can visit the CEQ website at http://www.whitehouse.gov/administration/eop/ceq/.

The White House has provided the following definition for green jobs:
*"Green jobs are jobs that provide products and services which use renewable energy resources, reduce pollution, conserve energy and natural resources and reconstitute waste."*

Other examples of how the Federal Government is progressing in its efforts to provide assistance for green jobs all around the country, and placing an extreme value on solving the current economic and environmental issues facing our nation and the world include:

- Hilda Solis, a former Democratic Representative from California who was responsible for introducing The Green Jobs Act of 2007 (H.R. 2847) was appointed U.S. Secretary of Labor by President Obama. The Green Jobs Act of 2007 authorized up to $125 million in funding to establish national and state job training programs, administered by the U.S. Department of Labor, to help address job shortages that are impairing growth in green industries, such as energy efficient building, construction, and retrofitting; renewable electric power; energy efficient and advanced drive train vehicles; biofuels; deconstruction and materials use; energy efficiency assessment for residential, commercial, or industrial sector, and manufacturing of sustainable products using sustainable processes. Priority for these training programs would be given to veterans, displaced workers, and at-risk young people. **However, the Green Jobs Act of 2007 was never funded by the Bush Administration.**

- After the Green Jobs Act of 2007 was authorized, Solis was quoted as saying "As a nation that was built on innovation and technology, I know that we can achieve the goals of becoming energy independent and reducing our global warming emissions. But the strength of our nation's economy depends on the availability of a highly skilled and well-trained work force. This legislation is an opportunity to advance not only the energy security of our nation, but also the economic security of our families. Through targeted job training efforts, we can support both our nation's innovation and technological leadership and lift people out of poverty."

- The announcement that the U.S. Department of Labor will be requesting proposals for Recovery Act Competitive Grant Opportunities providing Green Jobs Training. It is anticipated that up to $500 million will be targeted at research, labor exchange, and job training projects that prepare workers for careers in energy efficiency and renewable energy as defined in the Green Jobs Act. $250 million will be targeted at other high growth and emerging industry sectors. The Apollo Alliance points out a key difference in the Recovery Act Training Program and The Green Jobs Act, "The Green Jobs Act stipulated that funded training programs would have to meet specific criteria that best support the creation of good, green jobs. For example, the Act would only fund multi-stakeholder training partnerships that include labor, community, and industry representatives. The $500 million Energy Efficiency and Renewable Energy Worker Training program does not explicitly include these guidelines."

- Hillary Clinton saying, "Climate change is not just an environmental nor an energy issue, but also has implications for our health, our economies and our security," as she prepared for her first trip abroad as the newly appointed Secretary of State.

- Clinton also appointed Todd Stern as the special envoy for climate change to help restore America's credentials and leadership in shaping environmental policy. Stern was the former White House assistant who was the chief U.S. negotiator at the Kyoto Protocol.

- Lisa Jackson, Obama's appointment as Environmental Protection Agency Administrator, began her talk at the Good Jobs Green Jobs Conference in 2009 with the statement: "Green jobs are a reality, not just an idea. Green jobs are the driving engine for economic recovery. As a result, environmental issues are now a central part of all discussions."

President Obama introduced his American Jobs Act of 2011 to Congress on September 12, 2011. This Jobs Act lays out the President's strategy to help get Americans back to work as well as help the USA's economy become stronger. The American Jobs Act of 2011 can be read in its entirety at the following website: http://www.whitehouse.gov/jobsact/read-the-bill.

Within the Act there are strategies to:
- Favor the production and use of American made goods and products
- Assist small businesses
- Assist veterans in finding and keeping jobs
- Preventing teachers from being laid off, and creating more jobs in education
- Support the modernization of public school buildings across the country, which includes green building requirements for these buildings
- Support the modernization of community college buildings across the country, which includes green building requirements for these buildings
- Invest in transportation infrastructure improvements
- Aid with redevelopment of abandoned and foreclosed-upon properties and stabilization of the affected neighborhoods
- Assistance for unemployed individuals and low-income individuals in finding and keeping well paying jobs

## American Recovery and Reinvestment Act of 2009

Ironically what is breathing life into the green economy is the depressed state of the traditional economy due to problems in the banking industry, downturns in the housing industry, and the increasing unemployment rate. The goal of this stimulus package is to invest in areas of the economy that will provide immediate jobs, new innovations, and support emerging industries in their efforts to grow. It just so happens that the green economy can drive all three of these desired outcomes. The American Recovery and Reinvestment Act of 2009 was a $787 billion stimulus package, to be spent over a two year period, developed by the Federal Government to help to deal with the current issues facing our nation mentioned above. The Act was signed into law by President Obama on February 17th, 2009. There are many programs funded by the stimulus plan that specifically promote green industries and green jobs. It is estimated that this stimulus plan will save and create around 3.5 million jobs in the United States. As you scan the description of the green elements of the American Recovery and Reinvestment Act of 2009 below, pay particular attention to the bold font we've added for emphasis.

1) How do these words line up with your passions and your target niche?
2) What can you learn about the future of your target industry from what's listed here?
3) What new ideas and directions come to your mind as you review the list below?

The wording for these bullets is taken directly from an email received from Congresswoman Anna G. Eshoo – California's 14th Congressional District. (Please note: We deleted provisions, tax cuts, and funding that do not address green issues. Our additions are shown in italics.)

**High Tech and Green Tech Provisions**
- $11 billion for **smart-grid** related activities, including work to **modernize the electric grid**.
- $6.3 billion for **energy efficiency** and **conservation grants**.
- $2.5 billion for **energy efficiency** and **renewable energy research**.
- $2 billion in grant funding for the manufacturing of **advanced batteries systems** and components and vehicle batteries that are produced in the United States.

I. Introduction to Green Jobs and Green Careers

- $6 billion for new loan guarantees aimed at standard renewable projects such as **wind** or **solar** projects and for **electricity transmission** projects.
- $1 billion for other energy efficiency programs including **alternative fuel trucks and buses, transportation charging infrastructure, and smart and energy efficient appliances.**

**Science and Energy Funding and Incentives**
- Federal **Building Energy Efficiency** - $4.5 billion
- Fossil Energy Research and Development - $3.4 billion *(degree of green depends on projects funded)*
- **Weatherization** Assistance Program - $5 billion
- National **Science** Foundation - $3 billion *(degree of green depends on projects funded)*
- Science at the **Department of Energy** - $2 billion, including $400 million to Advanced Research Projects Agency-Energy (ARPA-E)
- **National Oceanic and Atmospheric Association** - $830 million
- National Institute of Standards and Technology - $580 million which includes the **Technology Innovation Program**

**Energy Tax Credits and Funding**
- Advanced Energy Investment Credit: Establishes a new manufacturing investment tax credit for investment in advanced energy facilities, such as facilities **that manufacture components for the production of renewable energy, advanced battery technology, and other innovative next-generation green technologies.**
- **Plug-in Hybrid Vehicles**: Provides a tax credit for families that purchase plug-in hybrid vehicles of up to $7,500 to spur the next generation of American cars.
- Long-term Extension and Modification of Renewable Energy Production Tax Credit: Includes a three-year extension of the production tax credit (PTC) for electricity derived from **wind** (through 2012) and for electricity derived from **biomass, geothermal, hydropower, landfill gas, waste-to-energy, and marine facilities** (through 2013).
- Temporary Election to Claim the Investment Tax Credit in Lieu of the Production Tax Credit: Facilities that produce electricity from **wind, closed-loop biomass, open-loop biomass, geothermal, small irrigation, hydropower, landfill gas, waste-to-energy, and marine renewable facilities** are eligible for a production tax credit. The bill would allow facilities to elect to claim the investment tax credit in lieu of the production tax credit.
- Removal of Dollar Limitations on Certain Energy Credits: The bill would repeal the individual dollar caps. As a result, each of these properties would be eligible for an uncapped thirty percent (30%) credit.
- Clean Renewable Energy Bonds ("CREBs"): The bill authorizes an additional $1.6 billion for new clean renewable energy bonds **to finance facilities that generate electricity** from the following resources: wind, closed-loop biomass, open-loop biomass, geothermal, small irrigation, hydropower, landfill gas, marine renewable, and trash combustion facilities.
- Qualified **Energy Conservation** Bonds: The bill authorizes an additional $2.4 billion for qualified energy conservation bonds to finance State, municipal and tribal government programs and initiatives designed to reduce greenhouse gas emissions.
- Tax Credits for **Energy-Efficient Improvements to Existing Homes**: Promotes energy-efficient investments in homes by extending and expanding tax credits through 2010 for purchases such as new furnaces, energy-efficient windows and doors, or insulation.
- Transportation and Infrastructure Funding-The legislation will invest $8.4 billion for investments in **public transportation**. State and local governments will be eligible for an additional $1.5 billion in competitive grants for transportation investments. $9.3 billion will be invested in Amtrak, High Speed and Intercity Rail. The American Recovery and Reinvestment Act will allow **high-speed rail** exempt facility bonds to be used to develop rail facilities that are used by trains that are capable of attaining speeds in excess of 150 miles per hour.

As for the allocation of funding for the Green Jobs Training in the American Recovery and Reinvestment Act, the following table is provided by the Apollo Alliance in an article titled "Congress Approves Clean Energy Provisions of Stimulus; Consistent With Apollo Economic Recovery Act" which is dated February 13, 2009, written by Elena Foshay and Keith Schneider and can be found at the following address: http://apolloalliance.org/rebuild-america/energy-efficiency-rebuild-america/data-points-energy-efficiency/clean-energy-provisions-of-stimulus-are-consistent-with-apollo-economic-recovery-act/

| Green Jobs Training | <ul><li>$500 million for WIA training programs in the renewable energy and energy efficiency sectors defined in the Green Jobs Act.</li><li>$250 million to upgrade Job Corps training facilities serving at-risk youth while improving energy efficiency and providing career training in the energy efficiency sector.</li><li>$50 million for YouthBuild programs that rehabilitate affordable housing, including energy efficiency retrofits</li><li>$100 million for worker training as part of the Smart Grid investment program.</li><li>$250 million for high growth industries including advanced manufacturing.</li></ul>**Total: $1.15 billion** |
|---|---|

**Don't be discouraged if your target green niche doesn't appear in this list.** Most of these funds are going to technologies and renewable energies that will fuel the green economy. Furthermore, all of the companies that are going to do this work are going to need the same business infrastructure roles of any other business - human resources, training, marketing, sales, graphic design, legal, financial, etc.

**As you consider the possible openings and opportunities that will develop from this package, stay true to your interests and passions.** Stay alert to how these developments begin a ripple effect into other areas of the green economy. Below you can find valuable resources for keeping an eye on the developments of the American Recovery and Reinvestment Act of 2009.

**American Recovery and Reinvestment Act (ARRA) of 2009 Resources**
American Recovery and Reinvestment Act of 2009 website (http://www.recovery.gov/)
Washington, D.C. ARRA website (http://recovery.dc.gov/recovery/site/default.asp)
Maryland ARRA website (http://statestat.maryland.gov/recovery.asp)
Virginia ARRA website (http://www.stimulus.virginia.gov/)

For the specific breakdown of stimulus funding see the ProPublica's "The Stimulus Plan: A Detailed List of Spending" (http://www.propublica.org/special/the-stimulus-plan-a-detailed-list-of-spending) and the New York Times (http://projects.nytimes.com/44th_president/stimulus)

For federal tax credits related to renewable energy and energy efficiency visit Energy Star's website at: http://www.energystar.gov/index.cfm?c=products.pr_tax_credits#s1

The ICLEI-Local Governments for Sustainability's website for Economic Recovery Funding Updates provides resources and guidance for local governments, organizations, and individuals for accessing funding for programs in the ARRA 2009 (http://www.icleiusa.org/stimulusfunding)

Green For All and Policy Link have prepared a User's Guide that is very informative and analyzes different programs that were funded by the ARRA in an effort to help everyone make the best use of recovery dollars. You can access a free download of Bringing Home the Green Recovery: A User's Guide at: http://www.greenforall.org/resources/recoveryusersguide

The Apollo Alliance's "Recovery Act Information Center" includes in depth information about the ARRA, which includes articles specifically mentioning what the impact of the ARRA funds will be on green jobs around the country. Visit this website at http://apolloalliance.org/new-apolloprogram/data-points-nap/recovery-act-information-center-what-you-need-to-know/

The Center for American Progress's website called "The Nationwide Allocation of Recovery Funding" provides a map depicting the allocation of ARRA funding by state, as well as their best estimates at the funding available for different programs. Visit their website at
http://www.americanprogress.org/issues/2009/02/compromise_map.html/#methodology

The Progressive States Network has created a website called "Implementing the Recovery Plan: A Resource Guide for State Legislators and Advocates" which has a good assortment of resources including links to other websites related to the ARRA. You can view this information at http://www.progressivestates.org/pubs/stateside-dispatch/2009-02-19.

*Carol McClelland, Ph.D., a pioneering career-change consultant, has spent eighteen years helping thousands of clients, students, and readers discover fulfilling careers that align with their personal values. As the Founder and Executive Director of Green Career Central, Carol is once again on the leading edge of her field. In addition to defining and clarifying the ever-evolving world of green career possibilities for professionals, students, and career counselors, she and her team provide inspirational, effective ways to find your green niche, informative resources, and practical job search strategies to those entering the green economy. Carol is the author of Green Careers For Dummies (January, 2010) and Your Dream Career For Dummies (2005).*

# Recent Publications on Green Jobs and the Green Economy

In the wake of economic struggles, there are still many strategies and initiatives locally, nationally, and globally to bring us back into economic prosperity and into a clean energy revolution. This effort has been labeled the green economy, which carries hopeful implications. A green economy will require retrofitting our economy across the board to infuse environmental sustainability. The foundation of a green economy is built on energy efficiency, renewable power, conservation and recycling, sustainable modes of transportation, sustainable agriculture, and green job creation. Initiatives to stimulate the green economy are predicting success and some are starting to yield it. In order for a green economy to evolve, an enormous effort must be undertaken with a level of commitment that we know is possible, by all parties including governments, businesses, workers, community groups, etc.

Numerous publications, with varying perspectives and forecasts have recently been released which outline, encourage, and analyze the green economy. To offer insight into some of those publications, this article provides a brief summary of some of the major green job reports to date that analyze the green economy and its implications on jobs both locally, and nationally.

## National Green Jobs Publications

### State of Green Business 2011
GreenBiz.com
http://www.greenbiz.com/business/research/report/2011/02/01/state-green-business-report-2011

The *State of Green Business 2011* is the fourth edition of the annual GreenBiz report and provides an update on the emerging green economy and its impact on business culture. Over the past year, mainstream businesses have made a notable shift towards enacting long-term sustainability goals. Despite the economic downturn, results show that environmental initiatives are growing and expanding across all fields. This year's report tracks new sustainability commitments made by major corporate powerhouses and aims to measure whether or not these trends are producing real results.

The first part of the report provides an overview of the top ten sustainable business trends of 2011. The top trend observed listed: "Consumer Giants Awaken to Green". This newfound sense of increased corporate environmental accountability is attributed to recent stakeholder concerns, hedge risks of petroleum usage and carbon emissions, and the potential for increased operational efficiency. Environmental stewardship has also become a trend in itself, making corporate greening initiatives attractive to investors, job seekers, current employees, and customers.

The rest of the trends fall in line with the overarching theme of 2011: consumers are more conscious about their products, and companies don't want to miss the window of opportunity to target the eco-friendly bandwagon. Some of the other trends include zero-waste initiatives, greener transport, water footprints, and sustainable food.

In order to track progress, the report illustrates current data sets using the GreenBiz Index, giving each a score of "swim", "tread", or "sink". Indicators with favorable ratings ("swim") included paper and recycling rates, energy savings via Energy Star and energy efficiency software, accelerated investment in electric car technology, and increased green office space. The "treaders" and "sinkers" were mainly climate related, with underwhelming developments in carbon intensity benchmarks, carbon reporting, and

I. Introduction to Green Jobs and Green Careers

toxic emissions. Electronic waste also scored a "sink", with little to no progress in combating e-waste dumping in developing countries and lacking accountability for our own trash.

In the interest of green jobs, the report also includes a brief summary of the first annual GreenBiz Salary Survey, published in 2010. Rather than focus on the greater impact of green jobs on the economy, the Salary Survey focuses specifically on the emergence of senior executive positions fully dedicated to environmental oversight and stewardship strategies. Findings show that securing sustainability executive jobs depends heavily on education and experience. Over half of all vice presidents, directors, and managers hold a master's degree and earn significantly more than those with only a bachelor's degree. On top of schooling, nearly all of the vice presidents with chief sustainability status have at least 16 years of experience. Although these prerequisites sound steep, the payoff seems to be worth it. Average salaries for managers measure around 100K, while average salaries for vice presidents come out to nearly $200,000.

### *2011 Green Data for a Growing Green Economy: Labor Market Research of Green Jobs in the District of Columbia, Maryland, and Virginia*
Mid-Atlantic Regional Collaborative and ICF International
http://www.dllr.state.md.us/greenjobs/greenreports/

In 2009, the U.S. Department of Labor's Employment and Training Administration awarded the Mid-Atlantic Regional Collaborative with a competitive, four million dollar grant to produce the first labor market information (LMI) study of its kind. In full, the project consists of (1) a three-state survey on green employment, education, and training, (2) state-by-state green workforce and training research, (3) an online collaboration between DC, Maryland, and Virginia LMI, and (4) an unprecedented regional green jobs portal operating on real time.

Providing the foundation for the report was data gathered in the MARC Regional Employer Survey, conducted by ICF International in 2010. The survey collected feedback from 10,000 employers in the DMV area. The questions asked regarded current and prospective numbers of employees, current engagement in different green categories as outlined by the Bureau of Labor Statistics (BL), and ultimately sought to expose gaps—or opportunities—in the labor market. The survey revealed unique characteristics of each state, revealing areas for improvement in current education and skill training mechanisms. The state-specific information is especially useful for career centers and job counselors, who can then choose an appropriate point of focus for advising students and future employees in their corresponding regions.

One subtopic of the study is the relation of green job openings to education level. D.C. demonstrated the largest proportion of green jobs requiring a bachelor's degree or higher. Most green job openings in Maryland do not require a bachelor's degree but do require an associate's degree, or a high school diploma at the least. Virginia exhibited an even distribution of required education, supporting both service and production oriented green jobs. Because education level nearly always determines wages earned, one can observe high average green job wages in D.C. in contrast to comparatively wages in Maryland.

The report also discusses the concepts of labor market tightness and green labor market gaps. Labor market tightness can be calculated via the ratio of green vacancies relative to unemployment rates. These ratios were highest in Frederick County, Anne Arundel County, and Montgomery County in Maryland, and Western and Northern Virginia. The green labor market gap is defined as the difference between worker supply and the demand for such workers. DC, Maryland, and Virginia were all found to experience over-supply in most green jobs requiring a bachelor's degree or higher. Under-supply was observed in systems operators, equipment specialists, mechanics, and maintenance and repair workers.

This unique state-by-state analysis paralleled with the greater regional study effectively reveals areas of oversupply in certain areas, while discovering areas of undersupply in others. By mapping the data, MARC report identifies existing green career pathways as well as other pathways demonstrating stagnant growth. The information presented is perfect for use by career counseling agencies, colleges, and training programs to better equip job seekers with the tools they need to find the position most fitting to the individual and the region in question. The study is also a career literacy tool for anyone interested in entering the green workforce and lacking background knowledge in prospective wages and standard prerequisites.

### *Renewable Energy and Energy Efficiency: Economic Drivers for the 21st Century*
American Society of Solar Energy
http://www.ases.org/images/stories/ASES-JobsReport-Final.pdf

The American Society of Solar Energy (ASES) researched and compiled a report based on renewable energy and energy efficiency technologies and analyzed the impact they will have on the economy and jobs in the United States. The Report includes creating a working definition of the renewable energy and energy efficiency industry, which have typically been difficult to clearly define. The Report goes on to estimate the size and scope of the renewable energy and energy efficiency industry and then forecasts the growth of the industry thru 2030. And finally to validate its estimates and forecast, the Report uses a case study in Ohio.

Defining renewable energy and energy efficiency is a work in progress but for consistency, renewable energy includes: hydroelectricity, biomass, geothermal, wind, photovoltaic, and solar thermal, while energy efficiency includes parts of major sectors, including: buildings, vehicles, lighting, appliances, etc. Because the energy efficiency industry is so difficult to define, it is a challenge to formulate consistent findings; however, measuring energy efficiency within the major sectors listed above, ASES was able to present its results from the renewable energy and energy efficiency sectors from 2006 data.

The results reveal roughly $1 trillion in industry sales, 8.5 million new jobs, $100 billion in industry profits, and $150 billion in government tax revenues. Using those results from 2006 the Report creates several scenarios for 2030, which were the base case, the moderate scenario, and the advanced scenario. The advanced scenario forecasts $4,530 billion in revenue and 40,103 thousand jobs created in the renewable energy and energy efficiency industry by 2030. Continuing with the 2006 data, the case study in Ohio reveals $800 million in revenue in renewable energy along with 6,600 jobs, while energy efficiency contributed $50 billion in revenue and 500,000 jobs.

The results of the case study illustrate the immediate impact that this industry can have on local, state, and national economies. To sum up the potential of this ever growing industry, we can conclude that the renewable energy and energy efficiency sector will create millions of jobs, revive the manufacturing sector, reduce the vulnerability of fuel prices, promote new technology, enhance economic growth, and contribute to reducing trade and budget deficits.

### *Current and Potential Green Jobs in the U.S. Economy*
The United States Conference of Mayors and Global Insight
http://www.usmayors.org/pressreleases/uploads/GreenJobsReport.pdf

This Report was presented to the U.S. Conference of Mayors as an examination of the economic benefits of the green economy in regard to reduction in fossil fuels, increase in energy efficiency, and curbing of greenhouse gas emissions. The Report begins by outlining oil and gas consumption, electricity demand, and the green economy; it then moves into the background of green jobs, the number of existing green jobs, the areas of future growth, and then forecasts potential growth under certain scenarios.

To reinforce the significance of a green economy, this Report compares its estimates to the U.S. spending $240 billion or 2.3% of its GDP on oil and $120 billion on electricity. After analyzing the economic impact of those figures, it's a fair assumption that investing in a green economy will offer macroeconomic benefits that create jobs and increase productivity, which together will create a virtuous cycle. By examining specific metropolitan areas in the United States, the current green jobs by category include: renewable power generation, agriculture and forestry, construction and systems installation, manufacturing, equipment dealers and wholesalers, engineering and research and consulting, and government administration. The number of jobs estimated in the existing green infrastructure industry as of 2006 totals 751,051 workers.

When focusing on future growth in green jobs, this Report identifies renewable resources in the areas of electricity generation and transportation fuels as the catalysts for development. Renewable power entails wind, solar, hydropower, geothermal, and biomass, with hydropower being the most relevant today, but studies predict all forms of renewable energy to be utilized to greater capacity in the near future. The article also addresses energy efficiency standards and their implementation, which are becoming better understood and are more frequently being practiced. To sum it up: renewable power and energy efficiency along with renewable transportation fuels are the foundation of a green economy.

The 30 year forecast in this Report approximates that renewable power generation will increase 30% from 2008, which is extremely promising for green job creation. In conclusion this Report estimates the creation of 4.2 million green jobs within the 30 year forecast.

### *Green Jobs: Towards Decent Work in a Sustainable, Low Carbon World*
UNEP/ILO/IOE/ITUC
http://www.unep.org/labour_environment/PDFs/Greenjobs/UNEP-Green-Jobs-Report.pdf

The *Green Jobs: Towards Decent Work in a Sustainable, Low Carbon World* report was commissioned by the United Nations Environmental Programme as part of its green job initiative. The Report addresses a green economy from a global prospective and the impact it will have on countries, both rich and developing, all over the world. It starts by acknowledging the fact that although efforts are being made, a green economy is still just a theory on the brink of reality. Naturally the Report discusses what will drive a sustainable economy and workforce and identifies greater efficiency in the use of energy, water, and materials as the core objective; in that it provides workers with adequate wages, safe working conditions, job security, reasonable career prospects, and worker rights.

In order for a green economy to develop, evolve, and sustain, the world must focus on key policy issues that include: subsides, carbon markets, tax reform, targets and mandates, energy alternatives, product take backs, eco-labeling, research and development budgets, and international aid. Implementation of these policy issues would certainly stimulate economies, individually and collectively, and while doing so is attainable, it is also difficult. Considering green jobs, both now and in the future, six major industry sectors can be addressed: energy supply alternatives, buildings, transportation, basic industry and recycling, food and agriculture, and forestry. If jobs in these major industries flourish, we could potentially see 20 million jobs created across the globe by 2030. While there is great potential for each of these industries to develop and drive enormous good green job creation, global policies must have a focused agenda for a green jobs future. The major elements of that policy agenda revolve around business and government action, financing a green jobs agenda, worker training, and a smooth transition.

The timing of policy implementation, economic and social prosperity, and employment will depend in fundamental ways on a stable climate and healthy ecosystems. The possibility of a green economy is promising and it can prevail if the world commits to developing it.

*Green Collar Jobs: An Analysis of the Capacity of Green Businesses to Provide High Quality Jobs for Men and Women with Barriers to Employment*
A Report for the City of Berkley by Raquel Pinderhughes
http://www.greenforall.org/resources/An-Analysis-of-the-Capacity-of-Green-Businesses-to

This Report examines green collar job potential in the Bay area and throughout the United States. It identifies green collar jobs as being jobs for low income residents with barriers to employment and a green collar job being a blue collar job that improves environmental quality. The poverty, unemployment, and social inequality in the Bay area as well as other areas of the country is astonishing, but green job creation can address all three issues and have a profound impact on society if the quality of green jobs, suitability of green jobs, and interest in green jobs are considered by all parties. First, an employee must have the desire to work and obtain a green job, but an employer must also be willing to hire employees in this demographic that have barriers to employment. These jobs must also produce adequate wages, benefits, and work conditions. As the green job sector blossoms, employees will need employers to provide sufficient training programs.

The City of Berkley makes a strong case that these are not just jobs, they are careers that can be sustained all over the country. In this report, Pinderhughes, the author, lists 22 types of green collar jobs ranging from parks and maintenance to printing and furniture production. The point is to show that there is tremendous green job potential outside of what people typically categorize as green jobs. Even jobs that have not traditionally been seen as environmentally conscious are being reconstructed to contribute to environmental sustainability.

The target demographic for the green workforce is 18-35 year old men and women with barriers to employment. This population includes individuals who do not have a high school degree, have been out of the labor market for a long time, were formally incarcerated, and/or have limited labor market skills and experience. Despite those inhibiting characteristics, training, internships, and apprenticeships need to be available to provide employees satisfactory training to be successful. If employees, employers, governments, and communities remain optimistic and collaborate, this program will be a success because green employment opportunities do exist and are in demand.

While this case study directly addresses green job potential and demand in the Bay area, the same concepts and job possibilities exist in urban areas all over the United States. For instance, The Center for American Progress outlined a D.C. Green Jobs Initiative for Washington, D.C. and it found the same green jobs scenario to be true for the D.C. area as was the case in the Bay area.

*Green Recovery: A Program to Create Good Jobs and Start Building a Low-Carbon Economy*
Center for American Progress and University of Massachusetts Political Economy Research Institute
http://www.americanprogress.org/issues/2008/09/green_recovery.html
http://www.peri.umass.edu/green_recovery

This report by The Political Economy Research Institute at the University of Massachusetts, Amherst and the Center for American Progress focuses on the green job market in the United States through June 2008. The report breaks down green jobs in the U.S. into six categories and each category consists of ten different job types, ranging in skill level and earnings. The study reveals that many green jobs already exist and the green job market will continue to expand as we develop our green economy. The initiative proposed by the Report (the Green Recovery Plan) would invest $100 billion over a two year period and is estimated that it would create approximately 2 million jobs (sum of direct, indirect, and induced jobs), as well as stabilize oil prices, help fight global warming, and start to build a low-carbon economy. The $100 billion for this Green Recovery Plan would be funded as follows: $50 billion for tax credits, $46 billion in direct government spending, and $4 billion for federal loan guarantees. All the funding would come from the U.S. Treasury, but most of it would be funneled down to local and state governments to be dispersed as described in the Report for various programs and initiatives. Most investments would be made in public infrastructure based on the suggestions of the Report.

In July 2008 there were approximately 8.8 million unemployed individuals in the United States, accounting for a 5.7% unemployment rate. So, the Report states why it is so important for our investments to create jobs, especially those that contribute to a greener America, a greener economy, and a low-carbon economy. Green jobs provide workers with job stability, good wages, and benefits; a green economy should be sustainable, for the environment, but also for workers' rights and opportunities. As we work for economic sustainability and climate change, good jobs will be produced. All geographic areas of the country would be able to take advantage of this Green Recovery Plan, but to what extent and how they would do so will vary depending on the location. This is due to differences in climate, workforce resources, current economic drivers, and types of jobs and industries available.

This Report focuses on six job strategies including: building retrofitting, mass transit, energy efficient strategies, wind power, solar power, and cellulosic biofuels; it also examines 45 jobs within those categories which already make up 14 million U.S. workers, or 9 percent of our total workforce. Statistics were taken from 12 different states based on the number of people employed under each job category and the average wages for each.

The Appendix of the Report provides information on the methodology of how they came up with their estimates and projections, as well as specific data on how their Green Recovery Plan would benefit each of the 50 states. For Maryland, they predicted that the state would get $1.9 billion to spend, and that 36,739 jobs would be created, which would have brought the June 2008 unemployment rate of 4.3% down to 3.1% after the programs were implemented. For Virginia, they predicted that the state would get $2.7 billion to spend, and that 56,459 jobs would be created, which would have brought down the June 2008 unemployment rate of 4.2% to 2.8% after the programs were implemented.

### *5 Million Green Jobs – How We Can Address Climate Change and Strengthen the Economy by Putting Americans to Work*
1Sky
http://www.1sky.org/files/green-jobs-1sky-v2-october08.pdf

1Sky was created in 2007 to focus the power of millions of concerned Americans on a single goal: bold federal action by 2010 that can reverse global warming. The 1Sky Solutions are grounded in scientific necessity - they are the bottom line of what's needed to dramatically reduce carbon emissions while maximizing energy efficiency, renewable energy and breakthrough technologies. 1Sky's main initiatives at the moment are to create 5 million green jobs and pathways out of poverty by rebuilding and refueling America with a comprehensive energy efficiency mobilization. This includes immediate investments in a clean-energy infrastructure, reducing global warming pollution at least 35% below current levels by 2020, and at least 80% by 2050, in line with the best science available, and re-powering America by imposing a moratorium on new coal plants that emit global warming pollution, and replacing dirty fuels with 100% renewable energy.

This Report from 1Sky focuses on their ambitious goal of creating 5 million green jobs, while at the same time taking head on the challenges we currently face from global warming. It begins by mentioning that although global warming represents an environmental and economic crisis, it also presents us with a tremendous opportunity. However, it will take the bold political leadership and the support of many individuals and organizations. 1Sky defines a green collar job as a well-paid, career-track job that contributes directly to preserving or enhancing environmental quality. Green collar jobs have many benefits, including dealing with poverty, pollution, and global warming. They are also jobs that favor keeping these jobs within the USA as opposed to outsourcing them globally. Green collar jobs provide an opportunity to revitalize certain regions and neighborhoods, since these jobs are often community based. 1 Sky does state that most green jobs are not new jobs, but jobs that require a new skill set for workers.

The report points to industries such as renewable energy (ex. solar, wind, and geothermal), energy efficiency (office, residential, and manufacturing plant retrofits), and transportation (mass transit, alternative fuel vehicles) as great opportunities for green jobs. A key element to the green jobs movement is investment of funds, and incentives and tax credits. This is to level the playing field for renewable energy sources in comparison to the current coal, nuclear, and fossil fuel industries which continue to be huge contributors to global warming, and are very capital intensive, and not very labor intensive.

Several examples of successful green job programs around the country are highlighted including how a new wind turbine factory in Ebensburg, PA has created many green jobs and has been paired with local political leadership around renewable energy, how Vermont has heavily invested in energy efficient programs for buildings that are creating awareness of the issues related to energy usage, and are saving families, businesses, and schools millions of dollars on energy bills, and an innovative green job training program in Los Angeles, CA brought about by community support which provides academic coursework and on the job training that helps individuals with barriers to employment get connected with career pathways and the skills they need to have successful green careers.

It is pointed out that the transition to a green job economy will require a large amount of support and assistance in recognizing the needs of displaced workers in the current dirty energy industries, which would include activities such as training, providing health insurance, and retirement packages. The Report concludes by pointing out that those who will be hit hardest by global warming and economic turmoil are low income communities and we need to create an economy that is inclusive of these often neglected communities and provides them with pathways out of poverty in the new green economy.

### *Green Collar Jobs in America's Cities: Building Pathways out of Poverty and Careers in the Clean Energy Economy*
Apollo Alliance, Green For All, Center for American Progress, and Center for Wisconsin Strategy
http://www.apolloalliance.org/downloads/greencollarjobs.pdf
http://www.greenforall.org/resources/green-collar-jobs-in-america2019s-cities

The Report is a joint effort between 4 different organizations that have a unique insight into green collar jobs and the current developments with green collar jobs around the country. While the Report admittedly states that it is not an exhaustive report on green collar jobs in the United States, it highlights some of the major programs, and gives recommendations on how we can get more of these types of programs up and running, and support them so they can stay successful over time. This is a great resource for anyone looking to start a green collar job program at a local level. The foreword from Van Jones and Jerome Ringo calls for bold and committed action coupled with smart thinking, in order for America to lift people out of poverty. Throughout the Report there are highlights of successful green collar jobs initiatives and programs, including the following locations: Los Angeles, CA, Milwaukee, WI, Washington, D.C, Richmond, VA, Chicago, IL, Oakland, CA, South Bronx, NY, Baltimore, MD, New York City, NY, and Newark, NJ.

Although we realize that there is great opportunity in growing a green economy, it is essential to note that we will not be successful in doing so if we don't deal with the current problem of a shortage of a qualified and skilled labor force. This Report is intended to help us do just this. Green collar jobs are defined as "well-paid, career track jobs that contribute directly to preserving or enhancing environmental quality."

---

Green collar jobs are described as ranging in skill level and pay, tending to be local jobs, covering many sectors of the economy, including both new jobs and existing jobs that require a new skill set, and building a sustainable economy, where environmental goals go hand in hand with social and economic goals. Four steps to building an effective green collar job program in your community are listed as follows: Identify goals and assess opportunities; enact policies and programs to drive investment; prepare green collar workforce through training partnerships and pathways out of poverty; and leverage success to build political support for new initiatives.

Identifying goals and assessing opportunities involves gaining an understanding of what it will take to achieve your current or future goals for local economic development. A thorough analysis should be done that involves discussions with all the various stakeholders, identifying barriers to goal achievement, and identifying solutions to these barriers using existing local assets. Enacting policies and programs to drive investment involves finding connections between policies, local investment, and incentives to create demand for green products and services, and then encouraging everyone to meet this demand through the use of local businesses and workers, where the workforce development and training is geared towards specific job opportunities and pathways out of poverty.

Preparing a green collar workforce should be done in tune with existing workforce and economic development strategies should be linked to existing policies, programs, and investments, should provide opportunities for a range of workers, and should give access to family supporting and career track jobs. Training partnerships can involve private industry, community organizations, labor unions, educational institutions, and government agencies. The approach of creating a local Green Job Corps can be a great way to provide opportunities for low income residents and individuals who may not be ready to succeed in conventional vocational training programs, and the program would involve job readiness, skills education, and career counseling for these individuals. In order to leverage the successes of your green collar job initiatives it is important to track the progress of these programs by identifying key indicators of success such as the number of participants in the programs, number of good, green jobs created, involvement from various partners, policy achievements, and amount of funding supplied. Showing this data to potential future partners will go a long way.

***Greener Pathways – Jobs and Workforce Development in the Clean Energy Economy***
Center on Wisconsin Strategy, The Workforce Alliance, and The Apollo Alliance
http://www.cows.org/pdf/rp-greenerpathways.pdf

This Report was created to provide strategies for realizing the vision of a clean energy economy and how it relates to providing greener pathways through green job opportunities. It lists the type and quality of jobs needed, describes the skills needed to fill these jobs, and identifies opportunities for existing plants and their workers to seize the opportunity to be at the forefront of this movement. The Report focuses on 3 major industries which are energy efficiency, wind, and biofuels and identifies federal resources that can be used to help support state level green job initiatives.

Careful thinking is the foundation for successful policies, so it is essential to target specific sectors, use good data, and measure and evaluate programs. On top of that, workforce training programs must be linked to these policies, and the green jobs created must provide community benefit, build career pathways, and bring residents out of poverty. For the purposes of this report green jobs are defined as family-supporting, middle-skill jobs in the primary sectors of a clean energy economy - efficiency, renewables, and alternative transportation and fuels. Not only should we be interested in green jobs, but also really we want good, green jobs. A good job is defined in the report as paying more than a poverty wage, or more than about $10 an hour, offers benefits, at least health-care and ideally pensions, paid sick leave, safe working conditions, reasonable schedules, organizing rights, and a modicum of job security, and is one with an accessible pathway to advancement. The Report is quick to point out that green job workforce training programs shouldn't be inventing new programs, but rather using the platform of existing workforce training programs and resources to incorporate green skills and training.

Some interesting and sobering statistics provided in the Report are:
- More than one in five (22 percent) working Americans hold poverty wage jobs
- Close to one out of three (29 percent) working families in this country are low income
- A breathtaking 42 percent of minority working families are low income
- In a 2005 survey by the National Association of Manufacturers, 90 percent of respondents indicated a moderate to severe shortage of qualified skilled production employees such as machinists and technicians
- In a recent power sector survey, nearly half of respondents said that more than 20 percent of their work force - mostly skilled trades people - would retire within the next five to seven years

The Report mentions that green job training should be developed using a career pathways framework so that it provides a form of step ladder for people of various skill levels and experience to gain access to green industries. It allows individuals to move up the career ladder as well, so they can advance in their career paths gaining more experience and garnering higher paying jobs. Examples of these types of framework are provided in the Report.

The first industry that is discussed is energy efficiency. This industry has already shown tremendous growth in recent years, and is one of the easiest and quickest green jobs programs to implement. Energy efficiency also offsets more greenhouse gas emissions than renewable energy and alternative fuels combined. Energy efficiency jobs are not easily outsourced, so they tend to be local jobs. The Report focuses it discussion of energy efficiency on buildings, because of the opportunities available, and the large quantity of energy usage buildings account for in our country. Focus should be paid to cities with older building stock because these buildings are likely the most inefficient, and would provide the highest return on investment for energy efficiency upgrades. Energy efficiency policy mandates can go a long way to creating green jobs, as well as saving large amounts of money and energy. Energy efficiency jobs are often jobs that can be done by traditional construction workers who are taught the specifics of the skill set required for energy efficiency. A case study is provided from Los Angeles, CA to show how one successful energy efficiency program has been set up.

The next industry examined is the wind energy industry, and it was chosen due to its rapid and high growth profile in the U.S. and globally, its potential for economic growth in both urban and rural areas, and its promise of job creation in many different occupations including manufacturing, installation, and operations. The U.S. has led the world in wind power installation for the past three years, and because it still only accounts for such a small percentage of our energy portfolio, there is incredible opportunity for more growth. Wind energy has the potential to be a significant boost to the Great Plains because this area is one of the most fertile wind regions in the country.

Market driven policies and mandates for renewable energy production however have led to other areas of the country taking the lead on wind energy such as California and Texas. As of January 2008, D.C. had a renewable portfolio standard of 11% by 2022 (recently updated to 20% by 2020), Maryland has a renewable portfolio standard of 9.5% by 2022 (recently updated to 20% by 2022), and Virginia has a renewable portfolio standard of 12% by 2022. A key aspect of wind energy in the United States will be industrial capacity and transportation networks because of the large scale of the wind turbines. It makes no sense for us to ship these materials from all over the world when we could produce them domestically and reduce environmental and economic impacts from transportation of these materials. There are many opportunities for manufacturing wind turbine parts due to the existing bottlenecks in the supply chain. Wind energy jobs can help the declining U.S. manufacturing industry, and the wind industry has the potential to take existing jobs in construction and energy industries and convert them to wind energy jobs, as well as create new jobs that require a totally new set of skills.

The third industry that is described in the report is the biofuel production industry. Everyone knows that our supplies of fossil fuels are running out, and we have all seen evidence as to the enormous environmental impacts our large-scale use of fossil fuels has had on the planet. Biofuel production is another rapidly growing industry that has the potential for green jobs to be created. Biofuels are made largely from plant material and the two most common forms currently in use are ethanol and biodiesel. Since these are not petroleum-based fuels, they reduce carbon emissions and can be made domestically. There is a lot of research and development being done around the country and the world to test different types of biofuels. Some of the biggest barriers with biofuels are the effect they have on the food industry and successfully developing efficient large-scale production of these fuels while keeping costs competitive with the cost of conventional fuels. While the biofuels industry may not create an enormous amount of jobs, the jobs it does require and could create usually pay well, and it is important to note that most of these jobs would be in the Midwest of the country where it is often difficult for residents to find good, well-paying jobs. An example of biofuel initiatives in Iowa is also provided in the Report.

As for federal resources for green job programs, information is provided about the Workforce Investment Act and the Green Jobs Act that show the different areas of focus within the legislation and also the different programs that were to be funded by the federal government. While federal initiatives are important to the green job discussion and growth in our country, the report calls for action from policy makers on the state level, and provides a list of 12 principles to follow when creating green job legislation, which can also be used by policy makers on the city or county level. A case study of recent Washington state legislation for green job initiatives is provided.

### Greener Skills: How Credentials Create Value in the Clean Energy Economy
Center on Wisconsin Strategy (COWS)
http://www.cows.org/pdf/rp-greenerskills.pdf

The purpose of this report is to suggest a plan for developing human capital in a green economy. The main focus of this agenda is to encourage the creation of a national skill credential system, and develop a stronger, better-equipped green workforce to support it. The most essential problem that this report aims to address is the issue of skill distribution and training in the American labor market.

In the argument for national skill standards, a comparison is made between the American economy and other advanced economies abroad, namely Germany and Ireland, noting the lack of stateside credentialing systems that apply to all working classes. Because the source of resistance to skill standards is employers looking to reduce costs, broad-based public policy is needed to cement a foundation of basic analytical and social skill sets. The current enthusiasm for a green energy economy can help set the stage to gain ground on necessary reforms to American education and job training systems.

The report details eight criteria for a coherent skills agenda. Individually, all eight criteria have been implemented and observed in different parts in the U.S., but never simultaneously. Together, these criteria would ensure accessibility, increase mobility, provide skills appropriate for particular circumstances, and assurance of payoff. The criteria are as follows:
1. Mapping regional labor markets by careers, jobs, and skills, and defining the different skills needed for different job pathways,
2. Modularizing training to effectively train specific skill sets one-by-one,
3. Providing training in conjunction with real labor market demand,
4. Maximizing training accessibility,
5. Certifying skills through testing,

6. Aligning certification with employer-recognized skill standards,
7. Removing income as a roadblock to training, and,
8. Providing social services to maximize access even further.

One point of particular focus is that of national certification. International and national governing bodies often offer individual professional certification for workers. These types of certifications operate mainly in the advanced professional world, and are typically time-consuming and expensive. Yet, when earned, such certifications can be especially useful for professionals with two- or four-year degrees and considerable work experience. Clean energy credentials are not standardized, and a myriad of organizations offer training systems and certifications that are not always recognized across the board. However, some institutions offer third-party verification recognized by most notable industry leaders. The report provides a list of national certifications offered by various organizations in the clean energy sector. Offerings include certifications to become a solar thermal installer, carbon reduction manager, energy auditor, energy procurement professional, and LEED Green Associate, among many others.

Washington State serves as an exemplary case study for improving education and skill training. A leader in energy technology innovation and skill standards development, Washington has made great gains in upgrading community and technical education programs to broaden opportunities for energy industry careers. The Energy Industry Skill Standards Project, for example, combines efforts from labor unions, community and technical colleges, and employers to create benchmarked standards for career development. The initiative also specifies key work functions and skills and performance indicators to equip individuals with all the information they need to succeed.

The report emphasizes the importance of creating a workable, national skill standard in unlocking the future to a strong, clean and equitable workforce. Federal leadership must rise to the challenge and work to improve existing jobs and train workers where they are most needed. After solidifying current jobs and appropriately training individuals to work most effectively in those positions, then the conversation surrounding the creation of clean energy jobs must turn into action.

### *Going Green: The Vital Role of Community Colleges in Building a Sustainable Future and Green Workforce*
National Council for Workforce Education (NCWE) and the Academy for Educational Development (AED)
http://www.aed.org/Publications/upload/GoingGreen.pdf

If you are interested in the education opportunities for individuals to gain green jobs skills, then this is a great report to read. While a lot of focus is put on vocational training programs for green jobs, we also need to realize the opportunities to utilize our nation's existing network of community colleges, and 4 year institutions to prepare our green job workforce. This Report specifically analyzes the role of community colleges in this venture, and hopefully will aide in creating more green jobs programs at community colleges across the country. The NCWE and AED provide examples of successful programs and initiatives at community colleges around the country, information on which industries and professional currently offer the most opportunities for green jobs, and resources for further information on the topic of green jobs.

If you didn't realize it, there are many community colleges all over the country that have already made significant commitments to implementing climate solutions and modeling sustainability on their campuses. One of these initiatives is the American College and University Presidents Climate Commitment which commits the colleges and universities to various pledges related to sustainability and climate change. More and more colleges and universities are beginning to inject sustainable approaches to planning and construction of campus land, as well as turning their facilities into living laboratories to provide hands on educational opportunities to their students and their local communities. Specific initiatives highlighted from around the country include the use of on-site renewable energy for campus facilities, water conservation measures, LEED certified buildings, hiring full time sustainability managers for the school, offering classes as well as certificate and degree programs in green and sustainable studies, creating outdoor classrooms, and engaging community partners to create long lasting relationships.

The Report then goes into a discussion of why community colleges are so well positioned to help create a green economy and train green workers. It mentions that some of the major reasons are their connections with local and regional labor markets, and the flexibility to respond to emerging industries and their changing skill needs. Some of the major industries for which opportunities exist for community colleges to train workers include renewable energy, buildings and construction (energy efficiency), transportation, manufacturing, agriculture, and forestry. A lot of the jobs in these industries are what are called "middle skills" jobs which require more than a high school diploma, but less than a 4 year degree, so community colleges are the perfect opportunity to fill this need.

Profiles of many different programs in these areas of study are described in this Report to give readers a feel for just how many types of programs there are out there, and several collaboration programs are also listed that include multiple community colleges working together to provide needed skills to the green workforce. Six action steps for community college leaders to build a sustainable future are identified and are as follows: 1) Serve as a catalyst in your local area for educating diverse audiences about green and sustainable issues and skills, 2) Reduce your institution's carbon footprint and keep track of greenhouse gas emissions, 3) Make sustainability a defining feature of campus culture and use this framework to shape major decisions and planning for the campus, 4) Pursue and maintain partnerships with key stakeholders in your local community and share knowledge to continually adapt and create your academic programs to provide the needed education and skills for green jobs, 5) Collaborate with other colleges and universities around the country to share knowledge about green initiatives and programs, so you don't have to reinvent the wheel, 6) Promote your campus' successful green efforts through the media, and on campus so that everyone knows what you are doing and gets involved.

The Appendix of the Report lists many great resources to explore, and one I would highly recommend checking out is the Association for the Advancement of Sustainability in Higher Education (AASHE) website at www.aashe.org.

***The Economic Development Potential of the Green Sector***
UCLA Center for Regional Policy Studies
http://repositories.cdlib.org/cgi/viewcontent.cgi?article=1086&context=lewis

For those interested in the economics of how the green movement can create a green economy that is profitable and more in tune with the environment, this is a great report to read. The Report deals with policies and strategies that can establish regional economic development and job creation to grow the Green sector. Realizing that there is tremendous competition already underway both within the United States, as well as abroad for regions to become Green centers of economic development, the Report lays out recommendations for making wise choices, suggesting innovative economic development approaches, and understanding what the potential benefits are from taking risks related to the green sector. Ideally after reading the Report, a particular region would be able to use this information to become a leading center of production for green goods and services.

After reviewing publications and studies as well as current initiatives underway in cities and metropolitan areas, the Report identifies some of the areas of the country that have taken the lead on growing the green sector and are now recognized as national leaders. They include Chicago, Los Angeles, Portland, OR, San Francisco, Boston, Philadelphia, New York City, Seattle and Detroit. The Report states that green development occurs through a commitment of resources and leadership, particularly among key policymakers that bring significant attention and institutional resources to the green sector. Through quick and aggressive action a region can realize the goal of becoming a net exporter of green services and goods, meaning they export more of these goods to outside the region, then they import from outside the region.

For a region to be successful at establishing itself as a center for green services and goods, the Report suggests that it should realize economies of scale that reduce average costs when increasing the level of production, create a collaborative effort among firms and organizations in the area to share intellectual assets in an attempt to lead to innovation, and capture agglomeration effects so that your initial efforts will pay off and be sustained. Capturing agglomeration effects occurs by being a demand leader, and having a substantial local and regional demand. This can be done through successful marketing and public relations, taking calculated risks, and engaging firms to be active in cooperation and participation with green initiatives.

The next part of developing a green economic development initiative is to get an understanding of the existing resources in your region in order to identify strengths and weaknesses. The Report lays out an extensive list of areas of study which includes gaining a thorough understanding the regions' economic market, firms and businesses, universities and research institutes, political climate and leadership, history of environmental issues, past efforts in innovation, public / private partnerships, labor force, current regulatory framework, and challenges in transportation, land and housing. Once a region has a comprehensive inventory of all these different aspects of the region, it will be easier to see where the best opportunities are, and what the barriers that need to be removed are. Then strategies can be developed to involve all the necessary elements of your green economic development.

Some of the strategies that the Report suggests for capitalizing on the growth of the green sector are developing working groups to discuss and create plans and policies for green economic growth, provide financial incentives and infrastructure for investment in the green sector, remove regulatory barriers to green development, match training programs to labor needs in green industries, develop a set of metrics and timelines that can track your progress and show you where you are being successful and where you need improvement, and specifically assign individuals or an and office to be responsible for coordinating your green initiatives, who will engage all the other stakeholders in the process.

### Clean Power, Green Jobs
Union of Concerned Scientists
http://www.ucsusa.org/assets/documents/clean_energy/Clean-Power-Green-Jobs-25-RES.pdf

This is a report / fact sheet from the Union of Concerned Scientists (UCS) that is devoted to showing how creating a National Renewable Electricity Standard will boost the economy, and protect the environment. The UCS conducted a study to see what the effects would be of requiring all electric utilities to provide at least 25% of their electricity from renewable sources by 2025. Their findings were that this would create more green jobs, lower consumer energy bills in every region of the country, and reduce harmful emissions from power plants.

On the green jobs front, their study showed the potential for creating 297,000 jobs in manufacturing, construction, operations, maintenance, agriculture, forestry, and other industries by 2025 if we were to enact the renewable energy standard they propose. It isn't stated that all of these would be green jobs, but one can imagine most of them would be in the clean energy industry, so would qualify as green jobs. Compared to the amount of jobs and economic development created by the same amount of electricity from fossil fuels, there is no question that renewable energy comes out on top.

Besides creating jobs, the National Renewable Energy Standard would boost the U.S. economy by creating billions of dollars in new capital investments, new income for landowners who own the land where the energy is being produced, and property tax revenue. Requiring 25% renewable energy by 2025 would also save consumers about $64 billion dollars in electricity and gas costs by 2025. The typical household would save about $67 a year on electricity and gas costs by 2025. Other benefits would include drastic reductions in carbon dioxide emissions from power plants by 277 million metric tons annually by 2025 (also significant reductions in other harmful air pollutants such as mercury and sulfur dioxide), and reduce the amount of electricity generated from imported energy sources, which in turn reduces the transportation impacts of these deliveries.

The Report also displays a table that shows the cumulative electricity and natural gas bill savings for each state based on their projections for the 25% renewable energy standard by 2025.

***Green Jobs: A Pathway to a Strong Middle Class***
White House Staff Report from Middle Class Task Force Meeting on Green Jobs
http://www.whitehouse.gov/assets/documents/mctf_one_staff_report_final.pdf

This is the official report from the White House about the first meeting held by the Middle Class Task Force which is chaired by Vice President Joe Biden. The topic of this meeting was green jobs, and the Report describes the Obama Administration's interest in green jobs, and what they plan to do to help develop green job opportunities for the workers of our country. According to the report, the Obama/Biden Administration is deeply committed to reforming how we create and consume energy in America, and one part of this reform project is to promote the creation of green jobs. The Report defines a green job broadly as employment that is associated with some aspect of environmental improvement, but goes on to provide several more specific definitions from various individuals and organizations. After examining several definitions of green jobs, the report concludes that there are typically 3 key aspects of the green job definition, and they are: 1) They involve some task associated with improving the environment, 2) They should be good jobs that promote sustainable family wage, health and retirement benefits and decent working conditions, and 3) They should be available to diverse workers from across the spectrum of race, gender, and ethnicity.

An analysis from the Council of Economic Advisers (CEA) shows the comparison of wages for green jobs and standard jobs in the same industry. Because it is virtually impossible to tell exactly which jobs are green jobs at the moment, the analysis focused on industries and occupations that were considered highly green. Although the definition of green jobs is very broad at this point in time, the CEA analysis shows the following findings: green jobs compared to other jobs tend to pay more, are more likely to be union jobs, and are more likely to be held by men but less likely to be held by minorities or urban residents.

Several challenges to creating green jobs for everyone are identified as well. Specific funding from The American Recovery and Investment Act (ARRA) for green job programs include:
- Building thousands of miles of high tech transmission lines for electricity distribution (New "Smart Grid")
- Greening the federal government – converting federal government buildings to high performance, green buildings
- Investing in green retrofits – energy efficiency initiatives for buildings and vehicles
- Establishing a Clean Energy Finance Authority (CEFA) – encourage and fund clean energy projects
- Launching a Green Job Training Program – to teach American workers the skills they need for high quality green jobs

It is great to see just how many green job initiatives are currently underway around the country. The Report highlights a few of these through case studies of programs in Los Angeles, CA, and Washington State. Next the Report describes how the only way our country's green job initiatives will be successful is through partnerships between private and public entities. Working together to share resources and also identify, as well as provide funding opportunities is vital to the green jobs initiative. The Report identifies the 3 most successful and promising strategies to do just this. The first is the Clean Energy Finance Authority (CEFA) established by the ARRA. The CEFA has a loan guarantee program that ensures banks will recoup their investments if they lend to clean energy projects. Identifying funding from banks has been a huge hurdle for development of new projects in the existing economic turmoil, so this should be a big incentive for banks.

The second strategy is the Production Tax Credit (PTC) for Renewable Energy, which was created by the Energy Policy Act of 1992, and provides a tax credit of up to about 2 cents per kilowatt-hour for renewable energy generation projects. The ARRA extended this program for three years through the end of 2012, and helps make renewable energy generation cost competitive with fossil fuel generation. The last strategy is one that is not a federal government program, but rather a green sector development on a smaller scale called Milwaukee Energy Efficiency (Me2). It deals with funding for energy efficiency projects and is a public / private partnership in the City of Milwaukee, Wisconsin. The program uses various funding sources to provide the upfront costs for energy efficiency upgrades, which can then be paid back gradually by the property owner through the savings in their monthly energy bills. The repayments are attached to the property, so even if a current occupant moves the next occupant is responsible for taking over the repayment obligation.

The next topic in the Report deals with specific elements that need to be considered when developing green job training programs. It mentions that training should be geared towards a specific sector of jobs that is known to have a shortage of skilled workers, and training programs should also provide support services for disadvantaged workers to help them address barriers to employment.

Based on the overview of all the existing green jobs data, case studies, legislation, etc. the Middle Class Task Force came to the conclusion that the green job initiative would need the following components to be successful (each of which they provide an example of from existing initiatives in Philadelphia):
- A public mandate to achieve an energy conservation goal;
- Elected officials invested in meeting the goal;
- Private employers interested in creating green jobs to meet the new labor demands for environmentally-sound output;
- Financing sources who want to invest in the new initiatives, often involving federal loan guarantees;
- Extensive labor force intermediaries, including community colleges, union apprenticeship programs, and public/private training programs to serve as a linkage between employers and workers and ensure that green jobs are good jobs;
- Partnerships and coordinating mechanisms for all of the above.

Hopefully this meeting and this Report are just the beginning of what will be a long term commitment from the Obama/Biden Administration for green jobs in America!

Read the update from 2009 at the following link:
http://www.whitehouse.gov/assets/documents/Middle_Class_Task_Force_Green_Jobs_Update.pdf

***The Two-Year, Nine-Million-Jobs Investment: The 2030 Challenge Stimulus Plan***
Architecture 2030
http://www.architecture2030.org/downloads/2030stimulusplan.pdf

Architecture 2030, a non-profit organization based in New Mexico, was created by Ed Mazria, an internationally renowned architect in the green industry. Architecture 2030's mission is to rapidly transform the U.S. and global building sector from the major contributor of greenhouse gas emissions to a central part of the solution to the global-warming crisis. Their goal is to achieve a dramatic reduction in the global-warming-causing greenhouse gas (GHG) emissions of the building sector by changing the way buildings and developments are planned, designed and constructed.

Architecture 2030 is best known for The 2030 Challenge it developed. The 2030 Challenge recognizes the severity of the issues facing our planet around climate change, greenhouse gases, and energy use. The Challenge calls for the global architecture and building community to adopt the following targets:
- All new buildings, developments and major renovations shall be designed to meet a fossil fuel, GHG-emitting, energy consumption performance standard of 50% of the regional (or country) average for that building type.
- At a minimum, an equal amount of existing building area shall be renovated annually to meet a fossil fuel, GHG-emitting, energy consumption performance standard of 50% of the regional (or country) average for that building type.
- The fossil fuel reduction standard for all new buildings and major renovations shall be increased to: 60% in 2010, 70% in 2015, 80% in 2020, 90% in 2025 and carbon-neutral in 2030 (using no fossil fuel GHG emitting energy to operate).

These targets may be accomplished by implementing innovative sustainable design strategies, generating on-site renewable power and/or purchasing (20% maximum) renewable energy and/or certified renewable energy credits.

One of the latest projects Architecture 2030 has been working on is the development of a plan called the 2030 Challenge Stimulus Plan (Plan). It lays out how investments in the private building sector can not only create jobs, but also pay for itself in time, and create new revenue streams. This Plan has specific relevance to the green jobs and green economy movement that our country is currently involved in.

The plan begins by discussing why they have chosen to focus on the private building sector, rather than public infrastructure and the public building sector. Some of the reasons include:
1. The private building sector accounts for 93% of total U.S. building stock and impacts the entire U.S. economy. Building construction alone accounts for approximately 10% of the U.S. GDP. (These numbers were taken from the 2007 Building Energy Data Book published by the Energy Information Administration.)
2. The private building sector is currently in much more of a decline than public infrastructure and the public building sector.
3. The large amount of construction workers employed in every sector of the U.S. economy
4. The large tax base generated from new jobs as well as private investment and spending

The Plan essentially calls for a restructuring of the way we both renovate and construct private building stock, as well as the financial models we use for mortgages and depreciation rates based on the level of energy reduction targets set by the 2030 Challenge. The Plan calls for a 'housing mortgage interest rate buy-down' and a 'commercial building accelerated-depreciation program' to be started and funded. The idea is that the higher the target you meet, the more financial incentive there would be for the owner. This framework sets up a cycle where investment is made by the private sector to renovate and construct building stock, which then creates new jobs, as produces immediate revenue streams for our economy, protects our mortgage industry from failure, saves consumers money in the long run, and all while protecting the environment at the same time.

Residential buildings undergoing renovation or being newly constructed would have the opportunity for increased mortgage financing as well as lower mortgage rates should they meet the 2030 Challenge energy reduction targets. A residential building that is carbon neutral would get a significantly lower mortgage rate than a residential building that is only 30% less than code (based on IECC 2006 and ASHRAE 90.1-2004 code standards). For commercial buildings being renovated or newly constructed, there would be an opportunity to have an accelerated depreciation schedule should the building meet the energy reduction targets. A commercial building that is carbon neutral would get a significantly shorter depreciation period than a commercial building that is only 30% less than code (based on IECC 2006 and ASHRAE 90.1-2004 code standards).

The Report provides estimates on the number of jobs the Plan would create. Based on 1.25 million new and 2.1 million refinanced 30-year mortgages and 400 million square feet of new and 900 million square feet of renovated commercial building space each year, it is estimated that a total of 9,297,687 jobs would be created (includes 4.18 million direct jobs in the building sector, 4.81 million indirect and induced jobs, and 327,000 jobs from consumer spending). All projections and estimates are based on a two year plan. The Plan would cost approximately $192.47 billion ($96.235 billion each year for 2 years). These costs will be paid back in full each year through the new tax base from the jobs created as well as saving from reducing unemployment benefits. At the same time the Plan would "generate $1 trillion in direct, non-federal investment and spending while opening up a new $236 billion renovation market that could grow to $2.6 trillion by 2030, and over $5.47 trillion by 2069." The Plan would be easily implemented very quickly through existing federal programs, and would make very good use of the Stimulus money becoming available.

The Report ends by concluding that with a single investment in the Plan, "the U.S. can create millions of jobs, strengthen the U.S. economy, reduce CO2 emissions and energy consumption, and save consumers billions of dollars. Investing in the private building sector is the only investment that can accomplish all of these objectives."

***Multiply Your Stimulus Dollars: 14x Stimulus A Plan for State and Local Governments***
Architecture 2030, ICLEI – Local Governments for Sustainability, RESNET, and Veterans Green Jobs
http://www.architecture2030.org/downloads/14x_stimulus.pdf

Architecture 2030 has partnered with several other organizations (ICLEI – Local Governments for Sustainability, RESNET, and Veterans Green Jobs) to develop the 14x Stimulus Plan. The 14x Stimulus Plan is based on the national 2030 Stimulus Plan, but instead focuses on the state and local government level, rather than the federal level. The 14x Stimulus Plan proposes the following scenario: "What if there was a way for states, cities, and counties to leverage each $1 of federal stimulus money spent to generate $14 of private spending, create 14 times the number of jobs, reimburse the federal government $3, and get $1 back to boot? Well, there is a way, the '14x Stimulus' plan."

The idea here is the same as the 2030 Stimulus Plan, as the 14x Stimulus Plan proposes a way to simultaneously address energy and greenhouse gas issues while revitalizing the building industry from its current declining state. The 14x Stimulus Plan recommends that local and state stimulus money should be invested in a "local mortgage buy-down program that offers reduced mortgage interest rates contingent upon renovating or building to meet specific energy reduction targets." The idea is this – if an existing home or newly constructed home can meet one of the proposed targets for energy reduction (based on a HERS rating score and the IECC 2006 code standard) they would be able to take advantage of lower mortgage rates. Existing homes would also need to put in a minimum investment (specified in the 14x Stimulus Plan) in energy efficiency and renewable energy systems.

The investment in the private building sector generates large amounts of private spending as well as creates large amount of new jobs. The 14x Stimulus Plan also has many other benefits which include "reduced risk of mortgage failure, increasing home values, more disposable income for homeowners, jobs to those who will pay federal taxes, a new market for material and product manufacturers, and dramatically reduced home energy consumption and greenhouse gas emissions." This plan states that without a significant commitment to reviving the building construction industry, namely renovation and home building, we will not see any end in sight to the current economic downturn the U.S. is facing.

The beauty of the 14x Stimulus Plan is that it benefits everyone from the federal government to the local and state governments, as well as consumers and the planet. How many other investment opportunities are out there right now which can claim this high a rate of return? Local and state governments in the Washington, D.C. area should take a careful look at this type of initiative and determine which elements of the 14x Stimulus Plan make sense for us as part of our efforts to green the metro area.

## DC Publications with Implications for Green Jobs

There are several reports that have been released recently in Washington, D.C. that I feel have an impact on the creation of green jobs in D.C., so I wanted to highlight a few of them in an effort to show what some of the current barriers are, as well as suggestions for what can be done to show improvement. These are by no means the entirety of all the reports out there, but are ones that are essential that we understand the information contained in them. See page 56 of this Guide for a summary of the 'Green Collar Jobs Demand Analysis' report from the Washington, D.C. Economic Partnership.

### *Washington, D.C.'s 2008 Strategic Plan for Workforce Development*
DC Workforce Investment Council
http://www.dcchamber.org/clientuploads/WIC_StrategicPlan.pdf

For those who aren't aware, there is an organization called the DC Workforce Investment Council (DCWIC) which is a public-private partnership which provides information around workforce development in the District. They also provide training and education opportunities, and are tasked with developing strategies and publishing reports for workforce development in the District. One of the major reports that the DCWIC produces is the DC Strategic Plan for Workforce Development, which we will be summarizing briefly for the 2008 report.

The 2008 report, although not for the current year, is still a valuable resource to learn about some of the characteristics of the economy, the education and training of residents, and the types of jobs available in the District. Among these characteristics to keep in mind related to green job workforce development are:
- The economy in the D.C. Metro Area is predominantly an office based economy
- D.C. ranks highly nationally in the educational attainments of its workforce
- The D.C. Metro Area had the highest median household income of all metropolitan areas in the United States in 2006 - $78,978
- District residents who do not possess these high educational attainments have a harder time finding employment in the D.C. Metro Area than they would in other areas of the country
- In 2001, nearly 75,000 D.C. residents lacked a high school diploma, and 150,000 lacked basic literacy skills, which means D.C. has one of the lowest adult literacy rates in the country
- Competition is intense for jobs, and many applicants have high levels of educational training

I feel that all this is summed up very well in the Executive Summary of this Report, as follows:
"The result, as several recent reports have noted, is "A Tale of Two Cities," One group of residents is highly educated and benefits greatly from the metropolitan area's strong demand for such workers. The other group, with lower levels of education and skills, is too often excluded from the region's prosperity and find it difficult to obtain employment or family sustaining wages. The fact that most of the low-income workers struggling for fuller inclusion in the District's labor market are Black or Hispanic and live in Wards 7 and 8 suggests that it will be difficult for Washington, D.C. to overcome its history of segregation and polarization without substantial improvements in the employment opportunities for its less advantaged workers. This creates several sobering challenges for workforce development in the District of Columbia."

The Report next goes into some of the challenges that are faced in workforce development in the District of Columbia. The first discusses how D.C. has an extremely high percentage of jobs held by individuals with a BA, and a low percentage of jobs that are held by those with a high school degree or less.

Another challenge is that District residents have a difficult time competing with suburban residents and even those with college degrees for the less-skilled jobs in the District. Only about a third of the less-skilled workers in the District are District residents, while two-thirds are residents of the nearby suburban areas in Maryland and Virginia. The next challenge deals with the wages paid to less-skilled jobs. In general, these jobs have been found to not provide living wages to keep families above the low-income threshold (twice the poverty level). The Report provides this staggering statistic as well: Almost all low-income working families with children in the District are minority families (96 percent) and nearly two-thirds (64 percent) are headed by a single mother. The last challenge mentioned is that job growth projections for the District are much lower than those in the surrounding suburban areas in Maryland and Virginia.

Although a lot of the workforce development and job growth for D.C. looks grim on paper, there are still many opportunities in some industries such as the health, hospitality, banking, and construction industries. A lot of what it all comes down to, whether we are talking about green jobs or any other jobs, is a commitment from the local government to assist a large segment of its workforce to gain the education and skills needed to compete more successfully for the jobs that will arise in the District. This is where a comprehensive and well thought out strategy and plan for green jobs training in D.C. will be of the utmost importance.

After laying out the challenges that D.C. faces, the Report proceeds to show the DCWIC's vision for the next five years and beyond around workforce development. They are as follows:
1. Focuses on the youth in the District and attempts to increase the high school graduation rates, the percentage of high school graduates who are proficient in math and reading, connecting youth with D.C.'s university's early on, and provide Career Academies as an option for education and training.
2. Expand the availability of career pathways through education geared towards specific career paths, and which provide students with an industry recognized certification upon completion.
3. Provide a community college within the District to increase the postsecondary training capacity of the District
4. Help make it more feasible for residents to attend educational programs through assistance with financial aid and support services such as childcare and transportation.
5. Provide more integrated instruction that leads to employment and wage gains combined with basic skills programs. Basic skills programs without a specific focus on a career path aren't as successful.
6. Expand opportunities and programs for on the job training rather than just programs that provide in class training.
7. Connect customized training programs in the banking, construction, health, and hospitality industries with the projected job growth potential of these industries in the District.

8. Expand training for current workers to provide them with the knowledge and skills to keep up with the advances in technology and the global competition that is common these days.
9. Develop a Work Readiness Credential. This will show that an individual has the skills and knowledge to begin employment with a company. Too often, not having job-readiness skills keeps individuals from either finding a job, or from being able to hold a job.
10. Make the workforce investment system more integrated, more publicly known, and more cohesive so as to ensure the best success for all the related programs.

### *Sustainability Diagnosis for the Washington, D.C. Zoning Review*
Clarion Associates and Farr Associates
https://www.communicationsmgr.com/projects/1355/docs/Diagnosis%20Draft%2017.pdf

In November, 2008 the DC Office of Planning contracted 2 of the leading sustainable land planning companies in the country (Clarion Associates and Farr Associates) to perform a Zoning Review of current D.C. codes and initiatives in relation to the overall sustainability of the District. When the District of Columbia undergoes its next zoning ordinance update, it wants to make sure that sustainability is embedded in the zoning codes. A Sustainability Working Group has been created that is tasked with determining the necessary steps to do so. The report is intended to be used as a resource for the Sustainability Working Group during this process.

The report breaks down its analysis and recommendations into seven categories, which are:
• Climate Change
• Energy Conservation and Renewable Energy Production
• Integrating Land Use and Mobility
• Water Conservation and Greywater
• Slopes, Streams, Stormwater, and Hydrology
• Food Production/Security and Community Health
• Sustainable Businesses and "Green Jobs"

While much of the Report discusses other topics besides green jobs, Chapter 8 of the report specifically focuses on Sustainable Businesses and "Green" Jobs. Even the parts of the Report that do not reference green jobs, are still relevant to the green jobs discussion though because when discussing the sustainability of a city, all these different topics are interrelated and need to be looked at comprehensively. It is noted in the Report that to be successful, there will need to be a strong commitment from different District government agencies to work together on key issues, and it will take more than just having codes and regulations in place to enhance the sustainability of the District.

The section of the Report that discusses Sustainable Businesses and "Green" Jobs begins with some background information on what the current state of awareness is and potential for sustainable businesses and green jobs. It provides a working definition for both the terms sustainable business and green job. For the purposes of this Report, a sustainable business is a business whose products and/or services directly improve the environment, or businesses that provide green collar jobs. Green jobs are defined as career-track employment opportunities in emerging environmental industries as well as conventional businesses and trades, created by a shift to more sustainable practices, materials, and performance. The definition includes both lower and higher skilled employment opportunities that minimize the carbon footprint of all necessary inputs and directly result in the restoration of the environment, the generation of clean energy and improved energy efficiency, the creation of high performing buildings, and the conservation of natural resources.

The DC Green Building Act of 2006 is highlighted as one initiative that has great potential for creating green jobs in the District. D.C. has a high unemployment rate, and green collar jobs provide an opportunity for those who traditionally have employment barriers to find gainful employment and career paths. Green jobs could possibly help make D.C.'s industrial zones thrive and altering the zoning codes to provide assistance and incentives to green jobs and business could be one way to attract more of these to the District. Specific industries mentioned that have a high potential for green jobs in D.C. are Green Building construction, energy conservation, and renewable energy (primarily solar and biodiesel), environmental restoration, and storm water management.

While there isn't currently a comprehensive plan in D.C. for green jobs and sustainable businesses, there are many programs and incentives in place that could help grow these industries in the city. These programs and incentives include:
• Green Collar Job Initiative
• The Clean and Affordable Energy Act of 2007
• The Sustainable Business Network of Washington (SBNOW)
• The D.C. Energy Conservation Code
• The Tax Incentive Assistance Project (TIAP)
• D.C. Small Business Energy Efficiency Program
• District of Columbia Public Service Commission: Net metering
• The DDOE's River Smart Homes
• The District of Columbia Renewable Energy Demonstration Project (REDP)

After analyzing the existing D.C. Zoning Ordinance, the Report makes several recommendations as to how to increase the number of sustainable businesses and green jobs in the District. These include defining "green collar job", "sustainable and/or green business", and "eco-industrial" in the zoning ordinance, creating separate zoning districts for eco-industrial and green/sustainable industrial, permitting smaller recycling facilities in commercial districts and green and sustainable businesses in commercial and industrial zoning areas, and providing FAR bonuses for the dismantling of buildings relevant to the amount of waste diverted from landfills.

# Good Jobs, Green Jobs Conference in Washington, D.C. 2012

Within just five years of the first 'Good Jobs, Green Jobs' convergence in Pittsburgh, this annual forum has become one of the most premier green jobs conferences in the country. The conference draws thousands of union, environmental, business and elected leaders seeking to build upon a growing green economy while tackling pressing environmental issues. The BlueGreen Alliance Foundation hosts the conference each year, serving as a research-oriented non-profit group that aims to inform the public about developing solutions to environmental challenges that also create economic opportunities. The Foundation is also part of the larger, national BlueGreen Alliance, which partners with labor unions and environmental organizations to expand and improve the green jobs market.

In past years, this conference was held in one location. This year, the conference will be held in four different locations: Atlanta, Los Angeles, Philadelphia and Detroit, and is designed to focus the conversation at the local level. Topics scheduled to be discussed at the conferences will center on the following categories:

1. Infrastructure and Cleaner, More Efficient Transportation
2. Responsible Investment
3. Regional, State and Local Initiatives and Partnerships
4. Workforce and Economic Development
5. Clean Energy Manufacturing
6. Emerging Green Sectors
7. Business, Investment and New Markets
8. Renewable Energy and Energy Efficiency
9. Youth, Education and Green Schools - Building a Clean Energy Movement

At the 2011 Conference, many of the workshops voiced the importance of reinforcing work training and development programs that have proven to be successful. The theme of the conference also focused on the interaction between local, private sector and government interests. The workshops and plenary speakers strongly advocated for a strengthened grassroots movement, market opportunities for clean energy technology, and government-led research and policy change, all of which depend on one another. Keynote speakers included EPA Administrator Lisa Jackson, Director of the National Economic Council Gene Sperling, and Secretary of Transportation Ray LaHood.

After two days of workshops, plenary panels and keynote speakers, the 'Good Jobs, Green Jobs' Conference culminated in Green Jobs Advocacy Day. Also organized by the BlueGreen Alliance, the 2011 Green Jobs Advocacy Day gathered hundreds of labor union, environmental advocacy and trade organization representatives to lobby their delegates in Congress to take action on the demand for a green economy. Participants attended meetings at House and Senate office buildings, armed with copies of a report, titled *Invest in a Prosperous and Healthy America*. The report summarized the policies necessary to expand green jobs, develop efficient transportation infrastructure, and protect the health of communities and workplaces. The report can be downloaded for free here: www.bluegreenalliance.org/advocacy_day/resources?id=0007

The 'Good Jobs, Green Jobs' Conference is an especially useful resource for green job seekers mainly due to the participation of various green economy stakeholders. Stakeholder companies and organizations register as Conference Conveners, effectively representing groups ranging from academic institutions and community organizations to advocacy organizations and businesses. Conveners gain mass visibility of conference attendees, while contributing to promotional efforts of the overall Conference. At this year's conference, over 200 Conveners registered to promote the event and lend membership support. Here are just a few examples of key Convener organizations that participated in 2011:

**The BlueGreen Alliance** is the primary host and presenter of the 'Good Jobs, Green Jobs' conference every year. The BlueGreen Alliance was initially created in 2006 as a collaborative effort between the United Steelworkers and the Sierra Club. Now including groups such as the Natural Resources Defense Council (NRDC), Union of Concerned Scientists (UCS) and American Federation of Teachers (AFT), the Alliance merges union and environmental interests and strives for greater, better jobs in the green economy. Find out more about the BlueGreen Alliance here: www.bluegreenalliance.org

**The American Federation of Labor and Congress of Industrial Organizations (AFL-CIO)** is an alliance of over 50 national and international labor unions. Its community affiliate, Working America, utilizes research, education, lobbying, and community organizing to voice the needs of the working population and create tangible political change in favor of people over corporate special interests. Executive Vice President Arlene Holt Baker provided the opening remarks to a plenary panel on sustainable communities at this year's 'Good Jobs, Green Jobs' Conference. Learn more about America's union movement at www.aflcio.org.

**The Center for American Progress** is a DC based think tank committed to policy development and analysis. Founded in 2003, CAP aims to shape national debate with its progressive policy stances that value economic mobility, diversity, and quality of life. CAP President and CEO John Podesta moderated the first plenary panel of the conference, titled "Clean Energy Economy: Manufacture It. Improve It. Invest in It." The panel discussed the need for a clean energy agenda that builds energy efficient homes and offices, redesigns the electricity grid for smart renewable energy production, and facilitates domestic clean energy technology innovation. More information on CAP can be found at www.americanprogress.org.

These groups, in addition to over 200 others, represent a coalition of organizations across the country that promote and prioritize the green economy objective and expansion of the green jobs market. If you would like more information on past or upcoming 'Good Jobs, Green Jobs' conferences, visit the conference webpage at www.greenjobsconference.org.

# The Green DC Agenda and Sustainable DC
## By: Dan Triman

The Mayor Fenty administration set the District government in motion related to sustainability initiatives for the city, the largest of which was the Green DC Agenda, launched on Earth Day of 2009. Mayor Gray and his administration have expanded upon these efforts with the recent launch of the Sustainable DC Initiative in March of 2012. Both of these initiatives involve strong partnerships from District agencies such as the District Department of the Environment (DDOE) and the Office of Planning, and set goals for the city in various categories related to sustainability. The Green DC Agenda Initiative and the Sustainable DC Initiative mark the largest comprehensive effort from the District government in recent time to green the city and its operations.

## Green DC Agenda

Realizing the importance and responsibility of the role the District plays as a leader for our nation, Fenty listed combating climate change, conserving energy and water, preserving land and habitat, and promoting public transportation, and community redevelopment as the major environmental challenges of 2009. Following the mayoral turnover in 2010, the Green DC Agenda has continued to meet goals and create new initiatives across these issue areas under direction of the DDOE. The goal of the Green DC Agenda: To make the District one of the world's most sustainable cities, through cleaner, swimmable rivers; healthier air indoors and out; more beautiful streets, parks, and school grounds; and a vibrant, competitive economy.

The DDOE has had a major role in taking the lead in creating the Green DC Agenda. Developing the Green DC Agenda involved discussions and coordination with every one of the District government's agencies and departments. Through this dialogue, the DDOE has been able to lay out a detailed plan, which lists the most critical green initiatives, or Agenda Items, along with the responsible agency for managing each, and a timeline for completion. There are currently well over 200 Agenda Items listed at http://ddoe.dc.gov/service/green-dc-agenda-items. The categories that the Agenda items are broken out into are Air, Development, Education, Energy, Food, Green Space, Toxics, Transit, Waste, and Water.

The Green DC Agenda includes seven themes (a. Homes, b. Schools, c. Neighborhoods and Communities, d. Parks and Natural Space, e. Transportation and Mobility, f. Business, Jobs and Economic Development, and g. City and Government Operations) and two spotlights (a. Climate Change, and b. Anacostia River). For each of these themes and spotlights, the website provides information on the Vision (imagining what the ideal scenario looks like), the Key Agenda Commitments (specific action items that will get us where we want to be), and Current Success (existing programs and initiatives already underway that are providing green benefits to the city).

The District is also asking its residents to take the Green Pledge as part of the Green DC Agenda. This involves agreeing to specific green lifestyle changes such as planting a tree at your house, bringing lunch from home more often, and taking public transportation, walking, or biking at least once a week. Other features of the Green DC Agenda include the ability to make suggestions or comments to the District about the Agenda, and live chats with DDOE Director Christophe A.G. Tulou.

## Sustainable DC

In July of 2011, Mayor Gray announced that DC would undertake an ambitious initiative to create a comprehensive Sustainability Strategy for the District. The vision for the Sustainable DC initiative is "In just one generation - 20 years - the District of Columbia will be the healthiest, greenest, and most livable city in the United States. An international destination for people and investment, the District will be a model of innovative policies and practices that improve quality of life and economic opportunity. We will demonstrate how enhancing our natural and built environments, investing in a diverse clean economy, and reducing disparities among residents can create an educated, equitable and prosperous society."

The efforts led by the DC Office of Planning (OP) in partnership with the District Department of the Environment (DDOE), resulted in setting the framework for the District's quest to become the most sustainable city in the country. The District's sustainability plan resulting from this initiative sets clear indicators to achieve these goals and tie implementation directly to responsible parties, work plans and budgets with clear timelines. The official plan was released on April 24th, 2012 by Mayor Gray and is titled "A Vision for A Sustainable DC". The plan can be viewed here: http://sustainable.dc.gov/sites/default/files/dc/sites/sustainable/publication/attachments/sustainable%20DC%20Vision%20Plan%202.2.pdf.

The initiative kicked off with "Sustainable September," where the District invited active collaboration by residents, business owners and others to help develop a vision for sustainability. On the main Sustainable DC website, several resources were made available including a discussion guide which outlines an agenda for community meetings to discuss the issues in the Sustainable DC initiative, a calendar of events, and a place where you can submit your thoughts or comments to the initiatives' organizers. Mayor Gray launched nine different public working groups that examined best practices, existing conditions, and public comments. Over 700 people participated in the working groups throughout the winter of 2011 and 2012. The nine working groups led to the nine topics covered in the "A Vision for Sustainable DC" document as follows:
- **Built Environment**: Building and infrastructure relationships to transportation, energy, and water
- **Climate**: Gas emissions reductions and adaptation to a changing climate
- **Energy**: Energy use, generation, efficiency, providers, and financing issues
- **Food**: Local food production, distribution, access, security, and community benefits
- **Nature**: Natural systems, parks, habitat, biodiversity, and wildlife
- **Transportation**: Transportation systems, infrastructure, modes, efficiencies, access, and delivery
- **Waste**: Waste recycling, reuse, hauling and collection, composting, and waste to energy
- **Water**: Watershed protection, storm water management, water quality and reuse, and sewers
- **Green Economy**: Job creation, economic development, and local business development

Each of the nine working groups consistently mentioned the need to provide particular focus on community health and education, social equity between all Wards and economic opportunity to create green and sustainable jobs. There will be another round of public comment and meetings as the District government determines the final budget for these initiatives, as well as finalizes and begins to implement the strategies required to meet the goals listed in the "A Vision for Sustainable DC" document.

The major goals listed in the "A Vision for Sustainable DC" document are as follows:
1) **Jobs:** Increase by 5 times the number of jobs providing green goods and services
2) **Health:** Cut citywide obesity rate by 50%
3) **Built Environment:** Attract and retain 250,000 new and existing residents
4) **Climate:** Cut citywide greenhouse gas emissions by 50%
5) **Energy:** Cut citywide energy consumption by 50%; Increase use of renewable energy to 50%
6) **Food:** Bring locally-grown food within a quarter mile of 75% of the population
7) **Nature:** Cover 40% of the District with a healthy tree canopy: Ensure 100% of residents are within a 10-minute walk of a natural space
8) **Transportation:** Make 75% of all trips by walking, biking, or transit

9) **Waste:** Achieve zero waste by consuming less and reusing everything else
10) **Water:** Make 100% of District waterways fishable and swimmable; Use 75% of our landscape to filter or capture rainwater for reuse
11) **Green Economy:** Develop 3 times as many small District-based businesses; Cut city-wide unemployment by 50%

With all of the recent attention and buzz in DC around sustainability and greening the city, there should be significant opportunities for both individuals and groups already involved in green industries, as well as individuals and groups interested in getting involved in these initiatives. With various stakeholders in DC, including the public and private sectors, as well as community groups, and residents all working together towards a similar vision for the city, the District appears to be on track to become a national as well as international leader in sustainability. To stay informed of all of the latest developments related to the Sustainable DC initiative visit the main website at http://sustainable.dc.gov.

# Washington, D.C. at the Forefront of Green Jobs Research
## By: Andi Joseph

There is an emerging trend gaining momentum across America: the green movement. From pop culture to business practices to everyday life, "green" has become a familiar word in our vocabulary. The District of Columbia is helping shape the sustainability movement through legislation, greener building codes, and the private and public sector's adoption of greener practices. In fact, DC is a national leader in green building; the city has more existing and planned LEED-certified buildings than any other city in America.

The Washington, DC Economic Partnership (WDCEP) became engaged in DC's green movement through involvement in the Green Collar Jobs Demand Analysis, an initiative that resulted from an effort by the District of Columbia to analyze DC's demand for green jobs. Together with the DC Office of Planning and the Department of Employment Services, the WDCEP undertook the Green Collar Jobs Demand Analysis initiative ("the Initiative") in the spring of 2008. The Initiative was prepared by a team that included The Louis Berger Group, Inc., ESOP Advisors, Inc., and the Green Builders Council of DC with Momentum Analysis. It is one of the first comprehensive studies of its kind to be completed in the United States.

The purpose of the Initiative was to estimate the number of potential green collar job opportunities generated from Washington, DC's green policies or laws from 2009 through 2018, and to identify barriers, opportunities and best practices from around the country. The lack of a nationally recognized definition of a green job/ green collar job (the District uses both terms interchangeably) is a good example of how ambiguous this concept still is for both experts in the field and for the population at large.

For the purposes of the Green Collar Jobs Demand Analysis, green collar jobs are career-track employment opportunities in emerging environmental industries as well as conventional businesses and trades, created by a shift to more sustainable practices, materials, and performance. A green collar job includes both lower and higher skilled employment opportunities that minimize the carbon footprint of all inputs necessary and directly results in the restoration of the environment, generation of clean energy and improved energy efficiency, creation of high performance buildings, and conservation of natural resources.

The Initiative quantified the job demand generated by the District's Green Building Act, Clean and Affordable Energy Act and other green policy interventions, and has listed job categories, skills and education requirements for green jobs. DC's green collar jobs were forecasted for the current, two, five and ten year periods. The District could currently count approximately 22,280 jobs as green (this is a little more than three percent of the 702,000 jobs in DC), and from 2009 to 2018, as many as 169,000 green jobs could result from the District's green initiatives. It should be noted that in most cases, the green collar jobs captured in the Green Collar Jobs Demand Analysis are existing jobs with new skill requirements. The Initiative's findings assert a key message to District policymakers and the business community: DC must prepare its workforce with the skills necessary for green employment.

To ensure that future workforce development initiatives focus in the appropriate areas to take advantage of green collar jobs, the Green Collar Jobs Demand Analysis analyzed which industries contain the greatest opportunities across the District. The Initiative identified that within DC, construction, architecture, engineering and federal government are among the largest industries in which green collar jobs are found.

I. Introduction to Green Jobs and Green Careers

In order to better understand nationwide trends, best practices from across America were researched. Particular attention was given to the impact green agendas have had on labor demand in other US cities. To gain a local perspective, focus groups of individuals employed within the District were conducted to identify attitudes, needs and plans related to green collar jobs.

The Green Collar Jobs Demand Analysis has provided the foundation through which Washington can develop a comprehensive plan to address the need for green workforce development. Mayor Vincent Gray's executive plan for jobs and economic development in DC includes the institution of the District Green Initiative (DGI) and a Sustainability Energy Utility (SEU), both of which will create green jobs and support continued growth of an urban green economy. The DGI initiative focuses specifically on creating green jobs in parts of the District that often lack economic opportunity. Despite the economy's downturn in the wake of the completion of the Initiative, support at the both the national and local level for green projects strengthens the prospect that green employment will continue to be a catalyst for economic growth, both in the District of Columbia and across America.

*Andi Joseph, MSc, originally from Oregon, moved to Washington, D.C. in 2007. As Director of Research & Communications at WDCEP, Andi had the opportunity to become involved in DC's green scene through management of the Green Collar Jobs Demand Analysis.*

# Washington, D.C. Green Collar Jobs Demand Analysis
## By: Dan Triman

The previous article from Andi Joseph provides an introduction to the 2008 District of Columbia Green Collar Jobs Demand Analysis (Report) conducted by The Louis Berger Group, Inc., ESOP Advisors, Inc., and the Green Builders Council of DC with Momentum Analysis. Andi's article mentions the background information for the Report as well as some of the key findings. The following article is intended to provide further detail about the Report and what this suggests for green jobs in Washington, D.C. **All statistics, tables, and graphs within this article come directly from the Report**. I encourage everyone to take a look at the entire Report, which is available on the Washington, DC Economic Partnership (WDCEP) website at
http://www.wdcep.com/pdf/pubs/dc_green_jobs_report09.pdf.

The Report is one of the first of its kind in the country, and it focuses solely on the District of Columbia, not on the surrounding metropolitan region. Though the Report does provide a good basis from which to begin the discussion about green jobs in Washington D.C., the data included in the Report only provides estimates and projections, as well as recommendations, and more analyses should be conducted. It is clear that there are a number of existing green jobs in D.C., and there is potential for more green jobs to emerge in the near future. How this happens, and to what degree we are able to involve all parties in the District in this initiative is what needs to be determined. There needs to be short term as well as long term implementation of policies, funding for training, and development of green career skills for workers, as well as clearly identifying the projects, and businesses and organizations that can employ green job workers.

The District is interested in green collar jobs that will help create employment opportunities as well as promote a sustainable local economy. The District also recognizes the national trends towards green industries and jobs and would like to take advantage of the opportunities presented by these trends. A particular emphasis was placed on green collar jobs that wouldn't require high level training and would provide employment for individuals who have been traditionally considered hard to employ. The Report based its findings on several types of information including current D.C. government green policies or legislation, major real estate development projects, government capital investments, proposed green initiatives, and several focus groups of various groups with specific knowledge relevant to green collar jobs. The Report uses the terms "green job" and "green collar job" interchangeably.

The Report looks at the projections for green jobs in D.C. for the next several years ending in 2018. The first step in the process of determining what the forecast looks like for green jobs in Washington, D.C. is to set the context of the green jobs discussion through an investigation into the current status of various issues in Washington, D.C. If we don't know where we currently stand in regards to these topics and haven't identifies the key assets and barriers our city faces, we can't accurately predict which direction we need to head in the future. Among the issues that need to be clearly understood are: current workforce development programs, current strategies for economic development, unemployment rates and unemployment population demographics, educational and research institution resources, environmental assets and problems, existing health problems, supply chains for life essentials such as food and water, the city's built environment and infrastructure, existing business industries, green initiatives that have already begun in the city, existing green jobs, political leadership, and strategic public/private partnerships.

There are some important aspects of Washington, D.C. that should guide the planning for green jobs in the city. These are as follows:

I. Introduction to Green Jobs and Green Careers

- The economy is currently struggling both locally and nationally
- D.C. has the highest number of combined LEED registered or certified buildings in the nation
- There exists a large base of colleges, universities, and training centers in D.C.
- There is a large federal government presence in D.C.
- A significant amount of the building stock is older buildings
- D.C.'s rivers and streams are highly polluted and in need of major cleanup efforts and protection
- There is a high rate of alternative transportation in D.C. (biking, walking, public transit, etc.)
- D.C. does not have a large manufacturing industry base
- There are a lot of small businesses, as well as international and national organizations and businesses in D.C.
- There isn't currently much land being used for agricultural purposes in D.C. for food production
- Utility rates are increasing significantly
- D.C. has a wealth of experts in the green industry
- D.C. has high prevalence rates for health problems such as asthma
- The American Recovery and Reinvestment Act of 2009 contains provisions for new transit investments, weatherization of homes and offices, and the green retro-fit of Federal buildings, among other job creating provisions

## Existing Green Jobs in D.C.

Although there currently isn't an easy way to determine which jobs in the District would be classified as "green", Berger identified specific criteria by which jobs could be categorized as green for the purposes of the Report. Because of the high degree of subjectivity involved in the classification process, jobs were classified as either "green" or "possibly green" based on the degree of confidence with which a categorization was made. Berger underwent an investigation of the major industries and jobs in the District. They created a database of current green jobs to track the number of green jobs in the District, and provided a tool with which to continue to track green jobs in the District in the upcoming years. The investigation focused on 82 industries, which together account for 75 percent of the District's employment. The green jobs database allows users to estimate green employment in 301 industries (including government) based on the industry's size, occupational composition and other available industry-specific data.

In accordance with data from 2008, the Report estimated a total of 22,283 "green" jobs and another 3,167 "possibly green" jobs in the District. Adding these together, these jobs accounted for 25,450 total jobs, a little over 3% of the 702,000 jobs in the District at the time. The rationale underlying Berger's classification differs from industry to industry. The Report provides the following examples of green industries in D.C. to give an idea of the types of jobs that were classified as "green" and "possibly green":

Construction Industry – 5,491 "green" jobs (4,757 in architecture and engineering)
Federal Government – more than 5,300 "green" jobs (based on agencies mission, such as EPA)
District Government - 300 "green" jobs (Department of Public Works, the District Department of the Environment and the Department of Parks and Recreation)
Environmental, conservation and wildlife organizations - 1,672 "green" jobs
Loan officers at banks offering Energy Efficient Mortgages – 13 "green" jobs
Jobs repairing, selling or renting bicycles – 51 "green" jobs
Restaurant Industry – 506 "possibly green" jobs (based on assuming that 2% of all full-service and limited service restaurants adhere to sustainable practices)
Office-based green businesses – 5% "possibly green" jobs since no firm data currently exists. However, the District is currently compiling a list of green office-based businesses (e.g., service sector enterprises such as accounting, legal, real estate and marketing)

## Unemployment Data

The Report analyzed D.C. Department of Employment Services (DOES) data to get an idea of the rate and demographics of the unemployed population. The DOES data shows the following key statistics:

- 22,200 persons, or 6.4 percent of the District's labor force, were unemployed in June 2008
- About one out of every four unemployed in the District does not have a high school degree
- Persons 25 and younger account for 31 percent of the District's total unemployed, 11 percent in the 41 to 45 age group and 10 percent in the 31 to 35 age group
- About 39 percent of the District's unemployed have not worked in the past year, 14 percent of which have not worked in the past five years.

Specific populations of unemployed individuals were identified by Berger to possess skills which should be easily transferable to green jobs and these include those who were employed in the following occupations: 1) Building and grounds maintenance, 2) Installation, maintenance, and repair, 3) Production, transportation and material moving and construction.

## Major D.C. Green Initiatives

The Report analyzes several of the District's current green initiatives to determine what the green job potential is for each of these initiatives. This doesn't mean that these are the only initiatives that will create green jobs in the District, but because they are either already in place, or well defined they allow for a reasonable projection of what their effect will be in the next ten years. Below is a list of the District's major green initiatives that the Report analyzed and it shows the investments in these initiatives and the corresponding estimated # of green jobs created by each. All job projection estimates listed in the summaries were based on the "Conservative Scenario" which falls between the "Aggressive Scenario" and the "Pessimistic Scenario".

District of Columbia's Green Building Act of 2006
It established a phased approach (over several years) for high-performance building standards for the planning, design, construction, operation and maintenance of building projects. Established incentives for green building, such as expedited permitting and created a Green Building Fund and the Green Building Advisory Council. The Act requires commercial buildings to be certified, using the Leadership in Energy and Environmental Design TM (LEED) Green Building Rating System (http://www.usgbc.org), and residential buildings to meet Green Communities standards (http://www.greencommunitiesonline.org). Berger estimates this initiative will generate a labor demand for 121,200 workers and an additional 9,200 workers to operate maintain the newly constructed and retrofitted facilities from 2009 to 2018.

*Green Building Act Investments and Labor Estimates* [1]

| Total Green Building Projects | | |
|---|---|---|
| Scenario | Investment Amount *(in millions)* | Total Labor Requirements *(in person years)* |
| Aggressive | $21,057.6 | 149,429 |
| Conservative | $17,055.3 | 121,177 |
| Pessimistic | $15,054.1 | 107,051 |

---

[1] The Louis Berger Group, Inc. in association with ESOP Advisors, Inc. and Green Builders Council, DC/Momentum Analysis. "District of Columbia Green Collar Jobs Demand Analysis Final Report." - WDCEP research homepage. September 2008. 29 pp. Washington, D.C. Economic Partnership and the Washington, D.C. Office of Planning. 03/24/09 <http://www.wdcep.com/pdf/pubs/dc_green_jobs_report09.pdf >.

Clean and Affordable Energy Act of 2008

This authorizes the creation of a Sustainable Energy Utility (SEU), which will conduct sustainable energy programs. It also creates a non-lapsing Sustainable Energy Trust Fund to provide funding for this and other programs related to energy efficiency and renewable energy. It authorizes public spending, and should spur increased private spending in the economy by establishing benchmarking requirements for public and private buildings, increasing the solar energy requirement for electrical providers and allowing energy sub metering for commercial tenants. Within this initiative is a proposed energy audit program which encourages the seller of a residence to provide potential buyers with estimates of energy use by the residence. Berger estimates this initiative will generate a labor demand for 11,800 workers and 300 energy inspectors from 2009 to 2018.

*Clean and Affordable Energy Act Investments and Labor Estimates* [2]

| Scenario | Investment Amount (in millions) | Total Labor Requirements (in person years) | Average Annual Labor Requirements | Duration of Initiative (in years) |
|---|---|---|---|---|
| Aggressive | $33.6 | 198 | 40 | 5 |
| Conservative | $24.0 | 165 | 33 | 5 |
| Pessimistic | $14.4 | 132 | 26 | 5 |

District Department of Transportation (DDOT) Transit Infrastructure Projects

DDOT in coordination with other District departments is implementing numerous environmentally focused projects that will result in green collar jobs in the occupational categories of design, construction and maintenance. The projects that are either planned or currently in construction include: a Low Impact Development (LID) program which focuses on installation of storm water infrastructure improvements, including installation of storm water Best Management Practices throughout the District; numerous streetscape improvements; the Anacostia Demonstration Streetcar Project; and the retrofitting of school buses. Berger estimates that the DDOT's initiatives will generate a labor demand for 10,300 workers from 2009 to 2018.

*DDOT Transit Infrastructure Project Investments and Labor Estimates* [3]

| Scenario | Total Investment (in millions) | Total Labor Requirements (in person years) | Average Jobs per Working Year | Years of Work |
|---|---|---|---|---|
| Aggressive | $1,950.4 | 12,833 | 1,283 | 10 |
| Conservative | $1,560.5 | 10,267 | 1,027 | 10 |
| Pessimistic | $1,365.5 | 8,984 | 898 | 10 |

Wastewater and Water Treatment Infrastructure Improvements

The DC Water and Sewer Authority (WASA) is investing in several new projects as part of its overall Capital Improvement Plan (CIP). The major projects that are believed to create green jobs are the Combined Sewer Overflow Control Plan (CSOCP), to alleviate the existing problems caused when the District has a significant rain storm, and constructing new digester facilities for wastewater treatment which will reduce energy usage and help manage biosolids. Berger estimates this initiative will generate a labor demand for 1,500 workers from 2009 to 2018.

---

[2] Ibid., 24

[3] Ibid., 60

*WASA Project Investments and Labor Estimates[4]*

| Scenario | Total Investment *(in millions)* | Total Labor Requirements *(in person years)* | Average Jobs per Working Year | Years of Work |
|---|---|---|---|---|
| Aggressive | $308.0 | 1,872 | 374 | 5 |
| Conservative | $246.4 | 1,498 | 299 | 5 |
| Pessimistic | $215.6 | 1,310 | 262 | 5 |

### Proposed Photovoltaic Solar Trees Parking Lots Initiative

The District has a proposed initiative to install solar panels on parking lots throughout the District, serving the dual purpose of creating small scale clean energy farms and providing shade for parked cars. This would also provide an effective method for creating a highly visible display of D.C.'s commitment to creating a greener economy. The initiative would also use the solar panel installations to supply 1,380 homes with solar energy indefinitely. Berger estimates this initiative will generate a labor demand for 440 workers from 2009 to 2010.

*Solar Tree Investments and Labor Estimates[5]*

| Scenario | Total Investment *(in millions)* | Total Labor Requirements *(in person years)* | Average Jobs per Working Year | Years of Work *(in years)* |
|---|---|---|---|---|
| Pessimistic | $28 | 140 | 140 | 1 |
| Conservative | $88 | 440 | 220 | 2 |
| Meeting CAEA ("carve out") Requirements | $257 | 1,286 | 321 | 4 |
| Aggressive | $420 | 2,100 | 525 | 4 |

### Proposed Green Roof Program Initiative

The District has made a strong commitment to increasing the number of Green Roofs in D.C. over the past few years, and continuing these initiatives would potentially create green jobs in the District. The assumptions for generating the labor demand estimates were based in part on the study *REGREENING WASHINGTON, DC: A Green Roof Vision Based on Quantifying Storm Water and Air Quality Benefits* produced by the Casey Trees Endowment Fund and Limno-Tech Inc. in August 2005. (http://www.greenroofs.org/resources/greenroofvisionfordc.pdf). Berger estimates that this initiative will generate a labor demand for 11,800 workers from 2009 to 2018.

*Green Roof Investments and Labor Estimates[6]*

| Scenario | | Total Investment *(in millions)* | Total Labor Requirements *(in person years)* | Average Number of Jobs per Working Year | Years of Work |
|---|---|---|---|---|---|
| Pessimistic | Case 2 | $299.9 | 5,895 | 590 | 10 |
| Conservative | Case 3 | $599.8 | 11,791 | 1,179 | 10 |
| Aggressive | Case 4 | $899.6 | 17,686 | 1,769 | 10 |

### Watershed Restoration Projects Initiative

The Report points out that the District is conducting some of the most comprehensive watershed restoration projects in the country. These projects include the restoration of the following watersheds:

---

[4] Ibid., 61

[5] Ibid., 53

[6] Ibid., 63

I. Introduction to Green Jobs and Green Careers

Watts Branch, Pope Branch and Anacostia River. No specific projections on green jobs created from this initiative were listed in the Report.

Green Summer Jobs Corps Initiative
The Report states that the District has one of the first and largest municipal green youth employment programs in the country, called the Green Summer Job Corps. It was started in 2008 by Mayor Fenty and provided green summer jobs for nearly 400 youth between the ages of 14 and 21 in its first year.

## Green Jobs Forecast

The estimate of total aggregate employment demand per year attributable to District green initiatives and proposals begins at about 23,931 annual job opportunities in 2009, gradually decreases to a low in the 10 year study period of 3,600 in year 2016, and then begins to increase again. The District of Columbia government's existing policies and legislation and proposed initiatives identified in the Report could produce over 169,000 job opportunities between 2009 and 2018. Keep in mind that this may change due to a variety of factors in the economy, government regulations, schedules for rolling out initiatives, and development trends.

*Employment Demand Estimates for Green Initiatives (Based on "Conservative Scenario")* [7]

| DC Green Initiative or Proposal | 2009 | 2010 | 2011 | 2012 | 2013 | 2014 | 2015 | 2016 | 2017 | 2018 | Total Labor Required |
|---|---|---|---|---|---|---|---|---|---|---|---|
| Green Building Act of 2006 -DHCD Projects | 125 | 120 | 120 | 120 | 120 | 120 | 0 | 0 | 0 | 0 | 725 |
| Green Building Act of 2006 -Market Response | 10,849 | 6,147 | 2,151 | 1,522 | 873 | 108 | 108 | 108 | 108 | 108 | 22,080 |
| Green Building Act of 2006 -Required Public | 5,910 | 6,362 | 6,037 | 5,723 | 5,337 | 4,697 | 2,351 | 1,470 | 1,545 | 1,586 | 41,018 |
| Green Building Act of 2006 -Required Private | 4,881 | 7,564 | 9,466 | 9,634 | 8,875 | 7,074 | 4,963 | 642 | 2,045 | 2,221 | 57,355 |
| Green Building Operations | 18 | 165 | 423 | 634 | 837 | 1,011 | 1,232 | 1,600 | 1,637 | 1,637 | 9,194 |
| Energy Act of 2008-Benchmarking | 0 | 4,598 | 2,904 | 2,205 | 2,608 | 780 | 242 | 67 | 27 | 13 | 13,444 |
| Energy Act of 2008-Solar Energy Legal Requirement | 27 | 31 | 43 | 99 | 99 | 100 | 137 | 140 | 141 | 176 | 992 |
| Energy Act of 2008-Submetering | 44 | 44 | 33 | 33 | 22 | 22 | 11 | 11 | 0 | 0 | 219 |
| Energy Act of 2008-Sustainable Energy Utility Retrofits | 0 | 16 | 31 | 36 | 41 | 41 | 0 | 0 | 0 | 0 | 165 |
| DOT Infrastructure Projects | 695 | 640 | 1,329 | 2,507 | 1,919 | 1,919 | 1,210 | 16 | 16 | 16 | 10,267 |
| Waste Water and Water Treatment Infrastructure | 0 | 14 | 367 | 377 | 377 | 376 | 0 | 0 | 0 | 0 | 1,512 |
| Solar Tree Parking Lot Initiative | 220 | 220 | 0 | 0 | 0 | 0 | 0 | 0 | 0 | 0 | 440 |
| Green Roofs Initiative | 1,179 | 1,179 | 1,179 | 1,179 | 1,179 | 1,179 | 1,179 | 1,179 | 1,179 | 1,179 | 11,791 |
| | | | | | | | | | | | 169,202 |

Notes:
- The "Conservative Scenario" represents middle estimate between "Pessimistic" (low) and "Aggressive" (high).
- Further elaboration on scenarios provided in Figure 1.1 and Table A.2.

---

[7] Ibid., 19

*Estimate of Annual Employment Demand Range Based on Studied Initiatives and Proposals*[8]

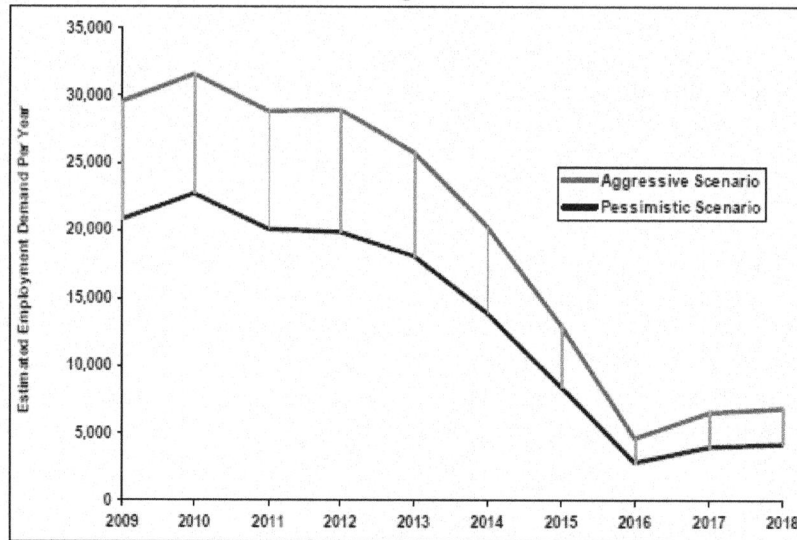

Source: The Louis Berger Group, 2008, based on data compiled by DC Office of Planning.

## Demand Estimates by Job Zone and Occupation

The Report identifies the following occupations as the 10 with the highest green job demand in the District:

- Carpenters (Job Zone 3)
- Construction laborers (Job Zones 1 & 2)
- First-line supervisors/managers of construction trades and extraction workers (Job Zone 3)
- Construction managers (Job Zone 3)
- Operating engineers and other construction equipment operators (Job Zone 3)
- Plumbers, pipefitters and steamfitters (Job Zone 3)
- Roofers (Job Zones 1 & 2)
- Electricians (Job Zone 3)
- Cement masons and concrete finishers (Job Zone 3)
- Painters, construction and maintenance (Job Zones 1 & 2)

The Report uses the Job Zone breakdown from the Occupational Information Network (O-Net) (http://online.onetcenter.org/help/online/zones) to classify green jobs into different categories based on level of preparation required. Below is a table that describes each Job Zone and provides the percentage of the Report's projected green jobs in the District.

Job Zone Percentages[9]

---

[8] Ibid., 20
[9] Ibid., 21

| Job Zone | % of Total | Job Zone Description |
|---|---|---|
| 1 | 15.75% | Little or No Preparation |
| 2 | 21.91% | Some Preparation |
| 3 | 42.30% | Medium Preparation |
| 4 | 11.78% | Considerate Preparation |
| 5 | 1.45% | Extensive Preparation |

As you can see from this table, thirty seven percent of the green job opportunities require little to no preparation, and thus have the fewest barriers to entry. Forty two percent of the green jobs produced will require a moderate level of preparation and typically require an associate's degree while a few will require a bachelor's degree or higher. Because the District wanted this study to place a priority on labor demand and occupational profiles of Jobs Zones 1-3, this doesn't mean that there will not be green job opportunities in Job Zones 4 and 5 as well. While Job Zones 4 and 5, those requiring more education and experience, might not have as many green jobs demand created from District green initiatives as Job Zones 1-3, there will still be some demand for new green jobs as well as new green skill sets in more technical positions such as energy auditors, architects, landscape designers and building commissioning agents.

## Best Practices From Around the Country and Recommendations

Another section of the Report focuses on how the District can model its green initiatives after successful green initiatives that have already been implemented across the country and provides recommendations on the next steps for the District to consider. While each case study provided shows a different opportunity for the District to develop new green jobs initiatives, it is critical to realize that the District's green programs and initiatives can use some of the components of these cases studies, but must be tailored to the specific characteristics of the District of Columbia if they are to be successful and sustainable.

Best Practices were focused on the following three priorities:
1. Focus on and reflect government leadership and involvement in Green Jobs program development and implementation.
2. Illustrate jobs efforts/programs that can be scaled to meet the growing future demands over time and support green business development, expansion and relocation efforts, as well as indicate the potential for near term positive impacts.
3. Illuminate successful efforts in the creation of entry level jobs for hard to serve populations, such as youth and ex-offenders.

Below is a short summary of each of the six best practices identified in the Report, as well as recommendations and case studies highlighted in this section of the Report:

Green procurement strategies
The Report suggests that the District Office of Contracting and Procurement should implement an Environmentally Preferable Purchasing Program similar to that of the U.S. Department of Defense green procurement strategy, which is the world's largest buyer. Other federal agencies such as the Environmental Protection Agency have also made great strides in green procurement. If District vendors were required to meet specific environmental standards and institute green supply chain and green IT efforts in order to supply the District with products and services, this would jumpstart the green products and services market in the District, as well as make District businesses competitive on a national and international level. The Report provides the following example of a typical supply chain for a product's life cycle as a framework for evaluating products: conception of the product, design of the product,

extraction of raw material for the product, processing of these raw materials, energy production involved in the product, the manufacture of the product, shipping of the product, marketing and selling at the wholesale and retail level of the product, consumer transport of the product, energy or operation of the product and disposal and recycling of the product.

Serving youth and ex-offenders in connection with green jobs workforce development programs
This Best Practice highlights successful programs on a national level from Green For All, and on a local level from the Ella Baker Center in Oakland, CA and the Center for Equal Employment Opportunities in New York City, NY. All of these programs focus on youth and ex-offenders to give them the needed workforce development training in an effort to provide them with pathways out of poverty, while at the same time creating a workforce that can help the community deal with environmental issues such as global warming. All of the programs provide key life skills training, as well as support services to participants to remove barriers to employment. The Oakland Green Corps was created and is maintained through a partnership between many community based organizations, unions, the city government, and private industry. The New York program focuses on recently released prisoners and gets them involved with job training programs immediately after they are released from prison, and uses a crew based model as opposed to having individuals placed separately at different jobs. Besides modeling District programs after these case studies, the Report also recommends that the District should partner with nonprofits that operate successful programs and encourage them to adopt green collar jobs as an area of focus.

Workforce programs involving renewable energy and energy efficiency training
The opportunity here is to identify near term demand jobs in the renewable energy and energy efficiency industries and develop training programs that will be poised to take advantage of District and Federal policies as well as Department of Labor funding such as the Green Jobs Act of 2007 (note that this was never funded, but the American Recovery and Reinvestment Act of 2009 was funded and provides approximately $500 million for green jobs training programs). The Report advises that veterans, displaced workers, and at-risk young people receive priority for these training programs. Several different programs of this type are highlighted from around the country including the Baltimore community's development of the East Baltimore Community Corporation which operates the Youth Construction Skills Program and the Ready to Work Grow Program. Recommendations in the Report include providing certification programs to give individuals industry credentials for green jobs, and to link training programs with employers so that employment is the direct outcome of the training programs.

Attracting new green businesses
The Report states that surprisingly there have not been many programs developed around the country to specifically attract green businesses to their region, with the exclusion of Pennsylvania, California, and to some extent Nevada. Pennsylvania has been successful in attracting businesses to spur their renewable energy industry including windmill builders, and biofuel storage and blending facilities through their investments and grant awards to spur this development. The Report recommends that since the District does not have a strong manufacturing presence, it should investigate the potential for using sectors that have a business base to attract green businesses. The specific example provided is for the District to utilize its substantial printing and printing supply industry to look into the possibility of converting these resources for the manufacturing of thin film "nano" solar cells such as has been done in California.

District Certified Business Enterprises presence in the federal and local government green marketplace
This Best Practice looks to ensure the success of District Certified Business Enterprises (CBEs) by establishing their presence in the federal and local government green marketplace. Specific projects that should be on the horizon that provide great opportunities are the environmental remediation of the Walter Reed Army Medical Center and the Potomac Annex. There should be up to 300 jobs available through the Department of Defense and US Army Corps of Engineers that CBEs could fill. These projects have already been allocated tens of millions of dollars for environmental remediation. As an example of how

I. Introduction to Green Jobs and Green Careers

this could be set up the Report provides a case study of Hunters Point Shipyard in San Francisco, CA. Recommendations in the Report include helping current and new CBEs certified under federal programs so they can compete for sub contracts on the above mentioned projects, as well as encouraging green redevelopment on these project sites as new projects are begun.

Green Business Certification Programs
Currently, there are very few green business certification programs in the country. It is recommended in the Report that the District creates a green business certification program similar to that of the Bay Area Green Business Program in San Francisco, CA. The Bay Area program provides assistance to businesses and public agencies to go beyond just meeting environmental standards, but instead making strides towards becoming a green business through initiatives to prevent pollution, conserve resources (water conservation, energy efficiency, waste reduction), and operate in a more sustainable manner. If a business meets the program's requirements, it is awarded a Green Business Certification. The incentive for businesses to participate in this program is that they can set themselves apart from their competition as truly green companies by using the certification in their marketing and advertising efforts.

## Focus Groups

The Green Builders Council of DC and Momentum Analysis conducted four focus groups in the summer of 2008 in DC, each of which had about 8 participants and lasted about 1.5 hours. The major findings of the focus groups were: there is little resistance to the green trend yet there is variation in comfort with "green" as a term, and as a trend; the underemployed need multi-faceted training; and the green trend will create few new jobs, but these jobs will require new skills. In general participants were willing to acknowledge that climate change is real and that environmental issues were important to the District. The term "green" meant different things to different focus groups and most participants mentioned their concerns about greenwashing. There was some difference of opinion on who should be responsible for providing training to the underemployed population, but most agreed that individuals needed life skills training as well as job track training. Through the focus groups it was identified that there isn't very good collaboration and partnership between employers and training providers. Also mentioned was the importance of workforce development programs specifying the difference between new green jobs being created and existing jobs that are just acquiring new green skill sets.

Based on the findings from the focus groups and follow up surveys sent to participants, several recommendations were provided in the Report for how the District can successfully move forward in creating green jobs within the city. These recommendations include making the green jobs discussion more inclusive of all industries, improve the dialogue between employers and training providers, provide sustainability education programs for those less familiar with green trends, provide incentives for renewable energy and green building, help publicize smaller green businesses and programs, create green economic zones, and focus on the positives of the District.

## Conclusions

There is definitely a lot of information to digest in the report, and hopefully after reading this summary you have been inspired to get involved in some way to help the District move forward in its efforts to become a national leader in green and create successful green jobs programs, as well as implement other green initiatives. In a few years, we should be getting inquiries from other cities about the District's green programs and initiatives and we should be seeing the District used as a case study in reports on green initiatives. You may have noticed that all the green job projections in the Report require some serious spending to achieve these results; we are talking billions of dollars! For this reason, it is vital that while knowing we want to act quickly and swiftly, we should do everything in our power to thoroughly analyze the best opportunities for investments in the green economy.

Luckily we have a significant amount of individuals and groups in the District who are committed to the cities' green agenda, and if we can all find a way to share resources, ideas, and experiences I have no doubt that the District will succeed in its efforts. But to do so, we need to ensure involvement from everyone in the District, because nothing is truly "green" or "sustainable" unless it is all inclusive of the entire population. The best thing you can do to get involved is start talking to others about your thoughts and concerns related to green initiatives in the District, and find others that you can work together with to have an even greater impact in the end.

I want to finish by commending the District in investing their time, efforts, and funding in not only implementing green initiatives, but also trying to gain a full understanding of the green potential of our city, and I think we are off to a great start. But as this Report shows, there is still a lot to do!

I. Introduction to Green Jobs and Green Careers

# Green Jobs Created from Green Certifications:
# A Washington, D.C. Example
## By: John Friedman

Green certifications can be a great way for companies to communicate the environmental impact of their products. But too often, they leave the public confused about what the various standards mean (to them and to the environment). Here's how environmental standards that actually mean something to consumers are offering avenues to job creation.

Remember back in school when you liked someone and wanted them to like you in return? It wasn't enough to tell them what a great person you were to get them to go out with you (in fact, that often backfired). Instead, you were better off if you found someone whom they trusted, and had that person say good things about you.

What does this have to do with corporate responsibility? The answer is simple: it is not enough to say that you are doing good things. It lacks credibility for two reasons. The first is that it is seen as self-serving. The second is because self-evaluating does not lend itself to comparisons (unless you're good enough to define the standards for your industry). One of the biggest benefits to third party validation is that it provides a solution to both of these dilemmas and actually provides the public with sound information on which to base their purchasing decisions. It is for this reason that auto manufacturers promote government and industry safety ratings rather than announcing, "~the safest car we have ever built", with the footnote explaining how and under which conditions that vehicle is considered the best.

In the area of corporate responsibility, there are a number of different standards and certifications. It is no wonder that the public is confused. As people seek to understand what the different standards mean (to them and to the environment), there are a few things that they should look for:

**Independence** - It was a running joke for many years that certain Olympic judges rated their country's own athletes higher and downgraded those representing nations with whom they had political differences. This was countered by the use of a panel of judges. The independence (honesty) of the process is also served by certifications that use independent auditors or evaluators. When auditors are not paid directly by those being audited but through an intermediary organization, the auditors are seen as being independent agents. There is an increasing need for people with skills in measurement, assessment, and evaluation.

**Credibility** - For a standard to be trusted, it must be a standard that people believe is a valid measurement of some dimension of environmental impact and performance. In the case of the environment, standards can be defined around such measurable elements as reductions in the use of water, energy and raw materials. On the output side, standards can measure and track reductions in pollution and emissions including carbon, sulfur, dust, chemicals and garbage/waste created. In the rush to be seen as green, some companies are rushing into the space and making claims that either cannot be backed up with hard scientific data or that only reflect a portion of the overall picture. In the social element, things are a bit more complex, as local cultures can often limit or define what can be done. But certainly companies should be held accountable for protecting the health and safety of their employees. They can, and should, move forward by measuring themselves in such things as living wages, child labor and protection, and equal opportunity based on ability.

**Meaningful** – Ultimately, it is the public that decides what is important to them and therefore meaningful as a standard. At times, I have been amused and astonished by the amount of effort some people put in to get and promote their professional credentials, basing it on what is important to them and their idea that the public understands and cares about the distinctions. We have all seen business cards with a string advanced degrees and professional associations following the individual's name, which may have little or no meaning to the layperson. While those who understand the degrees may be suitably impressed, it is a wasted effort for the majority of the public. In some cases it may be viewed as conceit. The nadir is when it is downright deceptive - such as when a person deliberately cites completely unrelated professional credentials in order to establish their bona fides from one area of expertise to indicate expertise in another. A few years ago, I was appalled when I discovered that a person with a Ph.D. was using their 'doctor' appellation to help them sell health products, counting on - and encouraging - the public to make the natural assumption.

**Understandable** – There is a reason why Good Housekeeping grants seals, why crash tests are reported in star rankings, why the <u>LEED certifications</u> contain differing levels based on different levels of performance. From our earliest childhood, we are conditioned to understand that there are different grades based on varying levels of achievement. The most understandable ratings (or rankings) communicate effectively because people intrinsically understand that something that earns five stars is "better" than one that earns four; a rating of "superior" is preferable to one of "good." It is interesting to note, however, that with rankings (i.e. 1 to 10) there is a base assumption that the difference between ranks is the same; where this may not be the case at all. Going back to the Olympics, the time between the first, , and third place runners is often measured in fractions of a second, whereas the eighth and ninth place finishers may have a comparative gulf between them. This misperception on the part of the public may provide the highest ranking programs, products, and services with an advantage that is out of proportion to the difference between them. Another area for career opportunities is for those with the ability to communicate effectively and with transparency about 'green' rankings.

**Based on Science** – Ratings must be based on things people believe in. Even simple basic measurements that quantify time (speed, longevity), quantity (number, fraction, or percent) often serve as proxies for quality or value. In the environmental space the value of social math - relating savings to something people find more relatable - is often an effective strategy for communication, but it can cloud the issue. Expressing the amount of $CO_2$ reduced based on an equivalent number of cars that it theoretically has taken off the roads may be fueling the major misperception by a third of Americans that personal automobiles are the greatest source of $CO_2$. In fact, forty-one percent of $CO_2$ emissions come from coal-fired electric power generation. The ultimate irony of this is that people who may gravitate to plug-in electric vehicles may think that they are helping to solve the problem while they are substituting tail pipe emissions (that they can see) for those from a far more polluting source. This example cries out for a standard measurement of carbon emissions across all vehicles (based on the same number passenger occupants) per mile, similar to the EPA mileage statistics. Climate science is therefore another career option with the potential for increasing opportunities.

**Public/open process** – Ever page through rankings by Consumer Reports, Good Housekeeping or US News & World Report? One of the things that these trusted rankings have in common is the fact that the measurement criteria are clearly stated and explained (such as reporting the annual operating costs for each appliance measured). This aids in making the ratings understandable and also lends credibility to the standards and the entire process. The evaluation process must be open as standards and knowledge evolve. A terrific example of this: the standards for accrediting health insurance plans. New and revised standards are developed through expanding medical consensus and then go through a public comment period before they can be made part of accreditation. Here the opportunities lie with organizations that

I. Introduction to Green Jobs and Green Careers

develop and implement standards. They need to engage stakeholders, which increasingly requires social media expertise and skill.

The creation, adoption and implementation of comprehensive environmental standards will create new opportunities for companies and organizations that wish to demonstrate their softened impact on the environment. It will also create jobs, as we have seen. From data entry to data analysts, from standards development to testing, and in addition to all the 'green' jobs, there are a wealth of other roles that must have a green component or an understanding to be competitive in the job market today.

*John Friedman has more than 20 years' experience in internal and external communications and a decade in the area of corporate responsibility and sustainability. His background includes developing and implementing award-winning programs including stakeholder engagement, community relations, organizational development, change management, and strategic philanthropy. A frequent presenter and contributor on issues relating to corporate social responsibility as a business strategy, John is author of "The New PR," a guide outlining how companies must modify the way they communicate to meet stakeholders' changing expectations. He also serves on the board of directors for the Sustainable Business Network of Washington (SB NOW).*

# Getting a Green Education: The World Is Greening - Are You?
## By: Mark Starik

So, you've seen the movie *Wall-E*, the TV series *Planet Earth*, and the unending green commercials featuring T. Boone Pickens, GE Ecomagination, each of the major oil companies, and even Wal-Mart, so you get it --- the world is going green. Now you ask yourself --- where do I fit in, or even, how can I help? Besides recycling, turning off the lights, and walking more, a good way to join the green wave is to get yourself educated to make better sustainability decisions.

Luckily, in addition to movies, TV, and the internet, thousands of green educational opportunities await your selection, and these options are probably as varied as the individuals who explore them. So, one question to ask at the beginning of your green educational journey is "what do you think you need to learn?" This is probably related to another question: "what do you want to do with the information once you get it?"

If you are mostly interested in making better-informed purchasing decisions in your household, many organizations, such as Green America, have dozens of tips for green consumers on their websites, in their brochures, and at their events. Personal sustainability coaches are an increasingly popular option for would-be green consumers, as are the multitude of workshops sponsored by Whole Foods, Home Depot, and other "greening" companies.

If you want to incorporate sustainability into your career, once again, a wide range of options exists, from a short course on green building (say, for Green Associate or LEED Accredited Professional certification) to full-blown university degrees in sustainability science, technology, policy, and management, among many other fields. Of course, you'll want to explore what kinds of green skills, knowledge, and credentials are required of the career positions you seek. And, it nearly always is a good idea to talk to people who have the kinds of sustainability jobs you want as well as people who can provide career advice on how you can acquire what you need to get those jobs.

For those seeking green certifications, they are available through individual or sets of courses offered by various certifying-related organizations (such as Green Advantage), technical and community colleges, and 4-year degree-granting colleges or university programs (including graduate programs). If you are looking for a hands-on position dealing with, say, energy-efficiency or renewable energy technologies, you may want to investigate the first several of these options.

But, if you are seeking a managerial, big-picture, multi-faceted sustainability career, college or university degree programs related to sustainability are expanding significantly and often provide broader, more complex perspectives on sustainability topics. Some of these institutions of higher learning, for instance, have developed or are associated with sustainability research institutes or centers, with information generated by this research integrated into especially graduate-level sustainability coursework. So, the best piece of green career advice is to try to match what you want with what's available, and then check it out.

Some of the trends that you might find, especially if you are exploring the college and university sustainability market, are similar to those in other sectors of society. Sustainability often has both an environmental and a socio-economic component, so you might find that multiple "schools" within a university share or cross-list courses, so that students can get a more comprehensive view of, say, sustainability policy, than that taught only in "the policy school." You may also find that, along with the

I. Introduction to Green Jobs and Green Careers

increased interest in sustainability, as in society in general, information systems and a global perspective are highlighted, so you might expect that an increasing number of sustainability programs include Global Information Systems and Environmental Management Information Systems and provide sustainability information from both developed and developing country perspectives. While attention to sustainability is increasing in general in higher education, would-be students are still encouraged to be entrepreneurial in both locating courses relevant to their particular sustainability careers and developing their own customized courses, including internships, in this still relatively new area of study.

Speaking of internships and other "service-learning" approaches, after you find the appropriate sustainability educational path, make sure you leverage it effectively by connecting with various sustainability networks related to your interest. In addition to joining sustainability career-related groups, you might suggest to your instructor(s) that sustainability subjects related to your particular interests are included in the course syllabus, that sustainability-oriented guest speakers with whom you want to connect more substantively be invited into class as outside experts, that interesting sustainability sites be considered for course field trips, and that course projects include options for developing your own sustainability practical interests.

Finally, in managing your green career, you'll want to be able to locate the appropriate educational sources, so that you can access these and move closer to your "green dream" job. Luckily, the same rainbow of sustainability education options mentioned above is offered by many organizations in the Washington, D.C. region. First, many low-cost sustainability courses are available in the region, such as the non-profit organization courses offered by the Institute for Policy Studies and its "social action" SALSA program. Second, a recent phenomenon in education in general and in sustainability education in particular are webinars or on-line short courses on a wide range of topics, featuring expert speakers, including on sustainability. The Environmental Law Institute and the National Association of Environmental Managers are two of many D.C. area organizations that offer regular sustainability webinars. Of course, many area-wide sustainability organizations have publications, websites, trainings, volunteer opportunities, and events that include potentially helpful information for those seeking or advancing green careers.

If you are interested in longer-term courses with more sustainability breadth and depth, this region's residents can take advantage of the Consortium of Universities of the Washington Metropolitan Area, popularly known as "the Consortium" to which the 15 largest universities and colleges in the area belong, each of which offers from dozens to more than a hundred different sustainability courses. The beauty of the Consortium is that students can enroll in any of these educational institutions and take courses, including sustainability courses, at any of these Consortium schools. So, if you thought you wanted to take a global sustainability course from American University, a business sustainability course from George Washington University, and a sustainability science course from the University of Maryland, you would only need to enroll in one of these universities and, subject to perhaps some limitations, be able to take any or all of them.

In the Resources section of this guide is a list of area-wide sustainability education resources that readers may find helpful in developing their green careers. Given the excitement that the emerging green economy is generating, all of us would do well to identify how we can both encourage and take advantage of the coming "green wave". Hopefully, using this guide will be your first step in moving in those sustainable directions!

*Mark Starik, PhD, is a Visiting Professor of Management and Sustainability at the College of Business, San Francisco State University and Professor of Strategic Management and Public Policy, at the School of Business, George Washington University. Mark is also a co-founder of several organizations, including the Institute for Sustainability Education & Action, and the Academy of Management Organizations & the Natural Environment*

*(ONE) Division, and is a board member of several non-profit organizations, including the DC Solar Household Energy, Inc., and the National Environmental Education Foundation.*

*He researches, teaches, and advises organizations and individuals in the areas of Strategic Environmental Management, Environmental and Energy Policy, Environmental Entrepreneurship, and Implementing Solutions to Climate Crises. He is also interested in the connections among the fields of strategic management, business and public policy (including civil society), and sustainability, both domestically and internationally. His research includes publications in a wide variety of both academic and practitioner outlets, including the <u>Academy of Management Review</u>, <u>the Academy of Management Journal</u>, <u>the Journal of Business Ethics</u>, and <u>Business Strategy and the Environment</u> and in the proceedings of several international organization conferences.*

# Being a 'Green' Entrepreneur

## By: Anca Novacovici

So you are thinking about starting your own business in a 'green' arena? To many, the word 'entrepreneur' conjures up images of glamour and excitement. They see a picture of an energetic, forward-thinking individual with a big idea, one that is financed by venture capitalists and requires working long hours resulting in big monetary rewards a couple of years down the road. Being an entrepreneur in a 'green' field seems even more exciting – it's an opportunity to jump into a new sector, help shape it, and capture market share early on – it can feel like the Wild West when you look at how quickly this market segment is growing!

But not so fast! Make sure you think this through first and weigh the pros and cons. Though being in the 'green' sector sounds exciting, starting a 'green' business still requires many of the same skills that are required in starting a conventional business. Being an entrepreneur does require an idea that you believe in, and it will likely require long hours, but it need not require external funding and most of the time does not involve overnight success. Being a 'green' entrepreneur in particular means going into uncharted territory in many cases, and that the market can change from one year to the next, which means you must apply caution.

When I started Eco-Coach in 2006, there were not many environmental sustainability consulting companies, and though I knew there was a need for the services, the target market was unclear – small, medium and larger sized businesses required the services, but they were not clear on what they wanted or needed because the market was developing. As a result, we had to educate businesses on the benefits of going 'green' and help them determine what best would fit their needs. Today, it is a different market – most companies, at least in the D.C. market, are aware of the advantages of 'going green' and know the direction they would like to go in. This requires a different approach than before, as well as a slightly different set of offerings.

Whether working in a 'green' or conventional industry, being an entrepreneur requires many of the same characteristics, such as:

1. **An idea:** A good one! Something that you believe in and that you have researched and proven feasible – if you're not sure, make sure to ask others with experience to take a look at it. I had many great 'green' ideas, many of which would not have been feasible at the time that I started my company because the market did not exist for them.

2. **Content knowledge**: It is important that you or someone on your team has in-depth knowledge of the product or service that you are about to launch, or is committed to becoming the 'expert' on it. Eco-Coach combines my skills in management consulting with my passion for the environment – many of the previous ideas I had were not in a field I was familiar with, which is another reason I did not undertake them.

3. **Risk tolerance**: The ability to tolerate a certain degree of risk is required; this is not to say, however, that you should take risks just for the sake of it – any risk, monetary or otherwise, must be calculated and a mitigation strategy should be developed to address that risk. I consider myself more risk-averse than other entrepreneurs whom I know, but I am still considered risk-tolerant by others, so you do not have to be a Richard Branson type but you still need to deal well with uncertainty.

4. **Flexibility**: Things will not always work out the way you want them to, so you will need to know how to adapt and move on. You may start out with a business concept and need to change it to adapt to market demand (this includes taking into account economic conditions, customer demand, and competitor products). When we started out, we offered residential concierge services as part of our

offerings for individuals; however, this is something that did not have high demand or a high return, so we decided to withdraw it from our offerings.

5. **Perseverance**: The willingness to do whatever it takes to succeed – this also takes motivation and discipline.

6. **Leadership skills**: You will need to make tough decisions along the way, and help others see your vision and move them towards that point – it will not always be easy to do! This also involves putting your ego aside and bringing people on board who are have stronger skills and knowledge than you do in certain area.

7. **Support network**: This includes mentors, partners, significant others, and other successfully entrepreneurs – it is important to have others to bounce ideas off of and who support you in your endeavor. There are many great resources in the D.C. area, and I feel fortunate to have met many great individuals, both in and out of the 'green' sector, who have provided insight, guidance and support throughout.

Most of the traits described about can be developed, and to some degree, you may be able to choose the type of business you start based on the level of comfort you have with many of these. For instance, if you have a low risk tolerance and know that you are not too flexible, you can consider a franchise. If, on the other hand, you have a high risk tolerance and access to funding, you can start a business in a developing field, such as solar technology.

That being said, there are a few additional traits that the 'green' entrepreneur must have, though these are also important in other businesses:

8. **High ethical standards**: A company that provides 'green' products or services should practice what it preaches and follow the triple bottom line (people, planet, profits). It is sometimes easy to take short-cuts and/or use non-green products and practices. Although in the beginning, it may be necessary due to cost and resource considerations and in order to get the business off the ground (especially if you are working in your basement, which may not be as eco-friendly and energy efficient as you would like it to be!), in general it is important to incorporate these values into the company culture as early as possible.

9. **Analytical skills**: These are required for all entrepreneurs, but they are especially important in the 'green' sector, as this is a relatively new sector. This means that you must tread carefully – there is huge opportunity but there is also a higher risk for failure, because some concepts have yet to be tested out and proven. To lower your risk, be sure to look at many different scenarios and really think through the repercussions of each.

10. **Creativity**: As with the other two skills, these are important for any entrepreneur but are especially important in a new sector. Being a 'green' business and taking into account the triple bottom line is a great opportunity for re-thinking the way business is done, for taking responsibility for the impacts that the business has upstream and downstream, as well as internally.

You will hear many entrepreneurs say that if they knew at the beginning how much work they would have to do to run a successful business, they would have thought twice about doing it. That being said, the upside is that if you choose to start a 'green' company, you can make a living doing what you enjoy and help the planet in the process, so your time in well-spent in many different ways. I feel fortunate to do what I am doing and while there are also tough days, for the most part, I would recommend entrepreneurship to anyone who is in the mood for an adventure!

# Finding Your Green Niche in the Green Economy
## By: Carol McClelland

If you have picked up this Guide, you no doubt want to find a job sooner rather than later.

Although you might think your best strategy is to jump into job search mode immediately, the most effective thing you can do is create a clear picture of your green career goal.

The green economy is evolving and shifting at the moment. New policies, tax credits, and technologies will be influencing and molding the green economy for some time to come.

With all of the changes taking place in the green economy, it's impossible for one person to keep track of and make sense of all that is changing. Don't expect yourself to be able to scan the entire green economy to figure out where you fit.

The key to success is to identify your green niche so that you can focus your job search, gain traction, and land a position.
- The clearer you are about your green career goal, the more focused you will be.
- The more focused you are, the more effective your networking conversations will be.
- The more focused your outreach actions are, the more efficient, productive, and effective your job search will be.

If you don't take the time to focus your search, it's more likely you'll feel:
- Overwhelmed (What information do I focus on?)
- Confused (Which industry is best for me?)
- Paralyzed (What do I do next?)

Don't waste time spinning your wheels. Investing time up front, even if you are in a hurry to get a job, will save you time and money in the end.

## Knowing Your Passions Is the Key to Your Success

The sooner you uncover your unique tapestry of passions, skills, and experience, the sooner you can make significant progress with your job search.

Use this list of everyday activities to discover what you are drawn to in the green economy and the green movement. At this point in the process, don't worry about what will make money or what you are trained to do. Focus instead on what excites you!

1. **Read** -- What you are drawn to read gives you a tremendous source of clues about your passions. For a week or two, record the titles of all of the articles, websites, books, blogs, and magazine articles you are drawn to read. When I say drawn to read, I mean:
   - You are excited to read it
   - You feel engaged while you read it
   - If you try to pass over it, it stays with you until you return to read it
   - The content sticks with you long after you complete the article

2. **Volunteer** -- Where you are motivated to give your time, talent, and energy provides you with another source of insight. Even if you don't have time to volunteer at the moment, you can think about where you'd like to dedicate your energy. Don't limit yourself to the volunteer opportunities that are available in your local area, instead open your mind to opportunities worldwide!
   - What kinds of organizations excite you?
   - What causes are you drawn to support?
   - How do you want to make a difference in your community or the world?
3. **Talk** -- What do you like talking about--discussing, explaining, teaching, debating, and sharing? Pay attention to the topics that engage you in this way. The quality of your voice is very telling. If you speak faster, with more passion, with more energy, it's very likely you are talking about one of your passions! Have a notepad near by to record your discoveries.
4. **Learn** -- What you are driven to learn about will also tell you a lot about what inspires you. Perhaps you already know what you might want to study. If so, take some time to brainstorm all the areas you'd like to learn about. If the topics aren't top of mind, go online to your local community college, university, or green community center. Scan the list of courses and record the ones that interest you. You don't have to take the classes, just recognize that you are curious to learn about those topics.
5. **Solve** -- The problems you are drawn to ponder and solve are another source of clues about your passions. Do you try to figure out how to use less energy in your house or business? Are you driven to find better ways to recycle? Do you wonder why businesses are having a hard time jumping into the green economy? Anything you are intrinsically drawn to solve is a good clue to your passions.

## Now What?

When you look at your full list of interests and passions on paper:
- Does one topic pop out at you?
- Do any themes appear? Record the themes you see so that you have them at your finger tips.
- Feel free to combine ideas if you see something that fits together.

Identify your top three topics/passions. If one of your ideas doesn't pan out, you can always come back to your list to find another one to add to your exploration list.

By keeping your target passions in mind, you'll be able to focus your job exploration and job search to get results. You'll know:

1. **What to Read** -- If you've done any research on the green economy you know there's no shortage of reading material! In fact, if you try to read, process, and remember everything you come in contact with you'll soon be completely overwhelmed.

   Knowing your focus helps you determine what to read, what to scan, and what to ignore. Use your precious time to focus on the articles, websites, and blogs that will have a high payoff for your future.

2. **What Google Alerts to Set Up** -- Did you know you can set up a Google Alert to receive a daily email summary of all the online articles, blogs, and news items that mentioned your keywords?

   Simple to set up and free, it's a great technique to make sure you find all the latest news about your target niche. Just go to **http://www.google.com/alerts** and fill out the form on the right side of the page. For the best results, use quotation marks around the words in your keyword phrase.

3. **Where to Network** -- Just as there are too many resources to read, there may be too many places to network in some regions. Again, the key is to focus in on high payoff events, the events that will give

you the opportunity to meet those who share your interests and passions. You may need to attend a variety of events to discover which ones are most beneficial to you.

If you live in a region that doesn't have an abundance of green networking events, look online for discussion forums you can join. Another option is to explore social networking sites to find people with whom you can network.

4. **What Associations to Join** -- One of the most effective ways to plug into a highly focused network is to join a professional association. Use your favorite search engine to locate a professional association that fits your interests. Just plug in your keyword and add "association" to your search.

   You can learn quite a bit about a profession just by reading their web page. There's no need to join until you are sure the organization is the best fit for you. You may need to explore a few associations to find the one that is best for you.

5. **What Conferences to Attend** --Attending a conference is a wonderful opportunity to discover the latest trends, rub shoulders with key players, and meet face-to-face with colleagues and potential colleagues. The key is figuring out which conference(s) to attend. Knowing your green career goal will help you make that decision.

   If your budget is limited, consider purchasing a day pass for the exhibit hall. Or scan the conference website to determine whether presentations will be streamed on the site. Of course watching online doesn't give you the opportunity meet other people in your field, but it will give you the opportunity to learn about the profession and the inside scoop.

6. **Who to Target for Conversation** -- When you know your focus, you can be much more effective in your networking efforts. Being able to state your target green career with clarity and confidence will enable your network to provide you with highly targeted contacts and resources. Be strategic as you set up one-on-one meeting with key contacts. You'll be amazed at how your network will expand.

7. **How to Volunteer to Get the Biggest Bang for Your Time Commitment** -- If you are interested in plugging into the green network in your region, volunteering can be a high payoff activity. The key is to find a way to volunteer that uses your talents and strengthens your resume. One of the benefits of making this commitment is that you are likely to meet people who are well connected in the local green movement and maybe in your target profession.

8. **What Training to Engage in** -- When you know what goal you are shooting for and you've started the process of understanding what it takes to excel in your field, you'll begin to understand what training you'll need. Do you need to take a refresher course, get a certification, or commit to a full degree program? Knowing this information sooner rather than later allows you to move into your new green career as strategically as possible.

9. **What Companies to Target** -- As you take all of the actions listed above, start a list of companies that hire people in your target profession. Don't worry where the company is located. You can learn a lot about your entire profession by researching companies with a local, national, and even global presence. As you get closer to starting your actual job search, you'll know what companies you want to target.

10. **What Job Boards to Check** --Defining your target profession also allows you to find job boards that are specifically for those in your target profession. You can use these job boards to discover which

job titles are aligned with your passions, interests and talents, to expand your list of target companies, and, of course, to identify job openings.

Don't rely on job boards as your sole source of job openings. Remember only a small percentage of jobs actually get listed on job boards. Being active in your network, attending conferences and being known within your profession will also alert you to unadvertised positions. Imagine finding a job opening that's not widely known!

Finding your green niche is not an instantaneous process. Think of it as a big treasure hunt. The more clues you have about your passions, your desired work environment, and your green goals, the more likely you are to find the career you've been searching for.

Give yourself a couple of days, or weeks if possible, to explore your green niche. Immerse yourself in the process of discovering what you are passionate about, what you are drawn to. After you've used the activities described above to create an in depth list of your skills and interests, sit with your list to see what feels like the strongest pull.

If you need a job immediately, use your green niche as the ideal job you are striving to reach in the next five years or so. With that in mind, what decisions can you make about your current job search to put you in position to transition into your ideal job when the opportunity presents itself?

If you have some time to explore your options, take a bit more time to immerse yourself in your target green niche. The more you know about the industry, field, and profession, the easier it will be to make connections, see where your skills fit in, and make the connections with those who are hiring.

*Carol McClelland, Ph.D., a pioneering career-change consultant, has spent eighteen years helping thousands of clients, students, and readers discover fulfilling careers that align with their personal values. As the Founder and Executive Director of Green Career Central, Carol is once again on the leading edge of her field. In addition to defining and clarifying the ever-evolving world of green career possibilities for professionals, students, and career counselors, she and her team provide inspiration, effective ways to find your green niche, informative resources, and practical job search strategies to those entering the green economy. Carol is the author of the forthcoming Green Careers For Dummies (January, 2010) and Your Dream Career For Dummies (2005).*

# Career Transitions into Green Jobs
## By: Vicki Lind and Gail Nicholson

It's vital that you clarify your employment goals before starting to network and job search. Major green industries and occupations are listed in the first section of this Guide, and local green employers are listed in the third section of this Guide. Target one or two areas to explore based on your interests and values, and stay within them for a while. Remember, employers are looking for someone who can articulate a clear purpose and enthusiasm for the specific job they want to fill. At the same time, stay open to different ways of reaching your goal, and take advantage of available openings in a tight market.

## Conduct a Self-Assessment

As a starting point, take time to reflect on who you are. Many questions precede a viable career transition. You may explore best in conversation with those closest to you, or perhaps by keeping a journal. In any case, we strongly recommend that you commit some time and thought to the process. Start by asking yourself some questions, such as:
* What am I passionate about?
* What matters to me?
* What environmental issues call to me?
* What am I good at?
* What roles do I like to play?
* What do I still want to learn?
* Do I like to travel?
* How much money do I need?

You may have difficulty developing an inventory of your skills and strengths - many people do - but it's worth the effort. Get help from co-workers, friends, or a career counselor whom you trust and who sees you in a positive light.

Consider the type of work environment along with the salary and benefits that would best support you. Is a small business something you've considered? Or are your interests requiring you to stitch together a couple of jobs to create a patchwork career? Are you open to going back to school or getting some kind of training in order to reach your ideal job and lifestyle?

## Evaluate Your Current Status

Before you begin your job exploration, take stock of your current situation. You will want to ask many questions, ranging from the practical to the psychological, such as:
* Am I set up to meet my basic needs (food, clothing, shelter)?
* Am I emotionally ready to explore new job possibilities?
* Do I need to focus my attention right now to address built-up burnout, setbacks, or the priorities of others in my life?

Perhaps you realize that spending time in nature for rejuvenation is a priority. Or, you might find your energy and finances are in a good place, and you're chomping at the bit to get started.

## Prioritize Your Options

As you take time to reflect on your deeper purpose, write down two or three fields or job ideas that match your vocational self. The trick is to generate a few matches for your individual passions. For example, when you began, you may have considered ten options, from starting your own organic baby food company to being an environmental educator. At this point, it's time to select the top few categories. Don't worry if your ideas are a little vague within your chosen field. The next leg of the journey will help you further define and clarify your purpose.

## Explore Your Options

Now you can build on what you know and **begin researching** what you don't know about the possibilities that intrigue you most. Use your questions and concerns about your options to direct your exploration. Questions, and even fears, are important to pay attention to at this point, as they tell you the type of information you'll need to gain clarity and direction. They should not automatically be perceived as barriers or signs that you're on the wrong path. We have too many stories of the overnight success in our heads. Toss those stories out, and get back to following up on your questions and concerns about future career options. Information can be your best antidote to fear.

For example, let your interest in climate change point you toward organizations and individuals known in that area. Then ask questions about jobs suitable for someone with your skills and background, about the pay or the availability of work, and whether a current trend will take hold. Additional questions can be found on **Informational Interviews,** page 89. Continue your efforts. We all make errors in judgment; learn from them. Hopefully, some detours can be avoided by reading **Ten Common Mistakes**, starting on page 87. Patience is a needed ingredient at this stage.

### Grow Your Network

While there are many ways to learn about possible career paths, *talking with people,* both informally and in informational interviews, is the best way to scope out an emerging field, especially those rare niches that only exist locally. These discussions will be more meaningful if you prepare by researching on the Internet and checking out the green job resources in Section III of this Guide. Prior to informational interviews, ground yourself in the basics, pick up specialized vocabulary, and formulate your questions. To develop your questions, refer to the **Informational Interviews** section, where we've provided sample questions and guidelines.

**Consider who you know**. Many people are surprised to realize they know someone who can help directly or indirectly. Think about it. Do you have a friend, relative, neighbor, co-worker, ex-colleague, classmate, or teacher who could help? Maybe someone with whom you used to volunteer or a parent of one of your kid's friends might know someone who can fill in a missing link. Once you start hearing the same names and information, you'll know that you've done your homework.

Since it is people who hire people, start now. Introduce yourself and develop connections that will lead to people thinking of you when they hear about an opening or have one to fill. Folks don't usually remember someone they've met just once. They remember people they have worked with on projects and run into over and over again. It takes time to make an impression. If you have to deliver pizza to pay the rent while you volunteer on a committee to become known, hang in there. That's how most of us get started.

## Write Your Resume

It's helpful to bring along an ***updated resume*** as you begin making your rounds, interviewing the most relevant and available people. Work on developing one that reflects your current objectives, strengths/skills, and accomplishments. For examples using the latest hybrid format, which combines the chronological and the skills-based approaches, check **Resumes and Cover Letters** from local successful or current job hunters, beginning on page 94.

## Network According to Your Personal Style

***Networking for jobs is an ongoing social endeavor.*** We have to get ourselves out there again and again. It helps to approach it in a way that will allow you to initiate and sustain our efforts.

### Introverts

Some of us draw energy from inside and need to pull away from social contact periodically to recharge. The mythical version of networking as a constant push to instantly impress a room full of strangers is repulsive and draining for this type. If you feel the need, respect your inclination to go at a slower pace at times, ease into the process, and take breaks from the process.

Emphasize talking with people one on one or in small groups. Prepare questions ahead of time and avoid winging it. Learn to tolerate small talk as a necessary icebreaker to talking about what really matters. Successfully target the groups it makes the most sense to meet, and attend gatherings consistently, allowing time to observe at first and then gradually form relationships. Resist the pressure to talk with more people than you are comfortable with, and remember that you are talking with folks because it's the only way to reach your goal.

### Extroverts

Outgoing types, particularly those with business experience, often find it easy to pick up the phone or attend a conference to connect with potential co-workers. They draw their energy from people, places, and things, and lose energy and motivation if isolated for too long. So if you're a people person, new in town, and short on friends, make sure you get out enough to draw nurturance from the outside world. Your knack for making conversation could connect you with someone helpful almost anywhere.

With a high tolerance for meeting strangers and genuine interest in a wide variety of topics, this type may need to pay attention to being selective about what they attend to ensure staying on track with deeper interests. A natural draw toward an ever-widening circle is a strength in networking, but it may need to be held in check. Stay in touch with folks you've met recently, and deepen existing contacts so that you stay in their minds.

Whatever your approach, use the list in **Organizations for Networking and Volunteering** beginning on page 159 as a place to select key organizations, and note people you meet there. Develop a system for organizing the information you collect.

Keep track of your follow-up commitments in a calendar or notebook, so that no one is forgotten. If the stack of business cards you have collected has grown to the point that you can only remember a few faces, it may be time to thin the deck. Consider who you enjoyed meeting and is best connected in your areas of focus. This is a good time to add these selected contacts to your email address book. Dedicate time for follow-up, so they become part of your committed network.

## Take Small Steps Daily Toward Emerging Goals

Life and career transitions take time, technically the rest of your life. Develop an ability to envision possibilities for yourself, drawing on your personal life interests and values. Regularly step back and ask, "What small step toward my priorities could I accomplish today?" These small steps could include getting a journal, a business card, an appointment calendar, and clothes for an interview. Take time to create an attractive, functional workspace.

When you want to call someone and feel intimidated, take a small step and just look up that person's phone number. Put it someplace where you'll find it and call later. If you continue to identify your priorities, and inch along, catching yourself as you occasionally fall off track, chances are in your favor that something meaningful will happen.

## Create a Support System, Get Organized

Throughout the process, make your support system all you need it to be. Start or find a group of like-minded people, or meet informally but regularly with any number of friends and family. Focus on developing important relationships in the fields that interest you by volunteering and networking.

Prioritize and reprioritize where you're continuing to put your energy, as you better understand your deeper interests and values. As time goes on, engage the world on the mutual basis of what's important to you and those that you connect with. Successful people say that it's all in the follow-up, the persistence, and continuously picking yourself up. Definitely spend energy networking. It will replenish you, and as you offer encouragement and help to others, your vision becomes real.

Support your cohorts in developing routines that ensure your accountability, rest, personal space, inspiration, and creativity. In addition, your team can review resume and cover letters, as well as spot position announcements that call your name.

## Prepare to Go the Distance

As you prepare to go the distance, remember that this is paradoxically both a strategic and somewhat random process. Remove any blinders about what your success will look like, and examine preconceived notions about what it takes to make it. Expect a few surprises as your path unfolds. Be aware that when you come from your deepest interests and values, people tend to respond affirmatively and help you in totally unexpected ways. Stay open to catch those curve balls.

Set yourself up to interview, explore, volunteer, and generally hang in there 'til you get the call that puts money in your pocket and gives you a chance to make a difference. To go the distance you may need to keep your day job. Consider it temporary, and draw comfort knowing that your basic needs are being met and you still have time to explore and connect. If possible, work part time, to allow more time for pursuing your true interests. As always, live simply and reduce expenses to help create and expand your options.

Down the road, as your vision becomes something you are trusting more and questioning less, consider what you still need in the way of resources, routines, and activities, so that you have what you need to go after what matters. Experiment with your lifestyle choices in order to support and continue your efforts. Sometimes it just gets down to trial and error.

## Conclusion

Any life journey that is worth taking alternates between smooth stretches, peaks, and valleys. Whether you are searching for a new career or greening your current organization, your passion for sustainability is your fuel (with a little stubbornness thrown in).

There is great need everywhere if we are going to alter the current disastrous trends of over-using resources and polluting our planet. Every day, both at work and at home, note where you are most happy to make a contribution. This can fill a need for concrete action, and it could be a clue to your calling. Notice any time you are feeling particularly motivated and engaged. You can trust your experience to tell you that you are on the right track — that you are being called to.

**"The place where your deep gladness and the world's deep hunger meet."**
—Novelist and theologian Frederick Buecher

# Examples of Successful Green Career Changers

## Example 1: Dan Triman

Although I am currently self-employed as a green building and sustainability consultant, as well as an environmental educator, and a green roof contractor, the path I took to get here has been very unconventional. I want to share my story because I feel it is important to realize that there is no exact formula for finding your career path, but instead it is about making key decisions, maintaining a level of commitment to learning, and being ready to take advantage of opportunities as they arise.

During my college years, I attended the Green Festival in D.C., and I discovered a few green building companies. I had never heard of green building before, and was immediately drawn to learn more about this field. I did some research and looked into how I could potentially find jobs and a career in the industry. After I graduated, I made my first unconventional career decision when I took a job as a carpenter's assistant building houses in Takoma Park, MD. Not exactly the typical choice for someone who just completed their civil engineering degree. But to me it was more important to do something I enjoyed and to learn hands-on about the construction industry. I still use some of the knowledge from that job to this day. I really enjoyed my job and spent about 4 months working there, then spent the next 3 months traveling across the United States. On my trip, I discovered that there were a lot of places around the country where things were going on that I was very intrigued by. The place that caught my attention the most was Portland, Oregon.

When I got back to the D.C. area, I got a traditional civil engineering job. I figured I owed it to myself after four and a half years of college. While I worked there, I continued to research green building and I quickly found that Portland, Oregon kept popping up as the best place in the United States to get involved with and learn about green building. I decided to quit my job, and made another career choice that many people questioned. I moved clear across the country to Portland in order to immerse myself in their green community.

When I first moved to Portland, I was unsuccessful in my attempts to get a green job due to my lack of experience, and being from out of town. So I took a job at a civil engineering firm, which wasn't doing much sustainability work. I decided to make the best of the situation, spending my free time networking, volunteering, and educating myself about green building and sustainability. In just a few months' time I was able to make some great contacts, get involved with sustainability conferences, volunteer on some green building projects, and even become the Sustainability Manager for my office. In a little over a year spent immersed in Portland's green culture, I was able to get certified as a LEED Accredited Professional and a Sustainable Building Advisor. I even used my experiences to co-author the *Portland 2008 Green Guide to Networking and Jobs*. Just by getting to know the right people, asking the right questions, and showing that I was interested and knowledgeable about green issues, I was offered several jobs, all without ever having submitted any resumes or applications.

My next big decision came when I decided to move back to Washington, D.C., for personal and professional reasons. After making another unconventional decision to leave my full-time job in Portland without having another one lined up, I then spent my last two months in Portland as a full-time volunteer. Before I left, I wanted to feel like I had accomplished everything I had come to Portland for. I volunteered for over 10 different organizations and got valuable experience in a variety of green careers. I also used this time to start my green job research for the D.C. area and prepare my resume and cover letter. It was amazing how in just one year all my efforts in Portland had added so much more green experience to my resume and provided me with valuable supporting documents such as writing samples and presentations I had prepared.

I think in all I contacted about 50 companies in the D.C. area inquiring about job openings. A few companies were interested in talking to me, but the majority of the responses were that they weren't interested. It was a little difficult to job-search and network from 3,000 miles away, but I made every effort I could to start getting familiar with the people I would need to know when I moved back to D.C. I was fortunate that the annual GreenBuild Conference, which is the largest green building conference in the U.S., coincided with my move. I figured this would be a great place to meet and talk to at least a few green professionals from the D.C. area. I was able to set up three informal meetings with companies in attendance at the conference. Two of these meetings eventually led to job offers, but I didn't accept either of these offers because they weren't exactly what I was looking for at the time. However, this experience confirmed that I had some options for jobs in the green building industry in D.C.

Once I was settled in D.C., I followed up with all the companies I had spoken to previously and I eventually went on about six interviews. I also began to attend some local green events. I used the job searching skills I had learned in Portland, and after about a month or so of networking, researching, volunteering, and going on interviews, I decided to take a job as an independent contractor with a small, locally based engineering consulting firm, Indigo Engineering Group, which has a commitment to green building and sustainable design. They were ready to take the next step and further develop their green consulting services, which is where I came in. As their chief green consultant, I've been the project manager for LEED certification projects, led green building workshops and put together presentations, participated in several focus groups to discuss the state of the green building industry in D.C., helped to market and grow the company's green services, and helped develop Sustainable Action Plans for various cities and counties.

During my first experiences as an independent contractor providing green consulting services, I found that I really enjoyed the flexible schedule and the chance to do other part-time work on the side. I took advantage of this opportunity and secured a research internship with Eco-Coach, a D.C. based sustainability consulting company. Taking a position as an intern probably wasn't the typical move for someone with a full time job as a green consultant. But I knew it would provide me with an opportunity to get my foot in the door with the company, and it did in fact lead to my working part time as a sustainability consultant for Eco-Coach for the past several years.

I have been fortunate to find numerous green job opportunities in D.C., and I owe most of my success to what I learned during my time in Portland. I've been an independent contractor/consultant for the past 5 years now, and have worked for over 15 different companies, providing them with green consulting and contracting services. I have carved out a great professional network in the DC area. I have really enjoyed the flexibility and variety that being an independent contractor/consultant has provided me. I have recently become very interested in environmental education and working with schools and students to give them meaningful experiences related to nature as well as provide insight into environmental issues. I still continue to be very active in networking and volunteering and have found a few classes to take to continue my education. I am always on the lookout for new opportunities for jobs and learning.

Job searching is a totally different scenario in Washington, D.C., compared with Portland, due to the types of people living in each city and the nature of the cities themselves. Even so, no matter where you are, or what kind of job you are looking for, if you are committed to making an effort, showing others that you do good work, and that you are sincerely interested in green and sustainable issues, you will be successful in finding your own green job.

**Example 2: Anca Novacovici**

I'm an entrepreneur, and I love what I do! The path that led me to sustainability consulting, and to starting Eco-Coach Inc., was an indirect one, as it is with many. When I was in college, I was interested in the environment but did not see it as a potential career choice – I was told repeatedly that the environment and making money did not go hand in hand. My other interest was in diplomacy, which was my major, but after four years at Georgetown University's School of Foreign Service, I decided that, although I loved international relations, this was not the direction I wanted to take.

Since working with the environment was still on my mind upon graduation, but I knew I did not want to work in conservation or get a technical degree, I chose to work with an organization that sold green personal care and household products. This was in the mid-nineties, and the general public was not interested in hearing 'green' claims, i.e. that bottled water would soon cost more than gasoline, or that green personal care products were healthier and less harmful to the environment. I soon realized that selling products was not for me and that I needed to acquire additional (and different) skills if I wanted to achieve my goal of helping the environment as well as enjoy what I was doing. Because I was interested in working with businesses, had an interest in the international realm, and there were no degrees in sustainability offered at the time, I chose to obtain a Master's in International Management, from Thunderbird, the American Graduate School of International Management.

I certainly built my business skills in grad school. When I graduated, however, I found that the field of environmental consulting was still focused on more technical aspects, such as bioremediation and wastewater management. 'Sustainability consulting' per se still had not developed as a field.

The next stop on my journey was traditional management consulting. I reasoned that this would provide me with skills and knowledge that I could eventually tie back to working with businesses and the environment. I worked for a boutique consultancy – the individuals I worked with were great, as were the clients, and the work was challenging. Though I was doing work that interested me, and acquiring many skills (often through trial by fire), it was not satisfying on a deeper level. I succeeded in getting a recycling program started in the office but other than that, my work was not directly related to sustainability.

Then, one day, I was laid off. It was a bit scary at the time, but I decided that this was the perfect opportunity to start working independently. A short while later, I incorporated my own management consulting company. The jump was made easier by the fact that both of my parents were entrepreneurs, but it was still a risk. I mitigated it by starting a business in a field where I had previous experience and prior clients. I was fortunate in that I had clients from the start, and again, worked with some great people. However, the idea of working to help businesses lessen their impact on the environment was still in the back of my mind. I kept on trying to figure out how I would be able to do this, and came up with many different ideas, ideas that had not yet been brought to market to my knowledge.

Even though I had many ideas, I did not start another business. Why? I didn't see the market for it, at least not enough of one to merit full-time employment. The turning point was the day I saw one of the ideas I had toyed with being implemented by someone else. That idea, which at the time was quite innovative, was to help individuals quantify the environmental impact of their transportation use and offset it or at least a part of it. The company was TerraPass - I have them to thank for unwittingly giving me the final nudge to get started.

Though I had had many ideas, I chose to focus on sustainability consulting and coaching because I had the skills and interest to work with businesses and individuals, educate them about the environment, and provide them with tools to help them decrease their negative impact on the earth. When I started Eco-Coach Inc., I had a rather broad scope; that scope has changed somewhat over time, and it has also narrowed. I suspect the direction and scope will continue changing somewhat in response to the market and to the input we receive from our clients and consultants, but for the most part, the services that we are offering are more or less set.

I consider myself lucky because I am able to do what I love and work with some wonderful people who really want to make a difference. However, as you have read, it was not a straight line to get to this point and it is (and was) hard work. It is also a continuous learning process, and certainly an opportunity for growth. I have learned that in order to stay focused and be successful, you must find your niche, and that niche should be something that you enjoy but also something that challenges you to grow and sustains you financially. It may not be something that you jump into right away – you may have to take a step back and identify the skills that you need to develop in order to get to where you want to be. The good news is that if you keep the goal in mind, you will eventually get there. Good luck on your journey!

## Example 3: Tim Sandusky

My transition into the green economy has its origins in my college experience. It began as an intellectual pursuit that quickly translated into a conviction, ultimately setting me on my current career path. It began when I was entering college and read "Cradle to Cradle" by William McDonough and Michael Braungart, which was a formidable work for popularizing industrial ecology and green design. It was truly a life-changing moment as I devoured the book in a couple days. I thus entered college with an environmental mission. Even so, and odd as it may seem, I chose to major in humanities and augment that education with a minor in environmental studies.

My strategy was to develop a broad and irreplaceable set of researching, reading, critical thinking, and writing skills which I would employ in service for the environment. To this end, the humanities served me well. But I also fulfilled my humanities requirements with as many environmentally-related classes as possible. It was in this setting that I read Aldo Leopold's "Land Ethic" for a philosophy class. As one of the greatest conservationists in the U.S., his ethical arguments had a profound effect on my thinking. I brought these ideas with me to my literature, philosophy, religion, and environmental studies courses. It was these ideas which spurred me to action in extracurricular activities. I volunteered with other students to create our campus community garden. I co-wrote an article discussing the sustainability of new campus development. These activities were the manifestations of my studies; they were my way of translating knowledge into action.

However it was not until I read Wendell Berry that I developed a firm grasp of the connection between environmental health and economics. More than any other moment, the afternoon I began to read "Art of the Commonplace" is responsible for my belief in the necessity of changing our economics in order to restore our ecology. Berry's work gave me a sense of vocation. Although I wasn't exactly sure how I would accomplish it, my broad goal was to help design that new economy which was truly local, ecological, holistic, and just.

I was confident in my academic training, zealous in my mission, but overlooked the circumstances - I was the victim of bad timing. As I graduated college in 2008, the economy began to tumble. My search for jobs and internships was frustrated by my liberal arts academic background and lack of professional experience. Perseverance was essential through several months. Meanwhile I had gotten a job as a cook in the kitchen of an organic vegetarian restaurant. But after many resumes, cover letters, and interviews, I was offered a research internship with Eco-Coach, a sustainability consultancy in D.C. In this capacity, I have gained valuable experience researching the green job market in D.C. and performed some networking outreach. I have also greatly enjoyed researching and writing for their blog.

I had continued to pursue other opportunities though, and eventually moved on from the restaurant to an internship on an organic farm. I had always had an interest in the local organic agriculture movement, land use issues, and land conservation. Perhaps it was an unconventional career move, but for me it made sense. The farm produces vegetables and eggs for two D.C. farmers markets, and is situated on a large nature preserve in the mountains of Virginia. Besides the farm work, I've been fortunate to enough to gain new insights about growth and land use and made some useful contacts.

I have always tried to stay busy by finding relevant environmental opportunities. From extracurricular activities in college to multiple internships, I have been able to do this to a surprisingly effective degree. Currently, I am pursuing volunteer opportunities with a sustainable business organization in D.C. and a land conservation group in Virginia. Internships give work experience to help you narrow career aspirations - my internships have done just that. I have been able to realize my interests lie in the intersection of community design and economics. With this focus, I am preparing to apply to graduate programs in urban planning to study land use planning.

These opportunities have had other positive effects too. I have been able to develop a broad perspective on environmental issues thanks to a range of experiences. I have viewed the environmental movement from a white-collar, urban, and cosmopolitan perspective found in D.C.'s surging green community. But I've also been immersed in the life of an organic farmer, whose rural, blue-collar realities are just as important. I have gotten my hands dirty in the entire food process, from planting seeds of chard to preparing chutney made of organic ingredients. And soon, I anticipate researching and advocating the policies that govern sustainable land use.

There are several important themes that have dictated my career plans and training. I have aspired to create a skill set that is applicable to most careers. The refinement of basic skills like critical thinking and writing are necessary for professional development and creating pragmatic solutions to our environmental problems. I have tried to have a solid grasp of the intellectual reasons why I chose to pursue a place in the green economy. This gave me a solid foundation and workable criteria for choosing which opportunities to pursue. I have endeavored to immerse myself in a place, to know a certain area well enough to call home. It is very difficult to have a positive impact on the environment that is both lasting and effective without being rooted in a place. Admittedly, this has been difficult. But I've been able to locate most of my activities between central Virginia and Philadelphia, centering on D.C. And while I lack the positions of power that most have, I am as proud as anyone to be a part of the emerging green economy in D.C.

# Ten Common Mistakes

## By: Vicki Lind and Gail Nicholson

### Mistake #1: Having too many career options

Most of you are divergent creative thinkers with many interests and concerns about multiple environmental issues. We salute you. But it can drag out your transition since you'll need a separate networking strategy and knowledge base for each career interest. After an initial exploration, narrow down to at least one of the following areas: Natural Resources, Green Building, Energy, Transportation, Sustainable Business, Fish/Water, Food, or Education.

### Mistake #2: Not balancing inputs from your heart with inputs from your brain

It is important to start by listening to your heart to determine your deeper values and passions, the ones that will drive your career decisions. And it always makes sense to pursue what you are passionate about, even in a recession. If you find a job doing something you enjoy, there is a far better chance that you will be successful in the long run. However, keep in mind that finding a balance between your heart and the realities of the job market will take you further. This requires spending time doing your research! After you thoroughly analyze your odds, your timeframe, and your financial needs you will have a better understanding of what your options might be. But you have to be willing to put in considerable time and effort if you are considering a non-traditional job. They can be harder to find, define, and establish yourself in, but with the right balance between heart and mind anything is possible.

### Mistake #3: Being too literal in evaluating career options

Some jobs are intrinsically sustainable, even though they are not clearly labeled as such. For example, if you are an elementary school teacher, you can integrate sustainability directly into many subjects, from choosing stories in which people care for the earth, to using math story problems about how to save fuel. Similarly, if you manage a purchasing department, you may be able to choose recycled papers and healthier products without having the title of sustainability coordinator.

### Mistake #4: Expecting it to happen quickly

The stark reality is that it often takes two or more years to transition into a competitive field. This is particularly true if you want to change both your job function and type of organization you work for. Many people spend a year or more volunteering to position themselves before landing a paid position.

### Mistake #5: Failing to broadcast your specific skills and needs

You need a basic message that clearly states what you are looking for so that others can more readily help you. Then you need to actually use your message — a lot. For example, one individual found a lead that unexpectedly resulted in a job at a leading environmental engineering firm by broadcasting, "I want to meet people who work on air or water quality compliance issues. I want to use my eight years of business background along with my degree in environmental science. My strengths include being organized, a good writer, and passionate about creating a healthier environment."

### Mistake #6: Volunteering "promiscuously"

Targeted volunteering can be one of the most potent job search tools; indiscriminate volunteering may waste your time even if it promotes wonderful causes. Targeted volunteering means selecting volunteer activities in an organization that might hire you, or where you can meet many people who might hire you, or where you can learn a desired skill.

## Mistake #7: Expecting to date the prom queen

Many sustainability-oriented people are strongly committed to their ideal job in a company totally committed to sustainability. You increase your options by adding a less-visible company that is open to new sustainability initiatives.

## Mistake #8: Hiding volunteer activities on the second page

If you've recently volunteered in a green organization and it is relevant, a description should be included in the first page of your resume. This can be done if you label the section with your job history as "Professional Experience." Unless you just stuffed envelopes, it counts!

## Mistake #9: Submitting a one-size-fits-all resume

On the other hand, your resume needs to be targeted to each position or type of position. Readers don't have time to read through extraneous material that detracts from their focus on how you match their needs. Start with a summary of qualifications that match those identified in their position announcement. Using vocabulary directly from their listed responsibilities or qualifications may seem uncreative, but it can be the most effective approach because it is easiest for the hiring manager. Many firms now use software that scans text in the resume for keywords. They attach a score to each resume based on the density of relevant keywords. Only resumes that meet a particular threshold of key words are reviewed.

## Mistake #10: Doing it on your own

It helps to work with a career counselor, participate in a job club, and/or find a job-search buddy. Career development and job-hunting are emotionally draining; they require commitment to an ongoing process rather than starts and stops. You've heard, "When one door closes, another one opens." What they don't tell you is that it's darn lonely in the hallway.

Now that you're read this list once, reread it again. Is there a mistake you're making right now? Is there a mistake you need to be particularly careful to avoid?

# Informational Interviews
## By: Vicki Lind, Gail Nicholson, and Jim Cassio

Informational interviews are an integral part of the career exploration process. They allow you to access a new field and its key players. The answers you get can help you carve out a career path or target a resume to a desired job posting. That being said, keep in mind that this is not a starting point to the job search but is rather a way to refine which specific career field, industries and employers you will focus on. In this phase, it is not essential that the person you are interviewing has knowledge of direct job openings. However, a quality exchange may lead you to position openings as your search becomes more focused. Any new contact may be one degree of separation from the person who ends up hiring you.

To identify individuals whom you would like to speak with, determine the field or fields that you are interested in, and identify individuals who you know in those fields. You can do this by asking your friends and family, as well as former employers and other individuals whom you know through community or religious organizations, sports teams, etc.... Another great way of identifying potential interviewees is through online networks, such as LinkedIn. Although many LinkedIn contacts may not be local and the interviews cannot be done face-to-face, they are still extremely viable resources for learning about a career field and/or industry that may be of interest.

Use the following guidelines to help you prepare and stimulate your thinking:
- Schedule the interview either face to face or via phone.
- Determine which questions you would like to ask ahead of time, based on the goal of the interview (ex: find out about a potential career path, learn about the skills required for a specific job, or obtain additional information about a training program).
- You are most likely to get an informational interview if you've been referred by a mutual friend, colleague, or friend of a friend. This is called a "warm" lead.
- When you make contact, tell the person that you value his or her time and will bring some specific questions with you. Ask if it would be helpful to send the questions in advance. Preparing questions will help you shape the interview to meet your needs.
- Start by suggesting a 20-minute interview at this person's place of work or offer to buy them a cup of coffee at a place convenient for them. They will likely express a preference for one of those two options.
- If someone says that they do not have time, ask if you can have 5 minutes now or later, when it is more convenient. Also, if that person can't be of help, ask him or her to suggest someone else whom you might contact.
- Generally, you'll want to bring a resume, or send it ahead if they prefer. Another option is to ask if you could send a resume as follow-up to the interview. This way you have a reason for a second contact and can adapt your resume to what you learned in the informational interview.
- You will probably not get the answers to all of your questions. The purpose of an informational interview is to gather information and build rapport. If the person would be a valuable addition to your network, the rapport may be the most important component of the interview.
- At the end of the interview or when following up, ask them if there are others that they would recommend you speak to.

Choose four or five of the questions listed below that you would truly like to have an answer to; the whole list would take a few hours. Find a balance between thoughtful planning and allowing time for spontaneous exchanges.

- Tell me about your career and how you became a _____. (Keep in mind that, if you're interviewing a supervisor or manager of the type of position you're really interested in, they may or may not have actually worked in that position previously. Therefore, you may also want to ask them about that specific position.)
- What are some of the lessons that you learned – what would you repeat and what would you do differently?
- What education or training did you have when you entered this field, including any specific degrees or certifications? Is that typical? What skills, degrees or certifications are most likely to help someone advance in this field?
- Do you think that your organization is committed to sustainability? If so, in what ways?
- What are its plans for sustainability in the future? Have time and money been allocated to carry them out?
- Tell me about your typical workday. What are your most favorite/least favorite parts of the day? How much time is spent on the computer? How much interacting with people? How much outside of the office?
- Where do you see the field going? Where is the most job growth expected? (E.g. generalists or specialists, types of employers, geographic areas, etc.)
- Are there some specialties or job titles within this field or closely linked to it that I might explore?
- Are there any specialized skills or knowledge for which there is increasing demand?
- What are the entry, the mid-level, and the high salaries in the field?
- Are there any professional associations for this field that I should know about? Any local organizations with open meetings that I might attend? Journals that you recommend?
- May I contact you again if I have any additional questions or when I begin my job search?
- May I check back in with you in few weeks (or months?) to see if any new positions have opened up?
- Now that you know a little more about me and my goals, what do think my next step should be?
- Is there anything else that I should be aware of during my search?

During the interview, take notes and listen carefully. Spend more time listening than talking about yourself, unless the interviewee is interested and asks questions. Be sure that you ask follow-up questions and try to avoid repeating a question that they already answered. Stick to the time requested unless they clearly indicate they have more time available. At the end, if there's any doubt, ask if you can follow-up with them in case you have any additional questions or need clarification.

Follow up right away with a thank you in a format that is consistent with the culture of the organization. For example, a thank you to someone in a small, conservation-minded nonprofit might enjoy a hand-written note on a Sierra Club card; a person in a hip creative firm might prefer a witty e-mail. Hopefully, the thank you letter will be the first of many exchanges. Stay in touch and find ways to build on the connection. For example, if you see an article that might be of interest to the interviewer, send it along. You never know when someone who began as your informational interviewee may develop into a significant professional relationship, or even become your mentor. You may want to add to the contact log sheet below and use this as a guide to create your own. For instance, you may want to include who referred you to them, and the full mailing address.

Potential Informational Interviews:*

Name_____    Phone_____    E-mail_____

Name_____    Phone_____    E-mail_____

Name_____    Phone_____    E-mail_____

Name_____    Phone_____    E-mail_____

Name_____    Phone_____    E-mail_____

Name_____    Phone_____    E-mail_____

Name_____    Phone_____    E-mail_____

Name_____    Phone_____    E-mail_____

* Note: This contact log sheet is just an example to get you started. We recommend that you develop an Excel spreadsheet to track your contacts, which would include the following: the contact's name, mailing address, cell and office phone numbers, email address, date of first contact, type of contact, date of meeting, referred by, and notes to include information on the conversation you had with that person, as well as additional fields you feel would help you keep track of the individuals you speak with (ex: whether a thank you note has been sent after the meeting, etc…).

# Strategic Volunteering
## By: Vicki Lind and Gail Nicholson

Your volunteer choices will lead to employment to the extent that they provide opportunities: to 1) expand your network in a focused employment arena, 2) practice needed skills, 3) produce a work sample, 4) garner ideal references, and/or 5) become an inside candidate in the organization.

As we've noted, D.C. is filled with opportunities for rewarding volunteer work. We can easily fill up our calendars with a day at a creek cleanup, an evening of phone calls for a political candidate, and a weekend day building a straw bale house. When you're employed, these are excellent volunteer choices. But when you're competing in a crowded career field, you may need to think more shrewdly and strategically about volunteer activities. Even if you have considerable time available, it's not wise to make long-term commitments until you've reflected on what you learned earlier in the exploration process.

By analyzing job openings that interest you, and by conducting informational interviews, you can identify skills and experience that you lack - especially those you keep seeing in job postings. A volunteer experience or internship can strategically fill in for missing experience.

Your research and volunteer experience should help you identify key players and employers in your desired field. Volunteering in a situation where you have significant contact with one of these players will increase the relevance and potency of your references.

Your chances of being hired are dramatically increased when employers have been able to observe you and your voluntary contributions to the organization. For example, Susan moved into a position that opened up where she was volunteering. The position was not advertised, and they even reconfigured the job to better match Susan's skill set. When asked for advice for other job seekers, she stated her successful three-step process: "Number one is to figure out where you want to work and volunteer there. Number two is to impress them with how much you can do for them. Number three is to keep hanging around until they hire you." Three other successful career changers have generously shared the following stories of their successful use of strategic volunteering.

## Case Study: Erik Karuso

In the early stages of Erik's search, he wanted to build on his success in field-based outdoor education along with his Master's degree in environmental policy (see resume on page 102). He was disappointed that this background did not open the door to interviews for a broad range of environmental positions. After reflection and disappointments, Erik met with a career counselor and decided to narrow his career focus to preservation of outdoor spaces. This led to strategically volunteering for The Nature Conservancy for 30 hours per week for two months. His specific tasks were to support the project manager: research sites, engage property owners and other stakeholders, and prepare maps and informational material. These tasks had much in common with the duties listed in a position opening as the Project Associate at the Trust for Public Land's Chesapeake Bay Field Office. As you can see on Erik's cover letter (page 107), he refers directly to this correlation. Erik reports that he is engaged and excited to be at TPL, his first serious position in his chosen career. He credits both his "incredible good luck that the position opened up" along with his focused volunteer/internship selection.

## Where to Volunteer

Once you've decided on the type of volunteer position(s) that could help you better compete for your desired paid position, you need to locate an organization that will respect your contribution and offer you a true opportunity for professional development. There's no shortage of organizations that want your time, so you need to be selective.

1. **Post your specific need on a listserv or website in your arena of interest.**
   See the resources section for a list of listservs and websites. Be specific:
   • I seek to volunteer 15 hours per week in an organization that promotes justice for underrepresented populations. I wish to use my legal skills (new law degree) and/or my accounting background.
   • I want to volunteer evenings and Saturdays to use my background in graphic design and newsletters to support conservation of natural resources and wilderness. I can design brochures, ads, and possibly websites. Prefer SW Washington, D.C. location.

2. **Approach one of your targeted organizations.**
   Once you have a selected career arena, it's helpful to make a list of the organizations where you might like to work. For example, if your target is green building, you might select the US Green Building Council (USGBC). For example, Rebecca's top interests and values included promoting green buildings. She had some experience in marketing and communications, but none for green buildings. She contacted USGBC Maryland Chapter and offered to provide program management support after her traditional work hours. They were delighted.

3. **Volunteer for a professional association.**
   One of the easiest ways to access friendly people willing to give you informational interviews is through professional organizations. For example, Patricia was introverted and disliked small talk at events. She signed up to organize the display booths at a sustainability conference. She welcomed the assignment to contact key sustainability organizations to invite them to attend. As a result, her network expanded quickly.

## Volunteering: Conclusion

In addition to helping you find a job, volunteering can offer you:
• A place to contribute where you can forget you're unemployed.
• A place to locate people for informational interviews.
• A place to nurture your self-worth.
• A place to go when your days have no structure.
• A place to meet kindred spirits.
• A place to make a difference.

# Resumes
## By: Vicki Lind and Gail Nicholson

Resumes and cover letters have one goal: to get you a coveted interview. Like everything else, resumes and cover letters have styles that are in favor and those that are out of favor. Beware of using ineffective, outmoded advice: resumes are one to two pages maximum; resumes are either functional or chronological; resumes should include hobbies and state, "references available upon request."

For most job seekers, the best resume format is a blend of a functional resume (organized by functional strengths) and a chronological resume (organized strictly by date).

Your resume format will be predominately chronological if your most recent position is the most relevant to the prospective position. Chronological resumes often include a brief "summary of strengths" or "profile" section at the top (see Sample Resume #1). Use vocabulary to describe your accomplishments that lines up closely with the vocabulary listed as qualifications in the announcement.

If your most recent job does not show your pertinent strengths, start with a strong functional section (see Sample Resume #2). Julie Ann McMann did not want to present as a music teacher, the profession she is leaving. Instead, she wanted to show her long history of writing and research in both volunteer and paid positions. Even if you have a strong functional start, you'll still need a chronological work history with short descriptions of your accomplishments and responsibilities at each place of employment. Hiring managers express frustration with resumes that focus exclusively on broad transferable skills without reference to where/when the skills were used.

## Resume Tips

- Begin sentences with action verbs such as initiated, trained, organized, and motivated. End with quantitative or qualitative results.
- Tailor each resume to each position that you apply for. One strategy is to develop a master resume with about three pages of material. When you apply for a job, refer to the position announcement and edit your resume down to two pages, using the most pertinent material (make sure to print it out double-sided).
- Include hobbies and community activities only if these are relevant to the position.
- Professional organizations, community activities, or languages you speak, if pertinent, make great additions.
- Don't list references with or in the resume, unless requested. References are generally requested if you are invited to an interview.

## Measurable Accomplishments

Quantitative measurements are particularly important if your job target is in sales/marketing, development, or engineering. The following examples are from a resume of a development officer:
- Studied major donor demographics, wrote solicitation letters and contacted targeted donors; raised up to $20,000 per year above dues and increased average size of gifts.
- Increased membership renewal 7% in two years by tripling annual contact with members.
- Within three weeks of joining the organization, won confidence from the board by producing their first fundraising event and raising $35,000.

# Cover Letters
## By: Vicki Lind and Gail Nicholson

A cover letter is a one-page introduction that works in partnership with the resume. Its style can express your personality, and should ideally balance warmth with professionalism. In less-crowded fields, job seekers can often garner an interview using a cover letter that highlights the passion for the mission of the organization and applicable transferable skills. Today, to be effective, you must also show that you understand the employer's needs and that the skills that you bring to the table match these needs. You should ideally show how you can help their business in one or more specific ways.

When hiring managers are deluged with applicants, they may skip the cover letters until they have culled the resumes to a shorter stack of qualified candidates. Stress the major points of your cover letter in bullets at the top of your resume. We want you in that shorter stack where your cover letter will be read.

Draft a generic copy for potential cover letters. But don't write final copy until you know the position and the company that will receive it. Edit and tailor each cover letter (and resume). Always ask someone else to be a final proofreader – you do not want to apply for the wrong position or address the cover letter to the wrong company! Resumes and cover letters take considerable time, but the time spent is well worth it.

Some companies prefer an online application and do not request cover letters. A few concise, targeted comments can be sent in the copy of an e-mail. In order to decide if you need a full cover letter, read the company's directions very carefully, and follow them.

## Cover Letter Format

Dear _____ (get name if possible):

### Opening Paragraph
State the reason for your letter, including the job title of the position you are seeking. State how you became aware of the position: referral, newspaper advertisement, trade magazine, etc. The strongest referral source is a colleague or co-worker who is known and respected by the person screening or hiring.

### Second Paragraph
This paragraph summarizes your knowledge and/or prior experience with this organization. You want to convey that you have cared enough about this position to become knowledgeable about the organization. To demonstrate your research, you can refer to a new direction, a new project, or recent recognition that the organization has received. Website or newspaper articles are good sources.

### Third/Fourth Paragraph
In one or two paragraphs, reiterate and possibly expand on one or two skills, accomplishments, or characteristics from your resume. To select which points to emphasize, reread the position announcement to assess what's most important to the employer. Emphasize the value you bring to the organization's mission and challenges. Be sure to focus on how you can help them, not the other way around.

### Closing Paragraph
State how you can be reached. You may want to restate in one sentence what you can do for the organization. You can state your enthusiasm about meeting in person. You can also state that you will follow up within a few days to discuss the position.

Sincerely,

_____ (Your Name and Contact Information)

# Sample Resumes

**Sample Resume #1***

## Erik Karuso
567 Florida Ave, NW, Washington, D.C.
Phone: 123-5678; Email: erikkaruso@yahoo.com

## Professional Skills

**Commitment to the Environment** – Knowledge of and passion for advancing conservation and environmental sustainability, demonstrated in professional and personal engagements.

**Research and Analysis** – Meticulous and efficient research skills in public policy, academic, and journalism contexts; experience manipulating, analyzing, and interpreting data.

**Project Coordination and Support** – Able to conceive of and complete projects involving multiple collaborators, frequent input, and political or administrative complexity.

**Computer Skills** – Currently using ArcGIS; produced reports using Word, Excel and PowerPoint; extensive web research experience; familiar with Microsoft Access.

## Professional Experience in Conservation and Environmental Policy

**The Nature Conservancy** – Washington, D.C.                                          2/07-present
*Project Assistant (volunteer) in the Government Relations Department*

- Assisting TNC staff to identify, develop, and assess alternative sites for a proposed Virginia National Guard training facility. Tasks include networking with local government authorities, researching land ownership and acquisition possibilities, and engaging Virginia National Guard leadership to reconcile TNC conservation goals with the Guard's training needs.
- Testing and expanding TNC's conservation project database, ConPro.

**Janet Reilly for California State Assembly** – San Francisco, CA                     1/06-5/06
*Consultant on environmental policy for a political campaign*

- Consulted with candidate to shape an environmental platform and seek endorsements. Researched existing initiatives and developed positions on key issues such as transportation and air quality.
- Rapidly developed expertise in pending initiatives, legislation, and priorities identified by constituents. Authored responses to endorsement questionnaires from environmental organizations.

**City of Annapolis, Office of Sustainable Development** – Annapolis, MD              6/03-4/04
*Research Associate in the Policy, Research, and Evaluation Division*

- Developed a pilot research and evaluation program to target investment in sustainable urban development; conducted extensive interviews with funding institutions, municipal environmental managers, and policy researchers nationwide; tracked and developed funding sources for research.
- Compiled and analyzed citywide greenhouse gas emissions data and energy consumption trends, created visual representations of these trends for use by management, drafted a detailed report for City Council, and wrote an executive summary of this report for public distribution.
- Coordinated a multi-stakeholder assessment of the ecological benefits of green roofs. Initiated meetings, scheduled tasks, established benchmarks, tracked and sought funding opportunities, and maintained momentum on an effort involving multiple city bureaus and external partners.
- Crafted outreach and communication materials based on "frames" research and consultations with target audiences to deliver sustainability messages to the public.

**Freelance** – Washington, D.C. and San Francisco, CA                           periodically since 9/01
*Writer, researcher, and editor of works ranging from policy documents to popular guidebooks*

- Edited research publications (2000-01) on environmental and human rights performance in the oil industry for the Natural Heritage Institute (Berkeley, CA).
- Author of *50 Hikes in Alaska's Chugach State Park* and *Best Short Hikes in California's North Sierra* (both by Mountaineers Books), study guides for SparkNotes, Inc., and book reviews in the *Willamette Week*.

**Chesapeake Climate Action Network** – Takoma Park, MD                           12/01-7/02
*Researcher and Assistant Producer (volunteer), supported writing of press releases*

Researched, wrote, and edited stories and press releases on local green events. Tropics included energy efficiency, watershed management, and sustainable urban development.

## Education

**University of California, Berkeley** – Berkeley, California                           8/04-6/06
**Master of Arts** in American History (expected 2007)
Research focus on the history of the concept of sustainability, the history of federal natural resource policies in the American West, and Native American history.

**Oxford University** – Oxford, England                           9/99-9/00
**Rhodes Scholar; Master of Science** (2000) in Environmental Change and Management (with Distinction). Course work in environmental science, policy, and economics; GIS and data analysis. Dissertation examines the concept of ecological integrity as applied to recreation management in Canada's Banff National Park.

**Harvard University** – Cambridge, Massachusetts                           9/93-6/98
**A.B. in History and Literature,** *magna cum laude* (1998). Phi Beta Kappa.


**Sample Resume #2***

# Julie Anne McMann
Email: juliemcmann@gmail.com

## PROFESSIONAL SKILLS

**Commitment to Sustainability and the Environment:** Knowledge of and passion for advancing sustainability and environmental issues, as demonstrated in professional and personal engagements.

**Writing/research:** Versatile writer/editor capable of reaching diverse audiences. Experience with grant writing. Extensive background in research. Experience with generating press releases and public service announcements. Familiarity with AP style. Thorough command of the rules of English grammar and spelling. Foreign language facility in Spanish, French and German.

**Education:** Experienced teacher skilled in disseminating information and generating enthusiasm while engaging others. Proven success in classroom presentation.

**Computer Skills:** Extensive Web research experience; proficiency with Word and Excel. Familiarity with both Macs and PCs.

**Other Skills:** Creative approach to problem solving; motivated self-starter able work with little supervision. Comfortable with working alone or as part of a team.

## RELEVANT EXPERIENCE

*Grant writer* (volunteer) Environmental Defense Fund, Washington, D.C.          10/07-present
Write grants to fund scientific research on global warming, oceans and health for local advocacy organization.
*Writer/researcher* (volunteer), Arlingtonians for a Clean Environment, Washington, D.C.  9/07-present

Write and research content for online newsletter.

*Program Annotator*, National Symphony Orchestra, Washington, D.C.          2004-present
    Write and research program notes for National Symphony.

*Program Annotator*, Cascade Festival of Music, Bend, OR          2006-present
    Write and research program notes for Cascade Festival of Music.

*Contributor*, National Public Radio's "Performance Today," Washington, D.C.  2004-2005
    Provided scripts to introduce specific works radio program.

*Commentator*, National Public Radio's "Performance Today," Washington, D.C.  1997-1998
    Provided occasional commentaries on nationally syndicated radio program.

*Music Teacher*, International School of Music, Bethesda, MD          1996-2007
    Taught general and applied music classes to groups of children and adults aged 18 months to 80 years; also taught private voice and music lessons in a one-on-one setting.

*Writer*, Washington Post.com, Washington, D.C.          1996-2000
    Wrote features, profiles and reviews for the weekly performing arts section of the online newspaper; also edited monthly events calendar.

---

**EDUCATION**

| | |
|---|---|
| M.M., Boston University | 1996 |
| Language Certificate, Middlebury College German Summer Language Program | 1993 |
| B.A. Music with Honors, University of California at Santa Cruz | 1989 |

**Sample Resume #3***

# Rebecca Rozinski
Rebeccaroz@hotmail.com

## QUALIFICATIONS SUMMARY

- Experience and training in program design and management, communications, grant writing and administration.

- Proficient in all Microsoft Office applications and the Internet.

- Experience with In Design, Plone and Auction Pay.

- Fluent in German.

### RELEVANT EXPERIENCE

10/07 – Present   **CCAN (Chesapeake Climate Action Network),** *Columnist/Blogger*, Takoma Park, MD

Write weekly blogs for a website focused on global warming education in the Washington, D.C. metro area. My blog focuses on what is happening in the nation's capital in relation to 'going green'.

06/07 – Present   **US Green Building Council Maryland Chapter,** *Interim Assistant Director*, Baltimore, MD

Provide program management for a variety of education and outreach projects and events. Responsibilities include writing marketing language and programmatic correspondence, budgeting, coordinating/liaising with partners, sponsorship research and coordination, event coordination, building event Web pages, and programmatic research.

04/07 – 06/07   **Mid-Willamette Cooperative Weed Management Area,** *Website Content Writer (contract)*, Willamette OR

Conducted research and wrote content for the Western Invasives Network, a website for the early detection and prevention of invasive plant species in the Pacific Northwest. Content primarily included 53 quick fact sheets, 6 full fact sheets for invasive plants, and a news and events page. Designed 5 different outreach posters.

04/07 – 06/07   **World Wildlife Fund,** *Office Assistant (temporary),* Washington, D.C.
Provided assistance to the Communications Manager, including research, drafting communications materials, copy editing, maintaining the media database, media archiving, and recording meeting minutes. Wrote programmatic communications material. Developed and designed a partner directory. Performed various administrative tasks for staff, such as programmatic research, conducting phone calls, facilitating mass mailings, and managing databases.

11/06 – 03/07   **World Wildlife Fund,** *Communications and Development Intern,* Washington, D.C.
Assisted with the coordination of the 2007 Panda Ball Gala; helped WWF nearly double its net financial goal for the event. Managed contact lists. Researched donor prospects, drafted donor correspondence, made follow-up calls to donors. Tracked and maintained donations and ticket sales with Auction Pay database. Drafted auction catalogue; assisted with catalogue design. Coordinated event volunteers.

7/06 – 09/06   **Chilkat Guides, Ltd.,** *Operations Coordinator,* Skagway, AK
Facilitated tour operations. Created and organized sales records; prepared and facilitated financial settlements with cruise ships; produced end-of-day reports. Assembled and instructed clients for excursion departures. Collaborated on community development programs under the Ministry of Social Transformation, Culture, and Local Government.
- Major projects included: Developed, implemented, and co-facilitated an environmental club program in four primary schools. Wrote a successful grant for two of the clubs, which allowed one to renovate their school's greenhouse to generate funds. Managed the budget for said grant.
- Collaborated with a local educator to develop, implement, and coordinate a nonprofit organization for after-school arts education for children, which currently enrolls over 20 children. Wrote grant proposals and subsequently secured two significant grants.
- Collaborated with the Ministry of Forestry to develop a campaign to protect a threatened endemic bird. Mobilized 8 community members to form a council to undertake campaign initiatives.
- Created an activities chapter for a nationally distributed environmental education textbook.
- Organized and facilitated needs assessments and community meetings for a community outreach program in six (6) communities for the St. Lucia National Emergency Management Organization.
- Led the development, implementation, and coordination of an after-school tutoring and mentoring program between a primary school and a secondary school. Trained 12 student volunteers.
- Edited articles for a quarterly Peace Corps Eastern Caribbean magazine as the copyeditor.

**Friends of the Earth,** *Communications and Administrative Intern,* Washington, D.C.
Wrote and edited press releases. Conducted web research and developed website content. Assisted with the content and design management of the 2003 annual report. Created a program manual. Maintained the media database. Liaised with media experts.

**EDUCATION**

**University of Virginia.** Charlottesville, VA. May 2003
**B.A. in German Language and Literature. Minor in Religious Studies. 3.72**

\* These resumes are included to provide you with examples. Although they are based on actual resumes, the names and some of the organizations and locations have been changed to protect individuals' privacy.

# Sample Cover Letters

## Sample Cover Letter #1*

1234 Florida Ave. NW
Washington, D.C.

Ms. Jennifer Smith
Hiring Director
ABC Organization
555 Wilson Boulevard
Arlington VA

Dear Ms. Smith:

I am writing in response to the Internet posting for an Environmental Advocate position in Arlington, VA. I was very excited to see a position in which I could use my governmental and media background to promote environmental protection in my native state of Virginia.

I grew up camping, hiking and swimming in the Shenandoah Mountains. I have a heartfelt regard for Virginia's natural treasures. I consider stewardship of the planet to be a foremost responsibility for we humans who have the power to destroy it. The current "war on the environment" deeply troubles me, so I have decided it is time to turn my efforts toward more direct involvement in environmental protection.

I have been impressed with ABC's advocacy for pollution controls, renewable energy and forest preservation, and your success in building coalitions and marshalling public involvement. Congratulations on breaking the record for public comment on the Administration's mercury proposal!

In my 16 years working inside Virginia State government and with other governmental agencies, I have built relationships and partnerships to find common ground and solve issues. I began my career in television news, so I meet your qualifications for a candidate with over three years of media and communications, including inside knowledge of how the media works.

As the director of the Department of Human Services' Program for At-Risk Teens, I was the main lobbyist for Jobs for Teens during the 2003 legislative session. In a climate of severe budget cuts, I successfully advocated for continued funding for the program. I built relationships with lobbyists who represent groups that would benefit from the program and enlisted their support.

I would like to put these skills to work to promote environmental preservation and protection in Virginia. The ABC Environmental Advocate position appears to be a wonderful opportunity to do just that, and I am eager to learn more about it.

I look forward to hearing from you.

Erin Doe

* Personal information has been changed to protect the privacy of applicants.

**Sample Cover Letter #2\***

4/9/12

John Verde
Trust for Public Land
660 Pennsylvania Avenue, SE
Washington, D.C. 20003

Dear Mr. Verde:

I am excited to submit my application for the position of Project Associate at the Trust for Public Land's Chesapeake Office. For the past seven years, I have broadly explored environmental issues, and gained experience shaping environmental policy in government, journalism, and academic settings. Last year, I gave serious consideration to my career goal for the next ten years and decided to build on my environmental foundation to focus on a career in conservation.

In pursuit of this goal, I recently met with Harry Messler to learn more about TPL's work. I am also applying my research skills and policy expertise as a volunteer assistant to the government relation's staff at The Nature Conservancy. My specific tasks in supporting the project manager, researching sites, engaging property owners and other stakeholders, and preparing maps and informational material have much in common with the Project Associate's duties at TPL.

I am firmly rooted in the Chesapeake Bay and familiar with its geography, politics, and culture. I care deeply about protecting its open spaces and can think of no organization so aligned with my goals as the Trust for Public Land. I admire TPL's tight focus on a pragmatic mission - to put high-quality land in public ownership - and its entrepreneurial style. I'm especially drawn to TPL's vision of conserving land for people, from pristine ecosystems to urban brownfields.

I pursued my interest in making cities more livable as a research associate at the Office of Sustainable Development (OSD). At OSD, I juggled multiple projects entailing research, project support, and coordination. My principal tasks included devising a blueprint for a policy and research division, through which OSD could influence the city's sustainability agenda by conceiving, independently funding, and partnering with the private sector to carry out demonstration projects. I balanced research and administrative support tasks to move projects forward.

As my resume indicates, I took a detour from my work in sustainability to pursue a doctorate in environmental history. After weighing the rewards of historical research against my desire to make a tangible contribution to the health of the environment, I packed up my research and analytical skills and brought them home to Washington, D.C., with a newly clarified focus and the hopes of finding an entry position in a conservation organization. I'm confident that I've found the right position as Project Associate at TPL.

Sincerely,

Erik Karuso

\* Personal information has been changed to protect the privacy of applicants

# Job Search Checklist
## By: Vicki Lind and Gail Nicholson

Use the following checklist to help you in your job search. The checklist will keep you focused, organized, and well prepared for potential job openings. We have provided you with space to write in information as you go through your search. You might need to reference the checklist at a later time so use it as a worksheet, and if you feel you need to add any other items to the checklist, feel free to do so.

❏ Target your resume(s) to your career objective(s).

❏ Identify the people or groups you need in your support network and what you need from them (e.g.: connections, accountability, technical information, cheerleading, and empathy).

1._____
2._____
3._____
4._____
5._____

❏ Identify and review Internet sites most likely to post appropriate job openings. Bookmark and periodically review these websites for desirable employers.

1._____  2._____
3._____  4._____
5._____  6._____
7._____  8._____
9._____  10._____

❏ Analyze job postings for required/desired technical skills & build skills for jobs that you would like.

❏ Follow up (phone/e-mail/mail) with people in your network who are most likely to hear about job openings.

1._____  2._____
3._____  4._____
5._____  6._____
7._____  8._____
9._____  10._____

❏ Carry out strategic volunteering or an internship to build the skills and/or contacts that fit your career objective(s).

❏ Become active in professional organizations/groups that can provide job leads that match your career objective(s).

1._____     2._____

3._____     4._____

5._____     6._____

7._____     8._____

9._____     10._____

❏ Develop an interview strategy and practice PAR (problem, action, results) stories.

❏ Customize your cover letter and tweak resume for each position to which you apply.

❏ Research the organization prior to each interview.

❏ Interview with energy and enthusiasm!

# Evaluating and Researching Employers
## By: Vicki Lind and Gail Nicholson

### Revisit Your Values and Needs

To determine if an organization is a place where you want to apply, revisit your values and needs and from there, consider the match. Evaluate green practices across all aspects of the organization, including procurement (purchasing eco-friendly supplies), personnel policies, the facility, and overall corporate culture. Explore whether you must have a position in a department with an explicitly green purpose (for example, educating people about use of chemical cleaners in the home), or if you are fine with working in an eco-friendly organization but you do not have a 'green job' and instead you are the accountant, for example.

To facilitate the clarification of your values and your potential employer's values/actions, we have provided the checklist: **Criteria for Evaluating Employers: Values**, page 109 The first step is to review the values we have listed and to add any additional values that are important to you. Then, review the list to determine what is "very important," what is "desirable," and what is "not a priority" to you. Finally, choose the top five values that are most important and see how your rating compares against that of your potential employer's.

### Hypothetical Case Study: Pat
There are no absolutes to determine which organizations are green. Often you will find a shade of green that works for you, but not your neighbor. Suppose Pat, your neighbor in Northeast Washington, D.C., comes to you excited: she has just received a coveted job offer from Capital One, located in McLean, Virginia. You have mentored her toward an overall sustainable lifestyle. She now buys local, recycles religiously, and her family will be joining you for the beach cleanup. You worry that you will burst her bubble with some of your hard-core generalizations: "All multinational corporations are corrupt. I can't forget the sweatshop stories. Cubes are bad for the soul." You realize that these generalizations reflect your values - not her values. You also recall that many of Capital One's buildings are up to LEED standards, even though they are not certified.

You decide to support Pat in posing research questions to address her concerns about gas consumption in the hour-long commute. You help her brainstorm options: "Can you carpool? Can you take metro? Is Zipcar an option so that your family only needs to own one vehicle? Will you make enough to buy a hybrid?"

### Research
After you revisit your values, the next step is to research the green practices and plans of a potential employer. There are four key times to ramp up your investigation:
- The time you decide to apply.
- Prior to the interview.
- At the interview.
- Prior to accepting the position.

We offer seven suggestions for researching a potential employer. The first five suggestions should be done prior to an interview, as a part of the research you do to become a more informed interviewee.

---

1. Review the organization's web site, especially the mission statement. For example, a brief review of Eco-Coach's website shows that the company is committed to sustainability and providing green services for their clients. It is also clear that they have a significant amount of experience in the green industry and that have been a leader in sustainability consulting for several years.

2. Search back issues of the *Washington Business Journal* and the *Washington Post,* accessible through their respective websites. Search by the name of the business/organization to see what's been written about it by outside reporters.

3. Some larger employers have been reviewed by credentialing organizations that audit facilities and products, from construction to air quality. **Criteria for Evaluating Employers: Certifications and Affiliations** on page 111 provides links to many of these organizations.

4. Affiliations, sponsorships and advertising can reveal the organization's orientation. However, whenever an organization is paying for promotional activities, be cautious about green washing. The watchdog group CorpWatch (http://www.corpwatch.com) defines green wash as "the phenomena of socially and environmentally destructive corporations, attempting to preserve and expand their markets or power by posing as friends of the environment."

5. Use your network to get the scoop on your targeted organization's commitment to sustainability. If your closer contacts don't have sufficient experience with the organization, seek out contacts familiar with the company by attending green networking events sponsored by Live Green, SB NOW, Green Drinks or other networking organizations.

6. At the end of most interviews, you'll be asked, "Do you have any questions for us?" This is an appropriate time to ask one or two questions about their environmental practices. At this time, it is appropriate to state your interest in sustainability if you have not yet done so, but be sure not to push too hard by asking pointed questions (e.g., "How much has the company donated to which causes?" or "Can we get organic snacks from the vending machine?"). Hold on to those questions and focus on making the case for why you are the best person to meet this organization's needs.

7. After you have been offered a job is an excellent time to put forth any additional questions that you may have. You can ask for a meeting with your prospective employer and be quite candid without the risk of the offer being rescinded. It is in the best interest of both you and your employer that you are thoroughly committed to your new position.

# Criteria for Evaluating Employers: Values
## By: Vicki Lind and Gail Nicholson

Rate the following values for you and for your potential employers, based on the research you have done to date and any potential interviews you have had with them. Once completed, determine the top 5 values that are most important to you and see how your potential employer ranks on these. Repeat this with any other employers that you are considering working for.

Ratings:
Very Important (3)
Desirable (2)
Not a Priority (1)

| | My Values | Employer Values |
|---|---|---|
| **PURPOSE and PRACTICES** | | |
| Company provides green product line or services | | |
| Mission statement includes green objectives | | |
| Company has a sustainability policy | | |
| My department provides green product line or services | | |
| Green initiatives in organization's plan | | |
| Leaders discuss sustainability priorities | | |
| Charitable giving practices consistent with stated values | | |
| Eco-friendly office practices | | |
| Sponsor nonprofit environmental groups | | |
| | | |
| **FACILITY and SUPPLIERS** | | |
| Use alternative energy and/or energy conservation program | | |
| Green building (LEED certification) | | |
| Strong recycling program | | |
| Use green vendors and suppliers | | |
| | | |
| **HUMAN RESOURCE POLICY and CULTURE** | | |
| Support four-day week to reduce commute miles | | |
| Support some telecommuting | | |
| Support work/life balance | | |
| Paid staff time for community service | | |
| Employee participation in decision-making | | |
| Employee programs encourage 'going green' at work & at home | | |
| | | |
| **TRANSPORTATION** | | |
| Access to public transportation | | |
| Subsidize use of public transportation | | |
| Ability to car pool or use flex car | | |
| Bike friendly (showers, racks) | | |
| Company vehicles are biodiesel or hybrid | | |
| Preferred parking for energy efficient cars | | |

| OTHER VALUES IMPORTANT TO ME | | |
|---|---|---|
| | | |
| | | |
| | | |
| | | |
| | | |
| | | |
| | | |
| | | |
| | | |
| | | |
| | | |

# Criteria for Evaluating Employers: Certifications and Affiliations
## By: Vicki Lind and Gail Nicholson

Although there are certain certifications and affiliations that can be used to evaluate how 'green' an employer is, keep in mind that there are some employers that choose not to participate in any of these programs but have nevertheless taken steps to be eco-friendly. In addition, many of these certification and affiliations focus only on specific industries; your potential employer's industry may not have a certification, or the certification may not apply to the type of work they are doing. Therefore, in addition to asking them about the following affiliations and certifications, be sure to check their website and search the Internet for additional information on any sustainability initiatives they may have undertaken or are currently undertaking.

## Recognized or Certified by an External Organization

| | |
|---|---|
| Cradle to Cradle | http://www.C2Ccertified.com |
| EPEAT | http://www.epeat.net/ |
| Forest Stewardship Council (FSC) | http://www.FSC.org |
| GreenGuard Indoor Air Quality | http://www.GreenGuard.com |
| Green Seal | http://www.greenseal.org/ |
| LEED Certification | http://www.usgbc.org/ |
| (Leadership in Energy and Environmental Design) | |
| Scientific Certification System | http://www.SCScertified.com |
| 'Certifiably Green' Business | http://www.sbnow.org  (launching in 2009) |

## Advertising and Affiliations

Member of CERES, a voluntary Coalition for Environmental Corporate Responsibility
> http://www.ceres.com

Green America's National Green Pages (formerly Coop America)
> http://www.coopamerica.org/pubs/greenpages/

Member of The Natural Step  http://www.ortns.org/

Recipient of the Mayor's Environmental Excellence Awards in DC
> http://ddoe.dc.gov/ddoe/cwp/view,a,1210,q,499054.asp

Sponsor nonprofit environmental groups and conferences

# Greening a Non-Green Employer
## By: Vicki Lind and Gail Nicholson

As we've stated, thousands of local employers are waking up to the green mission. Rather than search for a new employer (or until you find a new one), you may be able to go grow a green career "where you are planted." Or you can seek a new employer who has recently become aware of the ethical imperative to make a contribution, and you may be the person who helps provide guidance and expertise during the seminal stages. This can roll at a dizzying pace or be very slow, as you first need to get oriented to the culture and people in the new organization.

If you're considering investing your time and effort into greening a potentially non-green employer, you need to first find out if they can "walk the talk." Have they allocated time and funds? Is there at least one champion with clout? Even if you think, "yes, the commitment is deep and genuine", there is still a host of reasons that progress may seem slower than the movement of a glacier (a sadly outdated analogy). You and other employees may be too busy carrying out the duties that drive the company's bottom line. You may have captured the ear of one crucial champion, but your "ear" gets transferred. Or, decision-making is centralized at a corporate office and your local site has limited autonomy.

One tactic for greening your current organization is to target positions within the organization that implicitly have more influence on purchasing or vendors. The following are some examples:
- Positions where you have the authority to purchase office supplies may allow you to introduce recycled papers;
- Positions where you are in charge of landscapes might allow you to buy organic fertilizers; and
- Positions where you plan events that may permit you to start composting waste.

## Green Teams

While you are earning the respect needed to garner influence, a great first step is to engage coworkers in starting a Green Team. These are groups of employees within a company or organization that meets periodically to discuss issues related to green and sustainable practices. Green Teams tend to focus on issues related either to daily in-house practices, or on how to incorporate more sustainable practices into their work. Examples of topics for daily activities include:
- Waste reduction (amount of paper used, recycling practices, purchasing practices);
- Employee transportation (daily commuting, business trips, etc.); and
- Office environment (natural light, thermal comfort, connection to outdoors, nontoxic environment, etc.).

Green Teams tend to be a relatively small group of employees, but the size of the Green Team depends on the size of the company and how many employees are interested in devoting their time to this effort.

Green Teams can grow out of informal discussion groups, usually scheduled during non-work time, to explore and educate yourself and others about sustainability, as well as to evaluate a more structured Green Team. Some Green Teams don't have formal authority in the organization, but can still act as a catalyst for more formal initiatives. Groups without authority tend to fizzle out. You can keep them from fizzling out by making the meetings fun, focus on how you can go green and save the company money, and establish some metrics to track progress.

Green Teams thrive when they have management support in several ways: Management can support holding meetings during work hours, which bolsters attendance and signifies their support. The effectiveness of Green Teams is bolstered when management takes the time to honestly define and clarify which issues are open for consideration. Most importantly, management can provide a venue for green teams to present recommendations to someone who has the authority to implement change. If you'd like to start a Green Team and don't know how to get started, or have one and would like more guidance, you can also contact Anca's company, Eco-Coach. They provide workshops and will also be providing webinars for Green Teams. Also, take a look at the book 'Sustainability 101: A Toolkit for Your Business', which also provides easy steps to get started around the office. We have used the information in that book for many of our clients and have found that it has helped them take the beginning steps towards a more sustainable organization.

# III: Green Jobs Resources

# Local Career Centers

You may not be aware that there are many career centers in the Washington, D.C. metro area that provide career services to individuals seeking employment. These career centers can be great resources for getting connected to possible employers, as well as career guidance and training to help you identify the types of jobs that fit your skill set or that interest you. We have provided the list below for you so that you can quickly identify which career center(s) are the closest to you, and can easily contact them to see how they may be able to help you in your job searching process.

## Green Job Clubs

While visiting your local career center, you might as well find out what information and services they can offer you! They might even sponsor a green job seeker's group that could be very helpful to you. Such "job clubs" give members an opportunity to get together on a regular basis to share information and job leads with other people looking for similar jobs, or jobs in similar industries. Job clubs often feature guest speakers and generally provide a very cooperative and educational environment for their members. If your local career center doesn't have a green job club, ask them to start a sign-up list to see how many people would be interested in participating in such a group. Even if a career center doesn't currently offer specific training and assistance in green jobs, the more people that start asking about these types of services, the more likely they are to look into implementing these types of programs.

## Career Center Locations

### Washington, D.C.

Washington, D.C. Dept. of Employment Services (DOES)
4058 Minnesota Avenue, NE
Washington, D.C 20019
(202) 724-7000
http://www.does.dc.gov/does/cwp/view,a,1233,q,538261,doesNav,|32064|.asp

**Full Service One-Stop Career Centers**
Bertie Backus Campus
5171 South Dakota Avenue NE, 2nd Floor
Washington, D.C. 20017
Main: (202) 576-3092
TTY: (202) 576-3102
Fax: (202) 576-3103
Hours of Operations: M-F 8:30 am to 4:00 pm

Frank D. Reeves Municipal Center
2000 14th Street, NW, 3rd Floor
Washington, D.C. 20009
Main: (202) 442-4577
Hours of Operations: M-F 8:30 am to 4:00 pm

DC Works! Southeast Career Center
3720 Martin Luther King Jr. Avenue, SE

Washington, D.C. 20032
Main: (202) 741-7747
Hours of Operations: M-F 8:30 am to 4:00 pm

**Satellite Centers**
South Capitol One-Stop Career Center
4049 South Capitol Street, SW
Washington, D.C. 20032
Main: (202) 645-4000
TTY: (202) 645-0022
Fax: (202) 645-5337
Hours of Operations: M-F 8:30 am to 4:00 pm

US Veterans Assistance Center, Veterans Affairs Regional Office
1722 I Street, NW, Room 335
Washington, D.C. 20421
Main: (202) 530-9354
TTY: (202) 576-3262
Fax: (202) 530-9359
Hours of Operations: M-F 8:30 am to 3:30 pm

King Greenleaf Center
201 N Street, SW
Washington, D.C. 20024
Main (202) 724-2050
TTY: (202) 724-1409
Fax: (202) 724-1407
Hours of Operations: M-F 9:00 am to 3:00 pm

Business Opportunity Workforce Development Center
2311 Martin Luther King Jr. Avenue, SE
Washington, D.C. 20020
Main: (202) 645-8625
TTY: (202) 673-6994
Fax: (202) 645-0366
Hours of Operations: M-F 9:00 am to 4:00 pm

**Montgomery County**

MontgomeryWorks One Stop Career Center
Montgomery Works has job search resources, recruitment and job fairs, workshops and training, job seeker services, and labor market information.
Phone: (301) 946-1806
Website: http://www.montgomeryworks.com/
Email Address: info@montgomeryworks.com
Hours of Operations:  M-Th 8:30 am to 5:00 pm; F 8:30 am to 3:00 pm

Sales and Service Learning Center
The MontgomeryWorks Sales and Service Learning Center are in Wheaton at the Westfield Shoppingtown, adjacent to JC Penney and the parking garage next door to H&R Block.
11160 Veirs Mill Road Suite LLH17

Wheaton, MD 20902
Phone: (240) 403-3600
Hours of Operations:  M-Th 8:30 am to 5:00 pm; F 8:30 am to 3:00 pm

Wheaton
Located in the Westfield South Office Building next to the Westfield Shoppingtown Mall. It is two blocks from the Wheaton Metro station behind the Circuit City store and next to the movie theater.
11002 Veirs Mill Road, 1st Floor
Wheaton, MD 20902
Phone: (301) 946-1806
Fax: (301) 933-4427
Hours of Operations:  M-Th 8:30 am to 5:00 pm; F 8:30 am to 3:00 pm

Germantown
Located in the Upcounty Regional Services Center.
12900 Middlebrook Road
Germantown, MD 20874
Phone: (240) 777-2050
Fax: (240) 777-2070
Hours of Operations: M-Th 8:30 am to 5:00 pm; F 8:30 am to 3:00 pm

**Prince George's County**

Prince George's County, Maryland One Stop Career Center
The PG County One Stop Career Center offers services for job seekers that include Maryland Workforce Exchange, job search assistance, skills assessments and training, workshops, and labor market information.  For more information visit one of the offices listed below.
Website: http://www.pgworkforce.org/

Prince George's County Economic Development Corporation Workforce Services Division
Largo
1100 Mercantile Lane #100
Largo, MD 20744
Phone: (301) 618-8425
Hours of Operations:  M-F 8:00 am to 5:00 pm

Laurel
312 Marshall Av. #504
Laurel, MD 20707
Phone: (301) 362-9708
Hours of Operations: M-F 8:30 am to 4:00 pm

Silver Spring
820A University Blvd. E.
Silver Spring, MD 20903
Phone: (301) 434-6453
Hours of Operations: M-F 9:30 am to 3:30 pm

## Arlington County

Arlington Employment Center
Job seeker services include career counseling, workshops and seminars, resume assistance, job search assistance, aptitude tests and training referrals, youth employment services, and assistance for seniors and those with disabilities.
2100 Washington Boulevard, 1st Floor
Arlington, VA 22204
Phone: (703) 228-1400
Website: http://www.arlingtonva.us/portals/Topics/Jobs.aspx
Email: jobseeker@arlingtonva.us
Hours of Operations: M-Th 8:30 am to 4:00 pm; F 9:00 am to 4:00 pm

## Alexandria

City of Alexandria Department of Human Services JobLink
The career center has a resource center for self-directed job searches which includes resume help, job bulletin access, and other resources. Assisted job search services include employment specialists, skills assessments, and interview skills.
1900 North Beauregard St., Suite 300
Alexandria, VA 22311
Phone: (703) 746-5990
Hours of Operations: M-F 8:00 am to 5:00 pm
Website: http://alexandriava.gov/humanservices/info/default.aspx?id=8372

## Northern Virginia

**Northern Virginia Workforce System Skill Source Group**
These career centers have skills assessment, career training, job placement, personalized counseling, interview and resume preparation, and job search assistance. Access to fax machines, computers, the internet, interview coaching, and all the job listings and job fairs in the area is also available. Offices are in Fairfax and Loudon Counties:
http://www.myskillsource.org/home/index.shtml

**Fairfax County**
Falls Church SkillSource Center
6245 Leesburg Pike, Suite 315
Falls Church, Virginia 22044
Phone: (703) 533-5400
TTY: (703) 533-5316
Hours of Operations: M, T, Th 8:30 am to 5:00 pm; W 8:30 am to 7:00 pm; F 10:00 am to 5:00 pm

**Lake Anne Employment Resource Center**
A SkillSource Affiliate
11484 Washington Plaza West, Suite 130
Reston, VA 20190
Phone: (703) 787-4974
TTY: (703) 742-0350
Hours of Operations: M-Th 8:00 am to 4:30 pm; F 10:00 am to 4:30 pm

**South County SkillSource Center**
8350 Richmond Highway, Suite 327
Alexandria, VA 22309
Phone: (703) 704-6286
TTY: (703) 704-6685
Hours of Operations: M-Th 8:30 am to 5:00 pm; F 10:00 am to 4:30 pm

**Loudon County**

**Loudoun Employment Resource Center**
102 Heritage Way, N.E., Suite 103
Leesburg, VA 20176
Phone: (703) 771-5934
TTY: 711 VA Relay
http://www.loudoun.gov/Default.aspx?tabid=1308
Hours of Operations: M, T, TH, F 9:00 am to 12:30 pm; W 9:00 am to 12:30 pm; 1st F of the month 1:00 pm to 4:30 pm

**Prince William County**

**Woodbridge Virginia Workforce Center**
13370 Minnieville Road
Woodbridge, VA 22192
Phone: (703) 586-6800
TTY: (703) 583-6850
Hours of Operations: M-Th 8:30 am to 4:30 pm; W 9:00 am to 4:30 pm

# Green Education and Training Programs

As mentioned in the article by Mark Starik in the first section of this Guide, a great way for you to advance your career in the green industry and make yourself more marketable when it comes to getting green jobs is to gain knowledge of specific issues, topics, and developments in your particular area of interest. Luckily, there are an incredible amount of opportunities and resources available to you. These opportunities will not only provide you with valuable knowledge, but they will also connect you with green professionals and experts in their respective industries.

The following list of education and training opportunities in the Washington, D.C. metro area will provide you with a good idea of the variety and depth of different ways that you can gain knowledge about green and sustainability issues if you are interested in doing so. The list includes college and university offerings, workshops, green collar job training programs, and online offerings. The list is not meant to include every single training or education opportunity in the entire D.C. metro area, but rather to give you a general idea of what the current opportunities are. There are always more and more of these programs and courses being developed as time goes by, so keep an eye out for new offerings as well. If there is an organization or institution you are specifically intrigued by, even if they aren't on this list, contact them and ask them if they know of any current training and educational opportunities you could take advantage of.

## Colleges and Universities

A great resource for information about academic programs with a sustainability focus is the Association for the Advancement of Sustainability in Higher Education (AASHE). They maintain a list of degree and certificate programs in North America that have a sustainability focus. Their website can be found at the following link: http://www.aashe.org/

### American University
*B.A. in Environmental Studies*
Core courses are taken in the natural sciences and social sciences. Auxiliary classes are taken from the College of Arts and Sciences, the School of International Service, and the school of Public Affairs. Internships with non-profit organizations and governmental departments in D.C. are encouraged.
http://www.american.edu/cas/env_std/programs/undergrad/undergrad.html

*Certificate Program in Environmental Assessment*
Designed for professionals seeking a more specialized education. A Bachelor's degree and several prerequisites are required for admission.
http://www.american.edu/cas/env_std/programs/certificate/certificate.html

*M.S. in Environmental Science*
Interdisciplinary degree taught by faculty specializing in natural products chemistry, marine science, environmental toxicology, ecology, conservation biology, environmental chemistry, and environmental statistics. The program is characterized by its small class size and ample faculty-student interaction.
http://www.american.edu/cas/env_std/programs/graduate/graduate.html

*M.A. in Global Environmental Politics*
Environmental politics, natural sciences, and economics are integrated to provide an interdisciplinary study of the causes of, and solutions to, environmental problems. Integrating theory and practical

experience with policy formation and implementation, the degree is seminar-driven and individually-focused to provide a comprehensive and personalized degree.
http://www.american.edu/sis/academics/fieldofstudy/gep.htm

## Catholic University
*M.S. in Sustainable Design*
Housed in the School of Architecture and Planning, it is a post-professional, two-semester degree that explores the theory and implementation of environmental stewardship in building. Courses cover greenhouse gas emissions, life cycle assessment, and energy, water, and materials topics.
http://architecture.cua.edu/academicprograms/mssd.cfm

## George Mason University
*Conservation Studies*
A non-degree program, undergraduate classes are offered through a partnership between the Mason Center for Conservation Studies and the Smithsonian Institution National Zoo's Conservation and National Research Center. Courses cover topics that include environmental leadership and conservation science.
http://mccs.gmu.edu

*B.S. in Global and Environmental Change*
This undergraduate degree is unique for combining coursework in traditional natural sciences with social sciences to study the various spheres and scales of environmental interactions.
http://www.gmu.edu/catalog/cos/environmental.html#global_and_environmental_change_bs

*M.S. in Environmental Science and Public Policy*
A professional Master's degree, it examines solutions to a wide range of environmental problems, with departmental focus on ecosystem, conservation, and sustainability science, policy, and management. Two tracks are available, environmental science and policy which is research focused and geared towards those seeking a Ph.D., and environmental management which develops skills usually found in a Master of Public Administration program.
http://www.gmu.edu/departments/espp/graduate/degrees/masters.html

*Ph.D. in Environmental Science and Public Policy*
The interdisciplinary doctoral program is for more advanced study into the scientific research and policy solutions of environmental problems. It consists of an interdisciplinary core, from which students choose one of two tracks, either environmental science or environmental policy.
http://www.gmu.edu/departments/espp/graduate/degrees/doctoral.html

*Environmental Management, Undergraduate Certificate*
Requiring 27 hours, this program explores the problems and solutions of environmental problems, as well as methods of analysis. Interdisciplinary core courses are augmented by earth science, biological science, social science, and methods requirements.
http://www.gmu.edu/departments/espp/undergrad/degrees/management.html#requirements

*Environmental Management, Graduate Certificate*
This six-course certificate is designed for professional development as well as preparation for a M.S. or Ph.D. in Environmental Science and Policy. The courses span the natural sciences, social sciences, and environmental methods.
http://www.gmu.edu/departments/espp/graduate/degrees/certificate.html#certificate

**George Washington University**
For a general list of the green courses offered at George Washington University visit the following website: http://www.sustainability.gwu.edu/courses.html

*B.A. in Environmental Studies*
Housed in the Department of Geography, it requires courses in the biological sciences, geological sciences, and geography. It is an interdisciplinary program, with a wide variety of courses also coming from the humanities and social sciences.
http://gwired.gwu.edu/adm/classroom/schools/majors

*M.A. in Environmental Resource Policy*
An interdisciplinary program designed for policy decision-makers who want to focus on environmental and resource issues. Analytical skills are developed though coursework in political science, economics, the natural sciences, and environmental law.
http://programs.columbian.gwu.edu/enrp/

*LLM, Concentration in Environmental Law*
This Master's law degree offers three tracks within the concentration. The Environmental Law track offers flexibility to tailor the program. The Government Procurement and Environmental Law track studies the contracting and environmental problems of government contracts at the local, state, and federal levels. The International Environmental Law track studies the increasing need for global cooperation on environmental issues.
http://www.law.gwu.edu/ACADEMICS/FOCUSAREAS/ENVIRONMENTAL/Pages/LLM.aspx

*Sustainable Landscapes, Graduate Certificate*
A year-long program at the Alexandria campus, this certificate program is appropriate for advanced landscape design students and design professionals. The program explores best practices in landscape conservation and sustainability while focusing on the small-scale landscape and neighborhood level.
http://nearyou.gwu.edu/sl/index1.html

**Georgetown University**
*Center for the Environment*
Housed in the Department of the Biology, the center administers the Environmental Studies Minor and the Environmental Studies track of the Science, Technology, and International Affairs major. As such, the center advises students and serves as a resource for faculty and their classes in the environmental programs. The center also hosts lectures and forums.
http://www1.georgetown.edu/centers/environment/

*Science, Technology, International Affairs, Concentration in Environmental Studies*
The foundation of this undergraduate major is in the natural sciences, all though it is housed in the School of Foreign Service. Interdisciplinary in its coursework, this concentration covers the intersection of environmental and energy issues on a global level.
http://www3.georgetown.edu/sfs/bsfs/majors/stia

*Master of Public Policy, Environmental and Regulatory Policy Track*
This policy track takes advantage of course offerings from other Georgetown schools to create an interdisciplinary study of the ability of government to deal with environmental problems. Courses cover regulation, environmental law, ethics, economic tradeoffs, human health, and environmental sciences.
http://gppi.georgetown.edu/academics/mpp/requirements/12433.html

*J.D. in Environmental Law*
The J.D. program at Georgetown offers a wide base in environmental law, including U.S. federal law, international environmental law, environmental research workshop, and natural resources law. Specialized courses and seminars are chosen depending on interest, in order to focus on specific laws or environmental issues. Related courses are also chosen to round out the program.
http://www.law.georgetown.edu/curriculum/tab_clusters.cfm?Status=Cluster&Detail=12

**Montgomery College**
*A.S. in Environmental Science and Policy*
This Associate's degree is designed for students to transfer to a four-year program to earn a Bachelor's degree in environmental science and policy or a related degree. It requires a foundation in natural sciences, physical sciences, and math. Electives are upper level counterparts of these courses.
http://www.montgomerycollege.edu/curricula/descriptions/cdscience.htm#sciepoli

**University of the District of Columbia**
The Environment and Natural Resources (ENR) unit of UDC CES provides the D.C. community with environmental education programs. These programs cover a wide variety of topics. They teach Horticulture, Water Quality, pesticide and pest management. They also provide agricultural literacy through their Agriculture in the Classroom program.
http://www.udc.edu/ces/enr/about.htm

**University of Maryland**
For a general list of the courses offered at University of Maryland related to sustainability, visit the following website: http://sustainability.umd.edu/content/curriculum/academics_courses.php

*Environmental Science and Policy*
An undergraduate major that is begun in the College of Agriculture and Natural Resources, it is science-based but multidisciplinary in its scope. Students go on to choose concentrations from the College of Agriculture and Natural Resources, College of Social and Behavioral Sciences, College of Chemical and Life Sciences, or the College of Computer, Mathematical, and Physical Sciences.
http://ensp.umd.edu/

*B.S. Environmental Science and Technology*
Housed in the Department of Environmental Science and Technology, this degree is concerned with solutions to environmental problems. It covers the health of ecosystems, the built environment, and humans. Students choose a concentration from Ecological Technology Design, Environmental Health, Soil and Watershed Science, or Natural Resource Management.
http://www.enst.umd.edu/Future%20Students

*Master or Ph.D. Environmental Science and Technology*
This research-driven degree is divided into three specializations. The Soil and Watershed Science track looks at the biogeochemical cycle of soil on scales from field to watershed. Ecological Technology Design trains students to incorporate natural systems into the built environment to solve environmental problems. Wetland Science studies how wetlands provide for ecosystems and built environments.
http://www.agnr.umd.edu/Academics/departments/ENST/graduate/index.cfm

*Master of Community Planning, Concentration in Land Use and Environmental Planning*
A professional Master's degree, this specialization trains students in the history and practice of metropolitan land use and its environmental impacts. It also includes law, economics, equity studies, and growth management. The program is also affiliated with the Center for Smart Growth Research and Education.

http://www.arch.umd.edu/planning/academics/degree_programs/master_of_community_planning

*M.S. in Environmental Management*
A professional Master's degree housed in the Graduate School of Management and Technology, its aim to provide the knowledge and practical skills for professionals in environmental management settings. Coursework topics include water, air, and soil environmental issues, such as pollution prevention, environmental impact assessments, and waste management.
http://www.umuc.edu/programs/grad/msem/index.shtml

*M.S. in Sustainable Development and Conservation Biology*
This degree aims to give its students an interdisciplinary approach to the biodiversity crisis. Solutions are considered by integrating human development and biological conservation needs. Policy resources in D.C. are utilized as educational opportunities, namely the federal government and numerous environmental non-profits.
http://www.life.umd.edu/CONS

*Master of Public Policy, Environmental Policy*
This concentration is firmly grounded in policy formation and implementation, and then built upon by study in ecological economics, growth management, international development, or other environmental issues. The interdisciplinary design of the program means students explore the scientific, philosophical, legal, ecological, and political intersections in environmental issues.
http://publicpolicy.umd.edu/degree-programs/master-of-public-policy/areas-of-specialization/environmental-policy

*Office of Executive Programs, Environmental Policy*
This program is a service to local, State, and Federal government and private organizations to develop public knowledge of environmental issues and create appropriate environmental policies. It utilizes the breadth of resources at the university, including four colleges and many centers. Past work has included creating case studies, conferences, and customized certificate programs.
http://www.publicpolicy.umd.edu/executive-education/environmental-policy

*Undergraduate Certificate in International Agriculture and Natural Resources*
Any student at UMD can pursue this certificate in conjunction with their major. It is intended to give students a global experience. As such, its requirements include language, study abroad, international aspects of the environment, sustainability and development, nutrition, and business.
http://www.umd.edu/catalog/index.cfm/show/content.section/c/1/ss/383/s/387

*Graduate Certificate in Environmental Management*
The program is for new environmental professionals looking to enhance their skills to work with others in the field. It consists of five courses that include environmental auditing, communication, assessment, law, and pollution and waste management.
http://www.umuc.edu/programs/grad/certificates/tech_env_mgmt_envmgmt.shtml

*Graduate Certificate in Ecological Economics*
An interdisciplinary certificate program from the School of Public Policy, the curriculum focuses on resource economics, ecological economics, and quantitative methods. It requires graduate level prerequisites and is often taken in conjunction with a degree program.
http://www.publicpolicy.umd.edu/prospective-students/Academic_Programs/certificate-programs

**Virginia Tech, National Capital Region Campus**

*Master of Natural Resources*
Located in the D.C. metro area, this degree focuses on urban ecology and sustainability of natural resources. The sustainable use of fisheries, wildlife, and forest resources are emphasized. The program is designed for professionals who want a natural resource education. It is a non-research degree and ideally suited for working adults. Admission is usually part-time, although full-time admission can be available and an online version of the degree is offered as well.
http://natrespro.nvgc.vt.edu/masters_nr.htm

*Certificate of Graduate Study in Natural Resources*
This certificate requires 12 hours of graduate study, 9 of which must be in the College of Natural Resources. There is flexibility in the program to meet professional goals. Additionally, the certificate works in conjunction with the Master of Public Administration program, which can have a Natural Resource concentration with this certificate.
http://natrespro.nvgc.vt.edu/certofgrad.htm

*Master in Urban and Regional Planning*
This interdisciplinary professional Master's degree is concerned with management and protection of natural resources in relation to human needs and the built environment. While the program is strongly based in science and technology, it is broad in scope with coursework in policy, law, planning, and economics.
http://www.uap.vt.edu/programs/gradprograms/uap-programs-grads-MURP.html

## Local Non-Profit Organizations and For Profit-Businesses

**Arlingtonians for a Clean Environment**
One-day workshops on a variety of topics are offered, including recycling training, backyard habitats, rain gardens, and 'green' kitchen and bath remodeling. Workshops are held weekday evenings or weekends in Arlington, VA.
http://www.arlingtonenvironment.org/getinvolved.htm

**Casey Trees**
Beginner classes provide a general introduction to trees and the urban forests of D.C., as well as hands-on training in tree care. Advanced classes provide education in urban ecology, green design, environmental stewardship, and community outreach. Tree Walks and Pruning Workshops are also offered. Casey Trees also offers a Green Jobs brochure with information about why green jobs are important and the benefits they can have for the District, which can be accessed here: http://caseytrees.org/news/media-kit/index.php
http://www.caseytrees.org/education/index.php

**Chesapeake Climate Action Network**
The Chesapeake Climate Action Network offers forums, workshops, and classes. Informational and discussion events are offered to the public on climate change politics, clean energy generation, and energy efficiency. Events are in D.C. and the metro area, on weekday nights or weekends.
http://www.chesapeakeclimate.org/getinvolved/events.cfm

**Common Good City Farm**
This workshop series is offered once a month at the recently developed Common Good City Farm in LeDroit Park in NW D.C. Common Good City Farm was formerly the 7th Street Garden and has now moved to their new, larger location on the site of an old school building. The classes will focus on gardening topics that will help you learn how to improve your gardening skills at home.
http://commongoodcityfarm.org/growinggardens

**The Conservation Fund**
The Conservation Fund, a non-profit focused on environmental conservation efforts, has a program called the Conservation Leadership Network that offers a variety of training courses that look at land planning and conservation issues. They offer both online courses as well as workshops you can attend in person. Current courses include Strategic Conservation Planning Using the Green Infrastructure Approach, and Balancing Nature and Commerce in Communities that Neighbor Public Lands.
http://www.conservationfund.org/training_education/catalog_of_training_courses

**Eco-Coach Inc.**
Offers classes, webinars and workshops on going green at home (ex: energy efficiency, water conservation, etc.) as well as seminars on being green at the office (ex: marketing green, starting a Green Team, introduction to the Natural Step). Eco-Coach will soon be offering certification for in-home eco-auditors and is also working with SB NOW on a green business certification program for office-based and retail businesses and will be training eco-assessors to help with the certification process. Check their website and sign up for the newsletter to get information on upcoming classes and certification programs.
http://www.eco-coach.com

**Environmental Law Institute**
The Environmental Law Institute offers both training course workshops as well as webinars that focus on environmental law issues. Check their website for updates on upcoming events.
http://www.eli.org

**Environmental Protection Agency**
*National Network for Environmental Management Studies*
This fellowship program for undergraduate and graduate students provides training and research opportunities directly related to their field of study. It is designed to encourage entry into environmental jobs through placement in EPA offices and laboratories. Financial assistance is provided through the program.
http://www.epa.gov/enviroed/students.html

**Environmental Support Center**
The Leadership and Enhanced Assistance Program, LEAP program is a two-year program which helps environmental non-profits to realize their organizational goals. The program helps create and improve organizational plans, including strategic, leadership transition, fundraising, business, marketing, and fundraising plans. It also refines management, personnel, and financial systems. The program takes place through approved consultants, and funding is provided for the majority of the program.
http://www.envsc.org

**Everblue Training Institute**
Everblue Training Institute is currently offering classes to help prepare individuals for the LEED AP test as well as other courses for getting more familiar with the LEED Rating Systems. The classes are offered in the D.C. metro area at George Mason University.
http://www.everblueenergy.com/leed-exam-prep-washington-dc.html

**Green Advantage**
Green Advantage offers training classes to prepare individuals for their Green Advantage Exam which accredits people as Green Advantage certified building practitioners. The training courses are offered in the D.C. metro area at various times during the year. Green Advantage has also just partnered with the National Job Corps Association to offer green construction trainings and certification to young workers at

the Job Corps centers across the country. This will train young people to have the skills needed to become involved in the green job movement across the country.
http://www.greenadvantage.org

## Green Building Institute

The Green Building Institute has many course offerings open to the public. As an institution that was created to promote sustainable building through education, a variety of classes are offered. One-time classes at the institute are on topics such as geothermal energy systems, zero-energy homes, post-oil building, and deconstruction. One-time classes are also taught at community colleges throughout Maryland during the semester. Topics for these courses cover design, waste, site issues, efficiency, and landscaping.
http://www.greenbuildinginstitute.org/pages/courses.html

## Greenspace

Greenspace provides access and resources for education, training, and technical assistance that are essential in order for the thousands of building professionals in the National Capitol Region to choose green practices and succeeds in implementing DC's and Montgomery County's Building Acts. Greenspace is building capacity throughout the development community and within government to transform the marketplace and accelerate the adoption of green building practices.
http://www.greenspacencr.org/

## Green Roofs for Healthy Cities

Green Roofs for Healthy Cities (GRHC) is based in Toronto, Canada and is the leading organization in North America for promoting green roofs and providing a network for green roof professionals to gain access to research, conferences, and training courses. GRHC offers a series of classes as part of their Green Roof Professional Accreditation Program. The current course offerings are Green Roof Design 101, Green Roof Design & Installation 201, Green Roof Waterproofing& Drainage 301, Green Roof Plants & Growing Media 401, Green Walls 101, Ecological Design for Green Roofs, Green Roof Policy, and Green Infrastructure. Classes are offered in Washington, D.C. several times throughout the year, and the courses are intended to lead towards a professional accreditation as a Green Roof Professional, a new certification made available for the first time this year.
http://greenroofs.org/index.php/eduprogram/upcomingcourses

## Institute for Policy Studies: Social Action and Leadership School for Activists (SALSA)

The SALSA program has many course offerings that will help you act globally and learn locally. So if you are interested in global issues and want to get involved in activism around social action, look into taking some of the SALSA courses.
http://www.hotsalsa.org/index.php?view=calendar

## Maryland Green Registry

The Maryland Green Registry is a voluntary self-certification program that provides tips and resources to help organizations become more sustainable. Housed in the Maryland Department of the Environment, the Registry requires facilities to share environmentally friendly practices and provide quantitative results. Joining the Maryland Green Registry is free, and membership includes technical and informational assistance on implementing eco-friendly solutions.
http://mde.maryland.gov/MarylandGreen/Pages/Home.aspx

## National Building Museum

The National Building Museum often offers programs and lectures around green building and construction topics. Many of these courses can provide you continuing education credits, as they are a

registered training provider with organizations such as the American Institute of Architect, the American Society of Landscape Architects, and the American Institute of Certified Planners.
http://www.nbm.org/programs-lectures/ongoing-series.html

**National Park Service**
The National Park Service offers a Professional Development Program at the Kenilworth Park and Aquatic Gardens. The program is available upon request, and takes place on-line, at the park, and at the school. Training can be provided for plant identification, environmental economics, development and use of learning gardens, pond and wetland construction, Chesapeake Bay watershed ecology, wildlife ecology, and monitoring natural environments.
http://www.nps.gov/keaq/forteachers/professionaldevelopment.htm

**Neighborhood Farm Initiative**
A non-profit project of American the Beautiful Fund, the Neighborhood Farm Initiative (NFI) is an organization of community members participating in small-scale food production. Located next to the Fort Totten Metro Station on the Red Line, NFI serves to increase community access to fresh produce, promote community-building, educate youth and adults on urban food production, and improve underutilized public green spaces.
http://www.neighborhoodfarminitiative.org/

**Smithsonian Institute**
*Environmental Research Center, Professional Development*
This is a workshop for K-12 teachers, who can learn about the center's research, the Chesapeake Bay ecosystem, and research pertaining to the bay's watershed. Training is provided to help teachers create outdoor learning environments related the Chesapeake Bay and its watershed.
http://www.serc.si.edu/education/teachercorner/prof_development.aspx

*National Zoological Park, Professional Training Course*
This program is meant to compliment professional training and is open to both U.S. and international professionals. Tracks include wildlife conservation and management, biodiversity assessment and monitoring, GIS training, and wildlife endocrinology.
http://nationalzoo.si.edu/SCBI/MAB/GMU/gradprofcourses.cfm

*National Zoological Park, Teacher Workshops*
One to three day workshops, two-month fellowships, and customized in-service training are available. Workshops include tree identification, ecological field studies, and biodiversity science in the classroom.
http://nationalzoo.si.edu/Education/TeacherWorkshops

**US Department of Agriculture (USDA)**
The USDA Grad School provides adult continuing education opportunities through career training, customized solutions, evening and weekend classes in D.C., certificate programs, and distance education. Courses and certificates cover a wide array of topics from business to paralegal to IT. Environmentally-related offerings include Environmental Studies, Horticulture, GIS, and Landscape Design.
http://www.grad.usda.gov

**US Green Building Council**
USGBC offers a series of online courses and webinars as well as one-day private LEED workshops for larger groups. Course curriculum focuses on general green building principles, introduction to LEED, and implementation of LEED standards. Webinars have included LEED for homes, LEED for schools, LEED for retail, green leases, energy efficiency for schools, and green renovations. Registration and a fee are required.

http://www.usgbc.org/DisplayPage.aspx?CMSPageID=283

**The Washington Gardener**
The Washington Gardener is a gardening publication for the D.C. Metro region written in full by local area gardeners. In addition to providing tips and examples of gardening projects that readers can apply in their own gardens, the magazine also hosts events such as seed exchanges and garden tours.
http://www.washingtongardener.com/index_files/UpcomingEvents.htm

## Online Education and Training

**Bainbridge Institute**
The Bainbridge Institute offers several programs related to sustainable professional development. They have 2-3 year MBA in Sustainable Business and also offer Certificate Programs in Sustainable Business and Sustainable Entrepreneurship & Intrapreneurship. These programs offer the opportunity to deepen your understanding of entrepreneurial and sustainable business practices that champion social justice, environmental responsibility, and profitability.
http://www.bgiedu.org

**Boston Architectural College**
Courses as well as certificate programs are available for distance learning at the Boston Architectural College. They have a Sustainable Design program that covers learning about the many ways in which buildings interact with the natural environment and the choices available to make that interaction positive. They currently offer about 15 different courses, all of which are taught by well respected, industry leaders in Green Building.
http://www.the-bac.edu

**Eco-Achievers**
Eco Achievers is an educational provider for the renewable energy and sustainable living community. They help people succeed in achieving sustainability in their home and professional lives through relevant and targeted e-learning experiences. They offer several courses online, many of which are USGBC accredited. Courses include: Home Energy Fundamentals, Achieving Solar, and Life Cycle Assessment for Designers.
http://www.ecoachievers.com/

**Eco-Coach Inc.**
As described above, offers webinars as well as live classes on going green at home and work. Soon to offer courses and certifications in both of these areas – see description above for further details.
http://www.eco-coach.com

**Environmental Protection Agency**
*Air Pollution Training Institute, APTI*
This program gives technical air pollution training to government and tribal environmental professionals. It is administered through classroom, telecourse, self-instruction, and web-based teaching.
http://www.epa.gov/air/oaqps/eog

*Drinking Water Academy*
This training program aims to aid government and tribal environmental professionals in implementing the 1996 amendments to the Safe Drinking Water Act. Classroom, web-based training, and training materials are provided.
http://water.epa.gov/learn/training/dwatraining/index.cfm

*National Enforcement Training Institute, NETI*
NETI offers training to government and tribal lawyers and technical experts in inspection, enforcement, and criminal investigations of environmental regulations. Online classes, an E-library, and resource center are available.
https://www.netionline.com/Default.asp

*Pesticides Worker Safety and Training*
This program provides training and certification to meet the EPA's Worker Protection Standard for Agricultural Pesticides regulations. It covers the preparation, application, and exposure to pesticides through state and tribal administration of the national program.
http://www.epa.gov/pesticides/health/worker.htm

*Superfund Training and Learning Center*
Training for the management of hazardous waste is designed for professionals, all though some resources are open to the public. Online courses, self-directed instruction, videos, internet-based seminars, and in-person training are available.
http://www.epa.gov/superfund/training/index.htm

*Watershed Academy*
The program is the EPA's training center for the implementation of watershed regulations. 50 web-based self-training modules are offered for free, with a certificate awarded after completion of 15 modules and self-tests. Webcast seminars and live on-line training courses are also available.
http://www.epa.gov/owow/watershed/wacademy

**National Association of Environmental Managers**
There is usually one webinar per month offered from the National Association of Environmental Managers. Topics covered include those that deal with environmentally and socially responsible business, sustainability policies, and environmental management.
http://www.naem.org

**OpenCourseWare Green Classes**
A new trend in the past several years has been colleges and universities making their class materials available online free of charge to the public. These are great resources for individuals who are self-motivated and want to find resources and course material, without actually having to sign up for these classes and pay money for them. You can search for OpenCourseWare offerings based on specific topics on databases such as OCW Finder (http://ocwfinder.com) and the OpenCourseWare Consortium (http://www.ocwconsortium.org).

Below are some of the most notable resources with OpenCourseWare:
Massachusetts Institute of Technology http://ocw.mit.edu/OcwWeb/web/home/home/index.htm
Carnegie Mellon http://www.cmu.edu/oli/index.shtml
Tufts University http://ocw.tufts.edu
Johns Hopkins http://ocw.jhsph.edu

**San Francisco Institute of Architecture**
This school offers many courses as well as programs in ecological design, green building, and architecture. While they offer classes on their campus in California, they also have a good number of programs and courses available online. The school is one of the few in the country that has such a strong focus on ecological design.
http://www.sfia.net

**Solar Energy International**
Solar Energy International is an organization based in the Colorado that is well versed in providing training on topics related to renewable energy and sustainable building practices. While the majority of their courses are offered in Colorado or other west coast locations, they do offer online courses on topic such as Sustainable Home Design, PV Design, Advanced PV Design, and Renewable Energy for the Developing World. These courses are offered over a 6-week period.
http://www.solarenergy.org/solar-training-renewable-energy-workshops

**Strategic Sustainability Consulting Webinars**
Strategic Sustainability Consulting, a green business consulting company, offers several webinars on a routine basis. These webinars are a great opportunity to learn about how your business can make strides to become more sustainable, as well as how to gain a competitive advantage in the green marketplace. Or if you are interested in how you can find a career in sustainability consulting or the green industry, there are courses for this as well. Current offerings include Introduction to Sustainability Consulting, Creating Better Proposals, Managing Client Relationships, Emerging Growth Areas, and Creating a Climate Change Strategy. Most webinars last about 1-2 hours.
http://www.sustainabilityconsulting.com/extra-resources/category/recorded-webinars

**US Department Of Energy**
*Workforce Development for Teachers and Scientists, WDTS*
Professional development opportunities through the DOE include research opportunities and fellowships for teachers.  Funding is provided to give teachers time in a DOE office to help create and refine education programs and aid education policy formation.
http://www.scied.science.doe.gov/scied/sci_ed.htm

*Office of Energy Efficiency and Renewable Energy, Building Energy Codes Program*
These educational materials provide information about state energy codes.  They include recorded webcasts, self-paced training programs, presentations, and a glossary.  The DOE also hosts an annual forum to advance knowledge of state energy codes and other building energy issues.
http://www.energycodes.gov/training

*Office of Energy Efficiency and Renewable Energy, Weatherization and Intergovernmental Program*
These webcasts are conducted by the Technical Assistance Project for State and Local Officials and cover a variety of topics related to energy efficiency and renewable energy. The webcasts are offered several times throughout the year, and there is an archive where you can view past webcast presentations.
http://www1.eere.energy.gov/wip/wap_resources.html

## Local Green Job Training Programs

**Casey Trees High School Urban Forestry Summer Internship**
Casey Trees, a non-profit organization in the District, has a mission to restore, enhance, and protect the tree canopy in the Nation's Capital. Every summer, Casey Trees hires high school students to serve as Urban Forestry Interns. These paid interns, selected from across the city, receive instruction about trees and tree care, then work outdoors in city neighborhoods caring for trees and teaching residents how they can help regreen D.C. Casey Trees has three goals for these interns: gain job experience; learn about a broad range of forestry and environmental careers, and be stewards for trees planted by Casey Trees.
http://www.caseytrees.org/education/high-school-summer-jobs/index.php

**Common Good City Farm**
This program is available to low-income families and individuals and teaches them gardening skills through hands on training in exchange for fresh fruits and vegetables each week. The program runs from May through October.
http://www.commongoodcityfarm.org/GreenTomorrows

**DC Greenworks**
DC Greenworks, a non-profit, is the national capital region's preeminent green roof advocate and educator, as well as a one stop shop for green roof consultation, design, and installation. DC Greenworks has a long history of providing training for individuals interested in green roofs, rain barrels, and other landscape contracting activities. They have recently received several grants for green roof installations and rain barrel installations which should provide opportunities for green job training for D.C area residents. DC Greenworks is one of the driving forces behind the green revitalization of the H St NE corridor in the District.
http://www.dcgreenworks.org

**Earth Conservation Corps**
The Earth Conservation Corps is a nonprofit organization that engages the strong minds and muscles of Anacostia's youth in the restoration of the Anacostia River. As corps members improve their own lives, they rebuild the environmental, social, and economic health of their communities.
http://www.ecc1.org

**Goodwill**
Goodwill of Greater Washington provides a number of training and employment services to people with disabilities and disadvantages in the Greater Washington, D.C. metro area, at no charge to students.
http://www.dcgoodwill.org/index.php?option=com_content&view=category&layout=blog&id=45&Itemid=186

**Green Pathway DC**
Green Pathway D.C. offers a ten-week job training program in the field of sustainable building. Hosted by Goodwill of Greater Washington and the Green Builders Council of D.C., the program includes general work skills training, weatherization training, and curriculum focusing on green construction.
http://www.dcgoodwill.org/index.php?option=com_content&view=article&id=109:green-pathway-dc&catid=46&Itemid=178

**Green DMV Program Greater Washington Green Jobs Corps**
The Greater Washington Green Jobs Corps trains individuals from disadvantaged backgrounds to help meet the demand for skilled workers to provide services in the green economy. Participants of the program are trained to weatherize homes, businesses and federal buildings, install solar panels and perform energy audits. These sustainable services will save millions of dollars in energy costs for the Washington Metropolitan area. Like cities across the nation, the greater Washington area faces a shortage of programs providing "green-collar" workforce development. This shortage will worsen as the green economy grows. The Greater Washington Green Jobs Corps is a green job training program with a focus on providing trainees with barriers to employment the skills, confidence and assurance that upon graduation they are qualified to enter the green labor market and compete with others for employment in the green sector.
http://www.greendmv.org/programs_greentraining.html

**Mayor's Green Zone Environmental Program**
The Mayor's Green Zone Environmental Program (GZEP) engages District youth by providing them with substantive green-collar work. Participants receive hands-on experience and educational programming

that introduces them to environmental issues and careers. Green Zone projects also have measurable sustainability benefits for all District communities. This program is a project of the District of Columbia Department of the Environment (DDOE) and part of the District's larger Summer Youth Employment Program. GZEP is based on a ladder scheme through which youth and residents can move up within the one these fields based on level of experience and education. The youth will select one of four topic areas to work in: Energy, Watersheds, Parks, and Trees. GZEP also seeks to hire qualified Team Leaders, Ward Managers, Site Supervisors, Payroll Specialists, and Procurement Managers. Projects will be provided through collaboration among DDOE, other District agencies, non-profit community groups and private enterprise. Examples of projects for the 2009 program include: Community outreach and surveys, tree maintenance and mulching, energy audits of District school buildings, and invasive plant removal at Kingman Island.
http://green.dc.gov/summer

**National Green Energy Council Green Job Corps Initiative**
The Urban Green Job Corps will educate this new workforce to meet these immediate needs first of transitioning to a green economy. It will also at the same time work with potential employers to ensure that the green collar jobs that they provide workers with are stable living-wage jobs with benefits. This will be done by supporting living-wage ordinances, long-term hiring contracts, and unionization options. Secondly, Urban Green Job Corps will work to ensure that green collar jobs are offered to workers with limited initial education and skills, and will strive for local hiring requirements, training for green collar jobs in high schools, work force training programs, certification programs, matching programs, and employer incentives. The Green Jobs Corps Initiative plans to help create a clean energy economy will stabilize our economy and our climate.
http://www.greenenergycouncil.com/job_corps_iniative/gjc_initiative_3.pdf

**ONE DC**
ONE DC has distinguished itself as one of a few organizations in Washington, D.C. that moves beyond service provision to build sustainable community capacity and leadership so that low-income people of color can speak for themselves. ONE DC promotes leadership that does not tell others what to do but helps them take charge to build their abilities and skills. Finally, ONE DC recognizes that leadership cannot exist without the support and power of the whole community. Central to ONE DC's leadership style is the identification and dismantling of systemic influences such as racism, classism, and sexism that manifest both individually and institutionally.
http://www.onedconline.org/

**The Recycled Building Network, Inc. (ReBuild)**
Rebuild is a nonprofit formed in May 2008 to acquire a warehouse that can accept used building material donations, sell the products as deeply discounted prices to the public, and use the proceeds to train unemployed and underemployed unskilled workers for "green collar" jobs. Beyond accepting unwanted building materials, equipment, and supplies, they enable builders and homeowners to claim a tax deduction for donating their unwanted material, and establish appropriate training curricula in green collar occupations. The proceeds are used to provide or subsidize unskilled workers to obtain appropriate industry licenses, certification, on-the-job training, and experience in green collar positions.
http://www.rebuildwarehouse.org

**Student Conservation Association**
SCA is America's conservation corps. Their members protect and restore national parks, marine sanctuaries, cultural landmarks and community green spaces in all 50 states. The SCA offers a variety of green job opportunities where individuals gain experience working hands on outdoors on environmental projects. There is a local SCA chapter in the D.C. area which has local opportunities.
http://www.thesca.org/about/offices/washington-dc

**YouthBuild**

YouthBuild is a youth and community development program that simultaneously addresses core issues facing low-income communities: housing, education, employment, crime prevention, and leadership development. In YouthBuild programs, low-income young people ages 16-24 work toward their GEDs or high school diplomas, learn job skills and serve their communities by building affordable housing, and transform their own lives and roles in society. YouthBuild has been involved with several Green Building initiative programs in the past few years that teach their program participants green construction skills, and they recently held a Green Home Construction demonstration on the National Mall in D.C. http://www.youthbuild.org

In the D.C. area, there are a few YouthBuild programs, such as the following:
YouthBuild Public Charter School (http://www.youthbuildpcs.org/)
Sasha Bruce Youthwork (http://www.sashabruce.org/programs/show/building-opportunities/youthbuild)

# Green and Environmental Career Resource Books

The books included below focus specifically on the topic of green jobs, to get you started and determine which direction you would like to head in. Once you have determined your area of interest, you will need to research books that are specific to that particular topic. Those books are not included in this list.

**Careers in the Environment**
By Mike Fasulo and Paul Walker
Paperback: 192 pages
Publisher: McGraw-Hill
Retail Price: $15.95
Career/Job Profiles: 44

**Career Opportunities in Conservation and the Environment**
By Paul R. Greenland and AnnaMarie L. Sheldon
Paperback: 272 pages
Publisher: Checkmark Books
Retail Price: $18.95
Career/Job Profiles: 69

**Careers in Renewable Energy**
By Gregory McNamee
Paperback: 208 pages
Publisher: PixyJack Press
Retail Price: $20

**Green Careers**
By Frank Marquardt
Paperback: 72 pages
Publisher: Wetfeet.Com
Retail Price: $24.95

**Green Careers: Choosing Work for a Sustainable Future**
By Jim Cassio & Alice Rush
Paperback: 350+ pages
Publisher: New Society Publishers
Retail Price: $19.95
Career/Job Profiles: 90 + over 65 "real people" profiles

**ECO Guide to Careers That Make a Difference**
By the Environmental Careers Organization (Beth Ginsberg and Kevin Doyle)
Paperback: 320 pages
Publisher: Island Press
Retail Price: $19.95

**Making a Living While Making a Difference**
By Melissa Everett
Paperback: 240 pages
Publisher: New Society Publishers
Retail Price: $24.95

**Green Jobs: A Guide to Eco-Friendly Employment**
By A. Bronwyn Llewellyn, James P.
Hendrix, K. C. Golden
Paperback: 240 pages
Publisher: Adams Media
Retail Price: $12.95

**Saving the Earth as a Career: Advice on Becoming a Conservation Professional**
By Malcolm L. Hunter Jr., David Lindenmayer, Aram Calhoun
Paperback: 216 pages
Publisher: Wiley-Blackwell
Retail Price: $19.95

**The Idealist.org Handbook to Building a Better World**
By Idealist.org with Stephanie Land
Paperback: 288 pages
Publisher: Perigree
Retail Price: $14.95

**75 Green Businesses You Can Start to Make Money and Make a Difference**
By Glenn Croston, PhD
Paperback: 328 pages
Publisher: Entrepreneur Press
Retail Price: $19.95

**The Green Collar Economy: How One Solution Can Fix Our Two Biggest Problems**
By Van Jones
Hardback: 237 pages
Publisher: Harper One
Retail Price: $25.99

**Hot, Flat, and Crowded: Why We Need a Green Revolution - and How It Can Renew America**
By Thomas L. Friedman
Hardback: 438 pages
Publisher: Farrar, Straus and Giroux
Retail Price: $27.95

**Strategies for the Green Economy: Opportunities and Challenges in the New World of Business**
By Joel Makower
Hardback: 290 pages
Publisher: McGraw-Hill
Retail Price: $27.95

**Break Through: From the Death of Environmentalism to the Politics of Possibility**
By Michael Shellenberger; Ted Nordhaus
Hardback: 344 pages
Publisher: Houghton Mifflin
Retail Price: $25.00

**Build a Green Small Business: Profitable Ways to Become an Ecopreneur**
By Scott Cooney
Paperback: 243 pages
Publisher: McGraw-Hill
Retail Price: $19.95

# Local Green Conferences

The following is a list of some of the major conferences in the D.C. metro area that focus on green and sustainable issues from the 2011 calendar year. While this list is not comprehensive, it should give you a good set of resources to find out what types of conferences were going on last year. We have included conferences that have already happened because often conference websites are good resources for identifying individuals, organizations, and businesses that are involved with a particular green industry that you may be interested in.

You will notice that there were probably many more green conferences going on in the D.C. metro area than you knew of. It can be difficult to keep track of conferences because there isn't really a central source that lists all these types of events. The best thing to do is to keep checking every so often on the Internet for upcoming events and conferences. If you know what specific industry you are interested in, try calling or emailing the trade association for that industry and ask them if they know of any conferences or events coming up in the near future. They should be able to at least point you to the right place to check for updates.

Going to green conferences is a great way to network with a lot of people at a time, since they are all gathered in one place for the day. Conferences can save you a lot of time doing research for green jobs, and they allow you to get face time with people you may not easily meet with otherwise. We realize that conferences can be very expensive to attend, so one suggestion we have is for you to find out who is organizing the conference, then contact them and see if they might be willing to let you volunteer for the conference in exchange for a free conference pass. This is a relatively common approach so don't hesitate to ask. Volunteering at conferences also shows that you have a personal commitment to green and sustainable issues and you can list these types of volunteering experiences on your resume. If you aren't able to volunteer, be sure to get the early bird rates for the conference by signing up early. Finally, if it is a multi-day conference and you only have a limited amount to spend, pick the day that you think would have the best networking or workshops that interest you and pay for a one day pass if possible.

Conferences tend to attract some of the biggest names in the industry that the conference is about. Before you go, make sure that you have spent some time researching what will be happening at the conference and who will be there. There can be a lot happening, such as speakers, workshops, trade shows and exhibit halls, and even free giveaways. Usually, a conference will post an agenda, a list of speakers, a list of exhibitors, and other information on their website before the conference happens, so take advantage of this information to plan for the conference. The more time you can put in before the conference to identify the specific people and companies that you want to talk to, the easier it will be to accomplish your goals when you are at the conference.

If you are in the process of looking for a green job, make sure that you take some resumes, business cards, and other materials with you that you could give to potential employers. Don't be afraid to approach the people at the conference and tell them why you are there, and what your particular interests are. Even if you don't find employment at the conference, be sure to get the contact information for at least a few people, so that you can follow up with them to see if they might be able to help you identify other resources that would be valuable for your job search or if they would be open to an informational interview.

**Energy Biz Forum**
Leadership of the energy industry and our nation convene to develop real solutions to our national energy crisis. The EnergyBiz Leadership Forum isn't just about listening to thought leaders and policy makers; it's also about engaging them in new and unique ways. In addition to keynote addresses by luminaries, the event is built to promote interactivity and audience participation with presentations and roundtables – the latter includes open Q&A sessions.
* February 27-March 1, 2011, Mandarin Oriental Hotel in Washington, D.C.
* http://www.energybizforum.com/
* Organized by EnergyBiz

**2011 National Bike Summit**
The National Bike Summit brings together stakeholders from user groups, industry, government, and elected officials from around the country to share their ideas and best practices. Industry superstars, innovative thinkers, and effective national, state and local advocates will help craft a persuasive case statement for bicycling. Discover the value and impact of bicycling in the critical fields of transportation, health, recreation, tourism, energy and the environment.
* March 8-10, 2011, Grand Hyatt at Metro Center, Washington, D.C.
* http://www.bikeleague.org/conferences/summit11/index.php
* Organized by Bicycle City

**The 51st Annual Washington Home & Garden Show**
This is the East Coast's largest home and garden show, with over 800 booths exhibiting products and services. Besides the latest for home and garden, the show also features landscaped gardens and themed garden settings.
* March 11-13, 2011 Washington Convention Center in Washington, D.C.
* http://www.washingtonhomeandgardenshow.com/
* Organized by Washington Home & Garden Show, Inc.

**Smart and Sustainable Campuses Conference**
The conference is a symposium on sustainability, including operational solutions, smart growth policies, and strategies for achieving climate neutrality for university campuses and students.
* April 3-5, 2011, Inn and Conference Center, University of Maryland in College Park, MD
* Organized by the National Association College and University Business Officers

**Powershift 2011 Conference**
Power Shift '11 brings 10,000 young people to Washington to hold our elected officials accountable for rebuilding our economy and reclaiming our future through bold climate and clean energy policy.
* April 15-18, 2011 Walter E Washington Convention Center in Washington, D.C.
* http://www.wearepowershift.org/
* Organized by Powershift

**Earth Day**
Like in years past, hundreds of thousands of people will come to the heart of the nation's capital to show their support for responsible environmental policy that helps us face the challenges ahead. Earth Day will bring together families, adults of all ages, civic leaders, entertainers and other community members to celebrate Earth Day and share a common commitment to make greener life choices and stem the tide of climate change.
* April 16-17, 2011, The National Mall in Washington, D.C.
* http://www.earthday.org/earth-day-2011
* Organized by the Earth Day Network

**The 7ᵗʰ Annual National Sustainable Design Expo**

The event exhibits the sustainable designs of the future by P3 (student) teams and non-profit and government groups. Design subjects are alternative energy sources, agricultural applications, green chemistry, green buildings, sustainable water use, and other sustainable design technologies.
- April 16-17, 2011, The National Mall in Washington, D.C.
- http://www.epa.gov/P3/expo/
- Organized by the EPA's National Center for Environmental Research

**11ᵗʰ Annual Food Safety Summit**

The Food Safety Summit offers food manufacturers, retailers, restaurant and foodservice professionals, non-profit executives, and members of the military, government and academia an opportunity to come together to discuss the practical and technical regulatory and scientific issues surrounding food safety in North America and around the world.
- April 19-21, 2011, Washington, D.C. Convention Center in Washington, D.C.
- http://www.foodsafetysummit.com/
- Organized by BNP Media

**The 4ᵗʰ Annual Global Marine Renewable Energy Conference**

International agencies, national and state governments, environmental groups, and associations are sponsoring this collaborative, and global conference on marine renewables. The conference provides an opportunity to learn and talk about performance measures, setting priorities for environmental studies, establishing international standards for operations, how public policy can be driven and how best to work with stakeholder groups, resource agencies, and regulators
- April 28-29, 2011, Almas Temple in Washington, D.C.
- http://www.globalmarinerenewable.com/
- Organized by the Global Marine Renewable Energy Conference

**The Roundtable of Science and Technology for Sustainability**

The Roundtable on Science and Technology for Sustainability provides a forum for sharing views, information, and analyses related to sustainability. Members of the Roundtable on Science and Technology for Sustainability include senior decision-makers from the U.S. government, industry, academia, and non-profit organizations who are in a position to play a strong role in promoting sustainability. The goal for the Roundtable is to mobilize, encourage, and use scientific knowledge and technology to help achieve sustainability goals and support the implementation of sustainability practices.
- May 5-6, 2011, Keck Center of the National Academies in Washington, D.C.
- http://sites.nationalacademies.org/PGA/sustainability/PGA_062619
- Organized by the National Academies

**The Blue Vision Summit**

The three key themes of the Summit will be: 1) Solutions that are working at the local, state and regional level and how to expand them. 2) Collapse of marine wildlife and the oil spill in the Gulf of Mexico. 3) Federal Legislation. How to build an effective national constituency for ocean governance reform will be discussed.
- May 20-23, 2011, Carnegie Institution for Science, Washington, D.C.
- http://www.bluefront.org/blue_vision_blog/welcome/
- Organized by the Blue Frontier Campaign

**2011 Aid and International Development Forum**

This event is an opportunity to raise awareness of your organization and network with key international aid, humanitarian relief and development stakeholders.

- June 8-9, 2011, Walter E. Washington Convention Center in Washington, D.C.
- http://www.aidforumonline.org/

## Federal Facility Energy Management

This conference will help governmental defense agencies share best environmental practices and integrate renewable energy solutions into their energy portfolios. Key conference speakers include representatives from the Office of the Deputy Assistant Secretary of the Navy, the Department of Commerce, and the Office of the Assistant Secretary of the Army.

- June 8-10, 2011, Westin Alexandria in Alexandria, VA
- http://www.marcusevans.com/marcusevans-conferences-event-details.asp?EventID=17826&ad=caffem&SectorID=33&me_cid=12049&Date=10/03/2011 21:44:32
- Organized by Marcus Evans

## Corporate Citizenship and Sustainability Conference

The event links topics such as corporate social responsibility and global business ethics to the success of global sustainability programs. Executives from non and for-profits, governmental organizations, public relations firms, community involvement projects, and business ethics and compliance groups are all invited to attend.

- June 9-10, 2011, Westin Georgetown in Washington, D.C.
- http://conferenceboard.org/conferences/conferencedetail.cfm?conferenceid=2297&subtopicid=10
- Organized by the Conference Board

## ACE11 World's Water Event: 130th Annual Conference and Exposition

The conference hosts water professionals from all over the world to discuss infrastructure management problems, newly advanced water treatment technologies, and water resources protection.

- June 12-16, 2011, Walter E. Washington Convention Center in Washington, D.C.
- http://www.awwa.org/ACE11/index.cfm?showLogin=N
- Organized by the American Water Works Association

## The 14th Annual Congressional Renewable Energy and Energy Efficiency Expo

This conference brings businesses, sustainable energy industry trade organizations, government agencies and research groups together to discuss the status of renewable energy and energy efficiency technologies. Presentations cover technical, economic, and environmental perspectives of energy technologies. The forum is free and open to the public.

- June 16, 2011, Cannon House Office Building at the U.S. House of Representatives in Washington, D.C.
- http://hydro.org/news-and-media/events/details/sustainable-energy-coalition-14th-annual-congressional-renewable-energy-and-energy-efficiency-expo/
- Organized by the Sustainable Energy Coalition

## 2011 Energy Sustainability Conference and Fuel Cell Conference

This conference provides a unique opportunity for researchers, engineers, architects, consultants, and policy makers to communicate about energy efficiency in the realms of renewable energy technologies and fuel cell development. Workshops and tutorials are offered for professionals and students.

- August 7-10, 2011, Grand Hyatt Washington in Washington, D.C.
- http://www.asmeconferences.org/ESFuelCell2011/index.cfm
- Organized by the American Society of Mechanical Engineers

## Congresswoman Eleanor Holmes Norton's Annual Job Fair

The event is a job fair with representatives from many private, federal and D.C. employers. The fair also provides workshops on interviewing, resume preparation, dressing for success, and completing federal and D.C. employment applications.

- August 9, 2011, Walter E. Washington Convention Center in Washington, D.C.
- http://www.norton.house.gov/index.php?option=com_content&task=view&id=194&Itemid=100
- Organized by the Government of the District of Columbia

**RETECH 2011: The Renewable Energy Technology Conference and Exhibition**
RETECH gathers renewable energy technology industry speakers and experts every year to provide business managers, engineers, and government officials with policy and finance updates on key alternative energy sources such as wind, solar, and geothermal. The conference includes a trade show exhibition of the latest renewable energy technology products and services.

- September 20-22, 2011, Walter E. Washington Convention Center in Washington, D.C.
- http://www.retech2011.com/
- Organized by TradeFair Group

**Capital Home and Garden Show**
Browse the products and services from hundreds of exhibitors. Included are presentations and workshops on greening one's home and garden, money-saving tips, and gardening advice.

- September 23-25, 2011, Dulles Expo Center in Chantilly, VA
- http://www.capitalhomeshow.com
- Organized by Marketplace Events

**Take Back the American Dream**
Partnering with Van Jones' "Rebuild the Dream" organization, the Campaign for America's future is hosting a grassroots conference to focus on strengthening movement-building strategies. The conference intends to provide an assessment of where the progressive vision stands in the areas of clean energy, healthcare, workers' rights, fair trade, education, equality, civil liberties, foreign policy and more.

- October 3-5, 2011, Washington Hilton Hotel in Washington, D.C.
- www.ourfuture.org
- Organized by the Campaign for America's Future

**GridWise Global Forum**
The GridWise conference is an international convergence of policy and corporate leaders, technology innovators, environment advocacy groups and consumers. GridWise promotes cross-collaboration between scientists, policy makers, and consumers, while endorsing further development of smart grids.

- November 8-10, 2011, Ronald Reagan Building and International Trade Center in Washington, D.C.
- http://www.gridwiseglobalforum.org/
- Organized by GridWise Alliance and the U.S. Department of Energy

**EcoBuild America**
A comprehensive conference, it consists of presentations, product exhibits, and a job fair. Businesses and sectors represented at the conference cover building information management, green design, high performance buildings and energy efficiency, sustainable sites, and business and practice management.

- December 5-9, 2011, Walter E. Washington Convention Center in Washington, D.C.
- http://www.aececobuild.com/
- Organized by AEC Science & Technology, LLC

**Transportation Research Board (TRB) 91$^{st}$ Annual Meeting**

The TRB Annual Meeting program covers all transportation modes, with more than 4,000 presentations in nearly 650 sessions addressing topics of interest to all attendees—policy makers, administrators, practitioners, researchers, and Transportation, Energy, and Climate Change.

- January 22-26, 2012 Marriott Wardman Park, Omni Shoreham, and Washington Hilton hotels, in Washington, D.C.
- http://www.trb.org/AnnualMeeting2012/AnnualMeeting2012.aspx
- Organized by the National Academies

# Green Job Posting Websites

The following is a list of websites where you can access job postings both locally as well as nationally. While some of these job posting websites focus specifically on green jobs, others are traditional job posting websites that occasionally have green job postings. In order to stay on top of the latest potential job opportunities, it is good to frequently check these types of websites, so when something you are interested in comes up, you will be aware of it right away. If you are interested in a particular green job industry, it might be beneficial to check the job posting websites that specifically focus on that industry, while if you are interested in a variety of green jobs in various industries, consider checking the broader, more general green job websites.

## Local Job Posting Websites (5 or more job posts per week)

### DC Jobs
Search for jobs in DC, VA and MD. Categories include environmental science/services, agriculture/forestry/fishing, non-profit/associations, and volunteer opportunities.
http://www.dcjobs.com

### DC Jobsite
A website with numerous resources, job seekers can use various search techniques, post a resume, and get job alerts and consultations.
http://www.dcjobsite.com

### District of Columbia Jobs
Besides job listings, the site offers resume and career resources. Job search tools include searching by agriculture/fishing/forestry and environmental categories.
http://www.districtofcolumbiajobs.com

### Jobfetch
A job source that covers PA, VA, MD, and D.C., it can be searched by industry, city, or keyword. Categories include agriculture/forestry/environmental.
http://www.jobfetch.com

### Job Central
As the website of the National Labor Exchange, it is a non-profit resource connecting job seekers and employers. Jobs can be searched by keyword, date added, or industry category including agriculture and environmental services and equipment.
http://www.jobcentral.com/c-Washington-DC-jobs.asp

### Washington, D.C. Diversity
Jobs can be browsed by categories that include agriculture/forestry/fishing and environmental science/services. Specific locations in D.C. and the greater D.C. area can also be targeted. Information and advice on the job process are available in their resources section.
http://www.washingtondcdiversity.com

**Washington, D.C. Job Source**

As a resource for D.C., MD, and VA area jobs, it includes industry as well as government and non-profit jobs. Search by keyword, location, or category. The site also includes job news and employer information.

http://www.dcjobsource.com

**Washington, D.C. Jobsite**

Searching their job database is open to all. However, members can sign up for job alerts, newsletters, and others benefits. The site has a careers resources section as well.

http://www.washingtondcjobsite.com

**Washington Post**

Search by category and location in DC, VA, and MD. Employers include the U.S. government, NGO's, and universities.

http://www.washingtonpost.com

**Washington Recruiter**

As a local job board, job seekers can post resumes, sign up for job alerts, or search jobs by keyword or category.

http://www.washingtonrecruiter.com

## Local Job Posting Websites (Less than 5 job posts per week)

**DC Government Employment Opportunities**

This is the District of Columbia's main website for employment opportunities. It is managed by the Department of Human Resources and provides job listings, as well as information on the application process.

http://www.dcop.dc.gov/dcop/cwp/view,a,1222,q,530365,dcopNav,|31656|.asp

**DC Networks**

Maintained by the District of Columbia government, this website is a comprehensive resource for job searching in the D.C. metro area. It provides job listings, as well as career center information, and education and training opportunities.

http://www.dcnetworks.org

**EcoTuesday**

EcoTuesday is a forum for sustainable business leaders to come together to network, collaborate, and engage with one another in a structured environment. There is a local D.C. chapter of EcoTuesday that meets once a month. EcoTuesday is planning on launching a green jobs listing section of their website in the near future.

http://www.ecotuesday.com/jobs

**Mid-Atlantic Regional Collaborative (MARC)**

Released in July 2011, MARC is the highly-anticipated cross-regional green jobs portal with free, real-time job search capabilities and recruitment resources for D.C., Maryland, and Virginia job seekers and employers.

https://www.marcgreenworks.com/

**United States Green Building Council - National Capitol Region Chapter**

USGBC NCR's Career Center is the green building industry's exclusive resource for online employment connections in the national capital region. It is free for all job seekers to use.

http://www.usgbcncr.org/careers

**Washington, D.C. Jobs Today**
Job listings can be filtered by job type, education level required, keyword, or post date. Users can also post resumes and get job advice and research.
http://www.washingtondcjobstoday.com

**Washington Times**
The listing is for the D.C. metro area, all though additional cities in MD and VA can be included. Categories include agriculture/forestry/fishing and environmental services. Search terms include managerial level, category, and location. Managerial level includes non-managerial, manager, or senior manager.
http://www.washingtontimes.com/about/jobs/

**WTOP Radio**
D.C. area job postings are in the classifieds section. They are listed by category, including environmental services.
http://www.wtop.com/

## National Green Job Posting Websites (5 or more job posts per week)

**Clean Edge**
This is a great source for clean–tech job seekers, employers, and recruiters. During their BETA period it is free to post jobs, so take advantage of this while the offer lasts. It also provides recent green job articles from around the country.
http://jobs.cleanedge.com

**Clean Loop**
This is another website that has been recently created, and offers jobs, news, opinions, and metrics on the cleantech industry. As well as providing listings for green jobs, it also has a blog that discusses various cleantech topics.
http://www.ventureloop.com/cleanloop/careers_home.php

**Clean Tech Recruits**
This job site is exclusively for the clean tech and renewable energy industries. Registration offers a host of opportunities to members, and their listings range from internships to senior level positions.
http://www.cleantechrecruits.com

**Cool Climate Jobs**
This website claims it is the best source for climate change, renewable energy, and green collar jobs in the United States and around the world. Judging by the number of job postings they have on their site, they might just be right!
http://www.coolclimatejobs.com

**Earthworks-Jobs**
They have international opportunities in a large array of categories including biological and physical sciences, design, agriculture, business, and policy. You can also get CV tips and post your resume.
http://www.earthworks-jobs.com

**EcoClub Ecotourism**
EcoClub is an online community that has international job and internship opportunities in ecotourism and conservation.
http://ecoclub.com/jobs

**EcoEmploy**
EcoEmploy provides a variety of services in the U.S. and Canada, including environmental job postings, an online employer directory, resume tips, career and salary information, and links to other similarly specialized sites.
http://www.ecoemploy.com/

**EHS Careers**
EHS offers extensive listings for environmental and occupational health and safety jobs. Create an account or search by type, industry, or location.
http://www.ehscareers.com/home.cfm

**Environmental Career**
The job listings range from tree care to climate scientists. The site offers a variety of services such as posting your resume, getting new jobs emailed to you, and a resource and help center.
http://www.environmentalcareer.com

**Green Biz**
This national green jobs database includes employers who emphasize green, clean tech, and sustainable business practices. Jobs are listed by date, but can also be sorted by skill category, such as accounting, art/media/design, engineering, etc.
http://jobs.greenbiz.com

**Green Careers Center (formerly Environmental Career Center)**
Green Careers Center is located in Hampton, Virginia and is specifically focused on helping green job seekers identify the right jobs for them, as well as helping them along in the process with excellent career guidance. Green Careers Center has over 20 years of experience in Environmental and Green Career guidance, and their website contains a section devoted to listing green job opportunities.
http://www.environmentalcareer.com

**Green Career Central**
This is one of the most comprehensive resources on the web for Green Jobs and Green Careers. Besides offering articles, career advice, and other extremely valuable resources for green job seekers, the site also has a Job Board where current green job vacancies are listed.
http://www.jobtarget.com/home/index.cfm?site_id=7288

**Green Dream Jobs**
This sustainable business job service lists a wide spectrum of green jobs. Jobs are listed by date, but listings can be searched by location, skill level, skill category, and/or keyword.
http://www.sustainablebusiness.com/index.cfm/go/greendreamjobs.main

**Green Energy Jobs**
Green Energy Jobs is a global resource for green energy job vacancies. The website also provides a Green Energy Career Guide that profiles different green energy industries, providing types of jobs in each, and specifics about what the industry does.
http://www.greenenergyjobs.com

**Green Job Scene**
This site contains job listings from many different sectors that incorporate sustainability into their operations. It also features a blog on green job developments.
http://www.greenjobscene.com

**Green Jobs**
Green Jobs lists job openings around the world in the renewable energy industry. You can search jobs by type of job, or location.
http://www.greenjobs.com/public/index.aspx

**Green Jobs Network**
The mission of Green Jobs Network is to connect people seeking jobs that focus on environmental and social responsibility with available opportunities and resources. You can search for jobs by sector, city, or state.
http://www.greenjobs.net

**GreenJobSpider**
GreenJobSpider allows job seekers to browse multiple green job resources in one search, streamlining the job search process. Green jobs, green careers, job webinars, and job trainings are organized separately into four different searchable tabs. You can search by job title, keywords, company, or location.
http://www.greenjobspider.com/

**Idealist**
As a resource for, and about, non-profits, it maintains a database of jobs, internships, and volunteer opportunities. Areas of focus which can be searched for include energy conservation and green living, environment and ecology, farming and agriculture, and wildlife and animal welfare. Other search categories include location, skill category, education level, and job type.
http://www.idealist.org/if/as/Job

**North American Association For Environmental Education (NAAEE)**
The NAAEE jobs database provides listings for job openings in the environmental education field all over the country. Each job posting also has a job description and a deadline to submit applications by.
http://eelink.net/pages/EE+Jobs+Database

**Orion Magazine**
Orion's job resource provides grassroots internships and jobs, the majority with non-profit organizations and farms. Opportunities range from sustainable agriculture to environmental education, economic justice to ecological restoration. Nationwide listings can be searched by keyword and location, or be sorted by skill category.
http://jobs.oriongrassroots.org

**Ornithological Societies of America**
The society's list consists of an entire range of jobs and internships related to the study of birds, many of which are research or field work oriented. The list is organized by its monthly update.
http://www.osnabirds.org/on/ornjobs.htm

**RenewableEnergyJobs.com**
This is a relatively new job posting website that covers renewable energy job opportunities all over the world. You can post a resume and cover letter on the site and you can search job listings by location, and job sector.
http://www.renewableenergyjobs.com

**Solar Jobs**
This is an excellent resource for anyone interested in the solar industry. It will help you get connected to industry professionals and companies, identify job opportunities, and provide solar career related resources.
http://www.solarjobs.us

**Sustain Lane**
Sustain Lane offers a green jobs website that provides job listings all over the country, but has a Washington, D.C. specific section for those interested in local jobs only.
http://www.sustainlane.com/local/washington-dc/jobs?proximity=50

**The Job Seeker**
This service includes environmental and natural resource jobs only. Some jobs can be viewed online for free, however a subscription includes the entire list.
http://www.thejobseeker.net

**The Student Conservation Association**
SCA is a conservation corps providing internships and crew member experiences all across the U.S. Opportunities are seasonal and typically in national and state parks.
http://www.thesca.org

**Tree Hugger**
Tree Hugger's job board lists environmental internships and jobs from non-profits and business. A wide spectrum is represented, including organic agriculture, community organizing, renewable energy installation, consulting, and marketing. Search by keyword and location, or sort by skill category.
http://jobs.treehugger.com

**United States Green Building Council**
The USGBC's Career Center website provides listings for green building jobs across the country. It also allows you to post an anonymous resume for companies to look at.
http://careercenter.usgbc.org/home/index.cfm?site_id=2643

**Water Environment Federation**
Job seekers can browse job listings, search by position level, have new postings emailed to them, and confidentially post their resume.
http://jobbank.wef.org/search.cfm

**Wind Jobs**
If you are interested in finding opportunities in the wind industry, definitely check out this site, as it lists wind industry job openings from all over the world.
http://www.windjobs.org/job-search

**Work in Green Industries**
Search for jobs in various green industries, from construction to legal to marketing and conservation. There is a fee for job posters and job seekers.
http://workingreenindustries.com/ www.work-green.net/

## National Green Job Posting Websites (Less than 5 job posts per week)

**American Water Resources Job Board**
This listing includes many local government and private engineering jobs. The list can be sorted by date, company, or location.
http://careers.awra.org/search.cfm

**Biodiesel-Jobs.com**
A similar website to Ethanol-Jobs.com, this website consists of ethanol jobs in engineering, operations, and business.
http://www.biodiesel-jobs.com

**BiologyJobs**
The listings include jobs in all life science categories. Register to post your resume and set up job agents to receive jobs matching your criteria by email.
http://www.biologyjobs.com

**Eco**
An eco forum for discussing various sustainability issues, and they are in the process of developing and launching their eco jobs website very soon.
http://www.eco.org

**EnviroEducation**
This website provides resources for those interested in environmental jobs and internships, which can be browsed generally or by specialty. Links also have information on cover letters and resumes, interviewing, and career development.
http://www.enviroeducation.com/careers-jobs/#careers

**Environmental Career Opportunities**
Jobs and internships are listed by category or state. Categories include a wide spectrum of environmental fields, including natural resources management, law, education, engineering, energy, and advocacy. Employers listed are from the non-profit and business sectors.
http://www.ecojobs.com

**Environmental Jobs**
Jobs are sorted by environmental science, advocacy and policy, renewable energy, environmental engineering, and health and safety. Listings are from non-profits, private firms, and local governments.
http://www.environmentaljobs.com

**Environmental Jobs and Careers**
This website lists environmental jobs in fields like land management, community organizing, and activism. Most employers are non-profits, all though some private firms are also represented.
http://www.ecoemploy.com

**Environmental Protection Agency**
The EPA provides a website that lists all their current job, internship, and student programs related to environmental careers. If you would like to work for the federal government, this is a good site to keep an eye on.
http://www.epa.gov/careers

**Ethanol-Jobs**
A similar website to Biodiesel-Jobs.com, this website consists of ethanol jobs in engineering, operations, and business.
http://www.ethanol-jobs.com

**Ethical Jobs**
This site has world-wide postings for jobs, internships and volunteer opportunities in eco-responsible and humanitarian fields. Specific categories include corporate social responsibility, green energy, and sustainable & organic farming. Most listings are password protected, but group memberships can be obtained by universities and organizations.
http://www.EthicalJobs.net

**Forestry Careers**
This website provides information on all types of forestry careers. It discusses specific career paths, educational opportunities, and career links.
http://forestrycareers.org

**Green Gigs**
Green Gigs provides jobs listings and resources for those looking for home-based work that is environmentally-focused
http://greengigs.blogspot.com

**Grist**
Grist's environmental job board consists of postings from green business and environmental non-profits. Jobs are listed by date, but can also be viewed by category or searched for by keyword and/or location.
http://jobs.grist.org

**Meaningful Work & Travel**
This website contains a list of worldwide jobs and internships that are focused on the environment and/or education. Employers on the list consist of non-profits, schools, and nature preserves.
http://www.meaningfulworkandtravel.com

**Misco**
This website is a list of international environmental jobs in industry. Resources include emails of new jobs, resume posting, and links to career and education information.
http://www.miscojobs.com/jobs/l_4/pg_1.htm

**MonsterTrak**
Part of Monster Worldwide, Inc., MonsterTrak serves college students and recent graduates with a searchable job database in addition to interview tips, networking opportunities with other entry-level job seekers, and other education resources.
http://college.monster.com/?wt.mc_n=monstertrak

**Pennsylvania Associate for Sustainable Agriculture**
PASA's employment section lists farm internships, apprenticeships, and jobs which are predominantly in the Mid-Atlantic.
http://www.pasafarming.org/employment

**Planet Connect Green Career Center**
While this site doesn't necessarily post job openings, it does profile various green jobs so that you can get an idea of what these jobs involve.

http://www.planet-connect.org/career_center

## Renewable Energy World
As a renewable energy industry resource, the job database focuses on the engineering, business, and project management opportunities with renewable energy-related firms and corporations. Search terms include keyword, job title, or location. Listings can also be viewed by skill category.
http://jobs.renewableenergyworld.com/careers/jobsearch

## Rodale Institute
The Rodale Institute, a leading research and advocacy organization for organic agriculture, has a classifieds page which includes farming internships and jobs.
http://www.rodaleinstitute.org/classifieds

## Society of American Foresters Career Center
This is the website for the Society of American Foresters, and it provides job postings for various forester positions including internship, private sector, government, and college and university opportunities.
http://careercenter.eforester.org/home/index.cfm?site_id=8482

## Society of Environmental Journalists
In addition to links to job opportunities, their website has information on environmental journalism education, careers, and awards.
http://www.sej.org/careers/index.htm

## Soil and Water Conservation Society
Besides searching for jobs, users can create an account. This allows you to save job posts, post your resume, and get website support.
http://careers.swcs.org

## Solar Energy Industries Association
Job resources include space to post a resume, job listings, job alerts, and job seeker accounts. Jobs that are listed span solar energy, renewable energy in general, and building opportunities. Employers include local government, academia, and business.
http://www.jobtarget.com/home/index.cfm?site_id=4204

## Solar Energy International
This site lists green collar jobs in renewable energy, predominantly in solar.
http://solarenergytraining.org/course/view.php?id=7

## The Wildlife Society Jobs Board
This job board mainly consists of scientific, academic, non-profit, and technician jobs for wildlife professionals. Search by keyword, location, or type.
http://www.wildlife.org/jobs/index.cfm?tname=jobsboard

## General National Job Websites with Washington, D.C. Subsections

## All Star Jobs
Browse the list, search by job title or post a resume. Jobs for the greater D.C. area are also listed.
http://jobs.allstarjobs.com/category/washington-dc-jobs.html

**Business Week**
Use a general keyword search in conjunction with a variety of search filters.
http://jobs.businessweek.com/a/all-jobs/list/l-Washington,+DC

**D.C. Craigslist**
Open forum job site which can be searched using keyword and/or industry.
http://washingtondc.craigslist.org/jjj

**Indeed**
This site can be searched by salary, title, company, location, job type, or employer-recruiter.
http://www.indeed.com/l-Washington,-DC-jobs.html

**Job Fox**
The public, private, and educational sectors are represented. The site takes applicants through a series of questions in order to match them with suitable employers.
http://dc-jobs.jobfox.com

**Job Openings**
The list of jobs can be sorted by category, including environmental jobs.
http://www.jobopenings.net/jobs_by_state.php?state=DC

**Jobs.com**
Jobs are listed by date and can be searched by keyword.
http://dc.jobs.com

**Monster**
Search for area jobs by keyword, occupation, job type, industry, company, or phrase.
http://jobsearch.monster.com/District-of-Columbia/Washington/get-jobs-12.aspx

**Washington Business Journal**
The journal has a job board which can be searched by keyword, category, or employer. Listings include entry-level positions and internships.
http://washington.bizjournals.com/washington/jobs

**Yahoo jobs**
This site provides a list D.C. jobs by date, but can also be searched by keyword or job category.
http://hotjobs.yahoo.com/jobs-l-Washington-DC

# Organizations for Networking and Volunteering

The Washington, D.C. metro area is fortunate to be one of the largest geographic centers of non-profit organizations that focus on environmental issues, as well as offer green and sustainability services. Since D.C. is the nation's capital, many nonprofits have their national headquarters located in the D.C. area. On top of this, there are also many international non profits that are located here as well. Nonprofit organizations offer job opportunities frequently and employ large numbers of people, so if you are interested in nonprofit work, then there is bound to be a green organization in the D.C. area working on the issues you are interested in.

Besides offering potential employment, non profit organizations also frequently present opportunities for volunteering and/or networking. As you read in the Career Guidance section of this Guide, networking and volunteering are valuable tools for anyone seeking a green job. If you are looking to meet people in your field of interest, or gain some on the job experience, then you should strongly consider contacting several non profits and seeing if they might be able to help you with your green job seeking process. While some non profits are better set up to handle taking on volunteers, even the ones that don't explicitly mention that they have this capability still might be willing to help you out. It can never hurt to ask, and often if they can't help you out, they may be able to refer you to another organization that does similar work that can.

We have compiled the list below to give you a good perspective of the wide range of non profit organizations that we would classify as green. While we feel that we have compiled a pretty extensive list of non profits in the D.C. area, this is by no means inclusive of every non profit organization in the D.C area that is green. It would be virtually impossible to compile such a list. For an organization to qualify as green by our standards they had to meet one or more of the following criteria: have a strong commitment to environmental issues, provide green and sustainable education services, be heavily involved in a green industry, or specifically devote a significant amount of time to protecting the planet and improving the quality of life on the planet.

## Volunteering

### 1Sky
1Sky was created in 2007 to focus the power of millions of concerned Americans on a single goal: bold federal action by 2010 that can stem global warming. The 1Sky Solutions are grounded in scientific necessity - they are the bottom line of what's needed to dramatically reduce carbon emissions while maximizing energy efficiency, renewable energy and breakthrough technologies. They also represent significant economic promise.
http://www.1sky.org

### Agua Fund
The Fund's mission is to improve the quality of life through support of work to protect the natural environment and to help the poor, disadvantaged, and underserved.
http://www.aguafund.org

### African Wildlife Foundation
The African Wildlife Foundation (AWF) works together with the people of Africa to ensure the wildlife and wild lands of Africa will endure forever. AWF is the leading international conservation organization focused solely on Africa. They believe that protecting Africa's wildlife and wild landscapes is the key to

the future prosperity of Africa and its people – and for over forty-five years they have worked to help ensure that Africa's wild resources endure.
http://www.awf.org

**Alaska Wilderness League**
Alaska Wilderness League was founded in 1993 to further the protection of Alaska's public lands. Alaska Wilderness League works at the federal level on a variety of issues affecting Alaska's wild land and waters. Currently, the League is fighting to permanently protect the Arctic National Wildlife Refuge as Wilderness, promote the sustainable future of the Tongass and Chugach National Forests, and check the unbalanced and potentially destructive development of Alaska's arctic waters and Western Arctic public land.
http://www.alaskawild.org

**Alice Ferguson Foundation**
The Alice Ferguson Foundation was established in 1954 as a non-profit organization chartered in the state of Maryland. Their mission is to provide experiences that encourage connections between people, the natural environment, farming, and the cultural heritage of the Potomac River Watershed, which lead to personal environmental responsibility. They introduce the Potomac River, a working farm, woods, and wetlands each year to more than 10,000 students from the Washington, D.C. metro area.
http://www.potomaccleanup.org

**American Council for an Energy Efficient Economy**
The American Council for an Energy-Efficient Economy (ACEEE) is dedicated to advancing energy efficiency as a means of promoting economic prosperity, energy security, and environmental protection. ACEEE fulfills its mission by conducting in-depth technical and policy assessments, advising policymakers and program managers, working collaboratively with businesses, public interest groups, and other organizations, organizing conferences and workshops, publishing books, conference proceedings, and reports, as well as educating consumers and businesses.
http://www.aceee.org/

**American Council on Renewable Energy**
The American Council on Renewable Energy (ACORE) works to bring all forms of renewable energy into the mainstream of America's economy and lifestyle. ACORE consists of paying members from every aspect and sector of the renewable energy industries and their trade associations, including wind, solar, geothermal, biomass and biofuels, hydropower tidal/current energy and waste energy. The scope of ACORE's membership also spans – among others – financial institutions, government leaders, educators, end-users, professional service providers and allied non-profit groups.
http://www.acore.org

**American Farmland Trust**
Founded in 1980 by a group of farmers and conservationists concerned about the rapid loss of the nation's farmland to development, American Farmland Trust (AFT) is dedicated to protecting our nation's strategic agricultural resources. Working with farmers and ranchers, political leaders and community activists, AFT has helped to permanently protect more than a million acres of America's best farm and ranch land. Their goals are to transform U.S. farm policy, protect the land through protection, plan for agriculture in order to ensure the viability of farms and communities, and keep the land healthy.
http://www.farmland.org

**American Forest Foundation**
The American Forest Foundation (AFF) strives to ensure the sustainability of America's family forests for present and future generations. AFF is committed to creating a future where North American forests

are sustained by the public that understand and values the social, economic, and environmental benefits they provide to our communities, our nation, and the world. They aim to increase public awareness and the skills needed for conservation, develop policies for conservation, enhance the viability of forestland ownership, and increase the number of forest owners who sustainably manage natural resources.
http://www.forestfoundation.org

**American Forests**
American Forests is a world leader in planting trees for environmental restoration, a pioneer in the science and practice of urban forestry, and a primary communicator of the benefits of trees and forests. Citizens concerned about the waste and abuse of the nation's forests founded American Forests in 1875. The organization is proud of its historic roots in the development of America's conservation movement and the new approaches the organization has developed to help people improve the environment in the 21st Century.
http://www.americanforests.org

**American Hiking Society**
As the national voice for America's hikers, American Hiking Society promotes and protects foot trails and the hiking experience.  As a recreation-based non-profit organization, American Hiking Society champions conservation issues, builds partnerships between public and private stakeholders, and provides critical resources to plan, fund, and develop foot trails.
https://www.americanhiking.org

**American Rivers**
American Rivers is the leading national organization standing up for healthy rivers so our communities can thrive. Through national advocacy, innovative solutions and our growing network of strategic partners, they protect and promote our rivers as valuable assets that are vital to our health, safety and quality of life.  Founded in 1973, American Rivers has more than 65,000 members and supporters nationwide, with a local office in Washington, D.C.
http://www.americanrivers.org

**America the Beautiful Fund**
America the Beautiful Fund was started in 1965 to encourage volunteer citizen efforts and to protect the natural and historic beauty of America.  The America the Beautiful Fund was born of a desire to preserve the national heritage by assisting community-level programs and projects to save the natural and historic environment and improve the quality of life. The America the Beautiful Fund now provides support and direction to volunteer community projects in all 50 states operating as a clearinghouse of ideas for thousands of community projects and as a catalyst for new ones.
http://www.america-the-beautiful.org

**American Tree Farm System**
The American Tree Farm System (ATFS), a program of the American Forest Foundation's Center for Family Forests, is committed to sustaining forests, watershed and healthy habitats through the power of private stewardship. ATFS has established standards and guidelines for property owners to meet to become a Certified Tree Farm. Under these standards and guidelines, private forest owners must develop a management plan based on strict environmental standards and pass an inspection by an ATFS volunteer forester every five years.
http://www.treefarmsystem.org

**American Wind Energy Association**
The American Wind Energy Association (AWEA) is a national trade association representing wind power project developers, equipment suppliers, services providers, parts manufacturers, utilities, researchers, and

others involved in the wind industry - one of the world's fastest growing energy industries. In addition, AWEA represents hundreds of wind energy advocates from around the world.
http://www.awea.org

## Anacostia Watershed Society

The Anacostia Watershed Society's goal is to make the Anacostia River and its tributaries swimmable and fishable, to restore and protect our local environment for the health and enjoyment of everyone in our community, and to bring together people across all walks of life to achieve this vision.
http://www.anacostiaws.org

## Arbor Day Foundation

The Arbor Day Foundation works for a world where trees and forests are abundant, healthy, and sustainable, and highly valued by all people.  By creating mass-media communications, providing low-cost trees for planting, and producing high-quality, easy-to-use educational materials, they work to make tree planting and care something in which nearly everyone can be involved. They also create mechanisms through which the average individual can directly support positive tree conservation and education projects. It is their constant goal to expand a person's desire to plant a tree into a lifelong enthusiasm for tree planting and care, and for positive involvement in conservation issues relating to trees.
http://www.arborday.org

## Arlington Coalition for Sensible Transportation

The mission of ACST is to educate the public and policy makers on the facts pertaining to local, regional, and state transportation issues in order to ensure that changes to local, regional, and state transportation plans and any significant expansion of road capacity affecting the Arlington and Northern Virginia area occurs only if it is part of specific comprehensive local and regional transportation plans. These plans must assess local and regional transportation needs; consider all reasonable alternatives (including public transit, pedestrian, bicycle, and other alternatives); preserve quality of life and community integrity; minimize impacts on the environment; be viable for local communities as well as the entire region; be cost-effective in the long term; and made with community consensus.
http://www.acstnet.org

## Arlington Initiative to Reduce Emissions

AIRE believes that to protect the health and economic well-being of current and future generations, we must reduce our emissions of heat-trapping gases by using the technology, know-how, and practical solutions already at our disposal. The Fresh AIRE – Arlington Initiative to Reduce Emissions began in 2007 to undertake the goal of emissions reduction in Arlington County.
http://www.arlingtonva.us/portals/Topics/Climate.aspx

## Arlington Outdoor Education Association

The Arlington Outdoor Education Association, Inc maintains the Outdoor Lab and provides environmental and science education to 9,000 children in Arlington Public Schools each year.  The Phoebe Hall Knipling Outdoor Laboratory is a 210-acre facility that supports the science program. It provides a place for environmental education for elementary and secondary school children, a place for children to do water study, to come face to face with creatures native to the area, and to walk through the woods learning about the plants and terrain.
http://www.outdoorlab.org/Home2.asp

## Arlingtonians for a Clean Environment

Arlingtonians for a Clean Environment (ACE) works to improve the environment of Arlington County. ACE partners with citizens, civic associations, government agencies, and business and professional

organizations to achieve and maintain a clean and sustainable community. ACE provides environmental education and volunteer opportunities to Arlington County residents.
http://www.arlingtonenvironment.org

**Association of Fish and Wildlife Agencies**
The Association of Fish and Wildlife Agencies - the organization that represents all of North America's fish and wildlife agencies - promotes sound management and conservation, and speaks with a unified voice on important fish and wildlife issues. They provide member agencies and their senior staff with coordination services that range from migratory birds, fish habitat, and invasive species, to conservation education, leadership development, and international relations. The Association represents its state agency members on Capitol Hill and before the Administration on key conservation and management policies, and works to ensure that all fish and wildlife entities work collaboratively on the most important issues.
http://www.fishwildlife.org

**Audubon Naturalist Society**
The Audubon Naturalist Society is the largest and oldest independent environmental organization in the Washington, D.C. region. Founded in 1897, the independent nonprofit society focuses its efforts in the Mid-Atlantic region. A pioneer in linking conservation activities with environmental education, the Audubon Naturalist Society fosters stewardship of the region's environment by educating citizens about the natural world, promoting conservation of biodiversity, and protecting wildlife habitat.
http://www.audubonnaturalist.org

**Audubon Society**
Audubon's mission is to conserve and restore natural ecosystems, focusing on birds, other wildlife, and their habitats for the benefit of humanity and the earth's biological diversity. Their national network of community-based nature centers and chapters, scientific and educational programs, and advocacy on behalf of areas sustaining important bird populations, engage millions of people of all ages and backgrounds in positive conservation experiences.
http://www.audubon.org

**Ballston Science and Technology Alliance**
Ballston Science and Technology Alliance (BSTA) serves those engaged in and interested in science and technology, to increase understanding of and to engage the general public in a dialogue about contemporary science and technology and its impacts on everyday life.
http://www.arlingtonvirginiausa.com/index.cfm/13059?CFID=14024564&CFTOKEN=40175890&jsessi onid=f03062d0670f71a1074a321178343b780646

**Bethesda Green**
Bethesda Green serves as a living model to sustain the current and future development of Bethesda by promoting energy efficiency, recycling, and a community-wide environmental ethic. Through their collective efforts - residents, business, and government - they aim to make Bethesda a better place to live and work.
http://www.bethesdagreen.org

**Beyond Pesticides**
Beyond Pesticides (formerly National Coalition Against the Misuse of Pesticides) works with allies in protecting public health and the environment to lead the transition to a world free of toxic pesticides. Beyond Pesticides has historically taken a two-pronged approach to the pesticide problem by identifying the risks of conventional pest management practices and promoting non-chemical and least-hazardous management alternatives.
http://www.beyondpesticides.org

**Building Owners and Managers Association International**
Building Owners and Managers Association (BOMA) International is a primary source of information on office building development, leasing, building operating costs, energy consumption patterns, local and national building codes, legislation, occupancy statistics and technological development. BOMA's goal has always focused on actively and responsibly representing and promoting the interests of the commercial real estate industry through effective leadership and advocacy, through the collection, analysis and dissemination of information, and through professional development. BOMA has been involved in educating building owners and managers about sustainable operations and maintenance practices for some time.
http://www.boma.org

**Brookings Institution**
The Brookings Institution is a nonprofit public policy organization based in Washington, D.C. Their mission is to conduct high-quality, independent research and, based on that research, to provide innovative, practical recommendations. These recommendations advance three broad goals: strengthen American democracy, foster the economic and social welfare, security and opportunity of all Americans, and secure a more open, safe, prosperous and cooperative international system.
http://www.brookings.edu

**Business Council for Sustainable Energy**
The Business Council for Sustainable Energy is an organization dedicated to implementing market-based approaches to reducing pollution and providing a diverse, secure mix of energy resources. Founded in 1992 by senior executives in the natural gas, energy efficiency, electric utility, and renewable energy industries, the Council offers a distinct, business-oriented perspective on energy, environmental and sustainability issues.
http://www.bcse.org

**Campaign for America's Wilderness**
The Campaign for America's Wilderness works to protect the nation's remaining wild lands in order to ensure an enduring legacy of wilderness for future generations. They join with state and local partners to raise public awareness of our special wild lands and to secure dependable, permanent protection for wild lands administered by the U.S. Forest Service, the Bureau of Land Management, and other federal agencies. Their work includes campaign planning and implementation, strategically placed resources for opinion research, communications and public education initiatives, grassroots organizing, electronic outreach, leadership training, and advocacy.
http://www.leaveitwild.org

**Capital Area Food Bank**
The Capital Area Food Bank is the largest, public nonprofit hunger and nutrition education resource in the Washington, D.C. Metropolitan Area. Each year the CAFB distributes 20 million pounds of food, including 6 million pounds of fresh produce, to over 700 partner agencies.
http://www.capitalareafoodbank.org

**CarbonfreeDC**
CarbonfreeDC is a grassroots initiative dedicated to mobilizing D.C. area residents on one goal: dramatically reducing local carbon emissions. This is accomplished by bringing together individuals, businesses, organizations and local government to learn about local opportunities to reduce carbon emissions, increase the adoption of renewable energy, cultivate volunteer-lead sustainable office initiatives, and galvanize citizens to share knowledge and resources.
http://www.carbonfreedc.com

## Carbonfund.org

Carbonfund.org fights global warming by making it easy and affordable for any individual, business or organization to eliminate their climate impact and hastening the transformation to a clean energy future. They achieve their goals through climate change education, carbon offsets and reductions, and public outreach. Carbonfund.org supports renewable energy, energy efficiency and reforestation projects globally that reduce carbon dioxide emissions and the threat of climate change.
http://www.carbonfund.org

## Casey Trees

The mission of Casey Trees is to restore, enhance, and protect the tree canopy of the Nation's Capital. Casey Trees plants trees, trains people to become Citizen Foresters, engages thousands of volunteers in tree planting and care, teaches students in District schools about trees, monitors the city's tree canopy and provides guidelines for better planting space design so trees will thrive in the city.
http://www.caseytrees.org

## Center for Clean Air Policy

Since 1985, the Center for Clean Air Policy (CCAP) has been a recognized world leader in climate and air quality policy and is the only independent, nonprofit think tank working exclusively on those issues at the local, U.S. national and international levels. Headquartered in Washington, D.C., CCAP helps policy-makers around the world develop, promote and implement innovative, market-based solutions to major climate, air quality and energy problems that balance both environmental and economic interests. Their goal is to significantly advance cost-effective and pragmatic air quality and climate policy through analysis, dialogue and education to reach a broad range of policy-makers and stakeholders worldwide.
http://www.ccap.org

## Center for Food Safety

The Center for Food Safety (CFS) is a public interest and environmental advocacy membership organization established in 1997 by its sister organization, International Center for Technology Assessment, for the purpose of challenging harmful food production technologies and promoting sustainable alternatives. CFS combines multiple tools and strategies in pursuing its goals, including litigation and legal petitions for rulemaking, legal support for various sustainable agriculture and food safety constituencies, as well as public education, grassroots organizing and media outreach.
http://www.centerforfoodsafety.org

## Center for a New American Dream

Center for a New American Dream is dedicated to helping support and nurture an American dream that revives the spirit of the traditional dream—but with a new emphasis on non-material values like financial security, fairness, community, health, time, nature, and fun. They envision both a nation and a world in which a healthy global ecosystem anchors a just society offering all citizens the freedom, the resources and the personal security necessary to pursue their dreams, connect with the natural world, and enjoy a high quality of life.
http://www.newdream.org

## Center for New Urbanism DC

The D.C. Chapter of the Congress for the New Urbanism is an educational organization whose goal is to reform the practice of real estate development and urban planning. Activities include promoting the Congress for the New Urbanism and the Charter of the New Urbanism; educating the public and other professional sectors on the benefits of new urbanism and smart growth; aiding in skills development of local area professionals; and facilitating communication and coordination among D.C.-area new urbanists.
http://www.cnudc.org

## Center for Progressive Reform

The Center for Progressive Reform is a research and educational organization with a network of Member Scholars working to protect health, safety, and the environment through analysis and commentary. They work to protect the environment, defend clean science, ensure food and drug safety, expose excessive secrecy in government, reform regulatory policy, and encourage corporate accountability and tort reform.
http://www.progressiveregulation.org

## Center for Responsible Travel

The Center for Responsible Travel is a non-profit research institution whose mission is to design, monitor, evaluate, and improve ecotourism and sustainable tourism practices and principles. Its policy-oriented research focuses on ecotourism as a tool for poverty alleviation and biodiversity conservation, as well as socially and environmentally responsible tourism practices.
http://www.responsibletravel.org

## Center for Small Business and the Environment

The Center for Small Business and the Environment's mission is to essentially mobilize the economic and political powerhouse that constitutes small businesses on behalf of environmental protection.
http://www.aboutcsbe.org

## Chesapeake Bay Foundation

The Chesapeake Bay Foundation (CBF) is the only independent non-profit organization dedicated solely to restoring and protecting the Chesapeake Bay and its tributary rivers. Since their founding 40 years ago, their goal has been to improve water quality by reducing pollution. Their well known motto, Save the Bay, has been the battle cry for that goal.
http://www.cbf.org

## Chesapeake Climate Action Network

The Chesapeake Climate Action Network (CCAN) is the first grassroots, nonprofit organization dedicated exclusively to fighting global warming in Maryland, Virginia, and Washington, D.C. Their mission is to educate and mobilize citizens of this region in a way that fosters a rapid societal switch to clean energy and energy-efficient products, thus joining similar efforts worldwide to slow and perhaps halt the dangerous trend of global warming.
http://www.chesapeakeclimate.org

## Citizen's Network for Sustainable Development

The Citizens Network for Sustainable Development (CitNet) is an independent, non-profit network bringing together US based organizations, communities, and individuals working on sustainability issues across the US. CitNet works in the local, regional, and global arenas to make sustainable development a reality. By supporting citizen-led activities in development, monitoring and implementation of sustainability initiatives, promoting civil society participation in important policy foray, and connecting individuals and organizations, CitiNet is helping build an ecologically sound and socially equitable and economically just world.
http://www.citnet.org

## City Blossoms

City Blossoms is an organization dedicated to working with schools, neighborhood groups, community centers and other organizations to create spaces for children to use their creativity and combined strength and skills to learn how to grow and maintain fantastic yet functioning gardens.
http://www.cityblossoms.org

## City Farm DC

City Farm DC (CFDC) is an urban gardening collective in D.C. CFDC organizes community outreach to D.C. residents who have never been exposed to growing or eating local, sustainably-grown food. They connect private landowners with outdoor growing space to willing gardening partners. With CFDC's guidance, Growers and gardeners agree on simple terms, split costs, share food harvests, and have access to a variety of CFDC programs.
http://cityfarmdc.org

## Clean Water Action

Clean Water Action is an organization of 1.2 million members working to empower people to take action to protect America's waters, build healthy communities and to make democracy work for all of us. For 36 years, Clean Water Action has succeeded in winning some of the nation's most important environmental protections through grassroots organizing, expert policy research, and political advocacy focused on holding elected officials accountable to the public.
http://www.cleanwateraction.org

## Clean Water America Alliance

The Clean Water Alliance (CWAA) is working to explore the complex issue of water sustainability and plan for the future by improving public awareness that advances holistic, watershed-based approaches to water quality and quantity challenges. They focus on exploring and analyzing issues of critical importance to the nation's ability to provide clean and safe waters to future generations, offering information and education to citizens and policy-makers on key issues, and recognizing organizations and individuals for innovation and outstanding achievements in the water quality and quantity arena.
http://www.cleanwateramericaalliance.org

## Climate Action Network

Climate Action Network (CAN) is a worldwide network of over 450 Non- Governmental Organizations (NGOs) working to promote government and individual action to limit human-induced climate change to ecologically sustainable levels. CAN members work to achieve this goal through the coordination of information exchange and NGO strategy on international, regional and national climate issues. CAN has seven regional offices which co-ordinate these efforts in Africa, Central and Eastern Europe, Europe, Latin America, North America, South Asia, and Southeast Asia.
http://www.climatenetwork.org

## Coalition for Smarter Growth

The Coalition for Smarter Growth's mission is to ensure that transportation and development decisions accommodate growth while revitalizing communities, providing more housing and travel choices, and conserving our natural and historic areas. They work with state and local governments in the District of Columbia, the Virginia jurisdictions of Arlington, Fairfax, Alexandria, Loudoun, and Prince William, and Montgomery and Prince George's Counties in Maryland. With residents of many jurisdictions in other parts of Virginia and Maryland wrestling with similar planning challenges, they will (whenever time permits) provide technical advice to these communities as well.
http://www.smartergrowth.net

## Community Greens

The mission of Community Greens is to catalyze the development of shared green spaces inside residential blocks in cities across the United States. They believe that the Community Greens approach presents the best opportunity to add usable green space to our cities by converting underutilized backyards and dysfunctional alleys into functional and beautiful shared green spaces that are owned, managed, and enjoyed by the people who live around them.
http://www.communitygreens.org

## Conservation International

Conservation International believes that the Earth's natural heritage must be maintained if future generations are to thrive spiritually, culturally, and economically. Their mission is to conserve the Earth's living heritage – our global biodiversity – and to demonstrate that human societies are able to live harmoniously with nature. Their work is based on cutting-edge science, comprehensive partnerships, and concern for human well-being. With these three principles guiding them, they safeguard valuable species, preserve the most important landscapes and seascapes, and support communities that care for and rely on Earth's natural resources. To reach these goals, they focus on three strategies: dedicating themselves to innovation, raising awareness about conservation, and maintaining business-like effectiveness.
http://www.conservation.org

## Consortium for Ocean Leadership

The Consortium for Ocean Leadership represents 94 of the leading public and private ocean research and education institutions, aquaria and industry with the mission to advance research, education and sound ocean policy. The organization also manages ocean research and education programs in areas of scientific ocean drilling, ocean observing, ocean exploration, and ocean partnerships.
http://www.oceanleadership.org

## Cool Capital Challenge

Cool Capital Challenge is a regional effort coordinated by businesses, government agencies, non-profit and community organizations, congregations and environmental entities that promote efforts to reduce carbon dioxide emissions and stop global warming.
http://www.coolcapitalchallenge.org

## DC Appleseed

DC Appleseed works to solve major public policy issues facing the District of Columbia. Recent environmental projects include the Anacostia Waterfront Initiative, restoration of the Anacostia River and evaluating lead levels in District drinking water.
http://www.dcappleseed.org

## DC Environmental Education Consortium

The District of Columbia Environmental Education Consortium (DCEEC) represents over 30 environmental education organizations operating in the District of Columbia. It is an inclusive network of teachers, D.C. schools, environmental education providers, and supporters from businesses, universities, and the political arena. DCEEC connects D.C. teachers with the vast environmental education opportunities available to them and their students.
http://www.dcnaturally.org

## DC Environmental Film Festival

A film festival in Washington, D.C., it features a wide variety of films that capture the earth's beauty and address the ever-increasing threats to life on earth. The 2009 Festival spotlights earth's final frontier, the ocean, source of all life, covering nearly three quarters of the globe but less known than the surface of the moon. Explore our water planet through the festival's 140 films, enhanced with the perspectives and knowledge of over 50 filmmakers and 72 special guests who will be on hand for the festival.
http://www.dcenvironmentalfilmfest.org

## DC Fiscal Policy Institute

The DC Fiscal Policy Institute (DCFPI) conducts research and public education on budget and tax issues in the District of Columbia, with a particular emphasis on issues that affect low- and moderate-income residents. By preparing timely analyses that are used by policy makers, the media, and the public, DCFPI

seeks to inform public debates on budget and tax issues and to ensure that the needs of lower-income residents are considered in those debates.
http://dcfpi.org

## DC Greenworks

DC Greenworks, a 501 c3 non-profit, is the national capital region's preeminent green roof advocate and educator, as well as a one stop shop for green roof consultation, design, and installation. They serve the Washington, D.C. community by providing training, tools, and techniques that utilize, protect and advance the environment. DC Greenworks sees a vital connection between economy and ecology, employment potential and environmental sustainability. They actively seek to discover, promote, and deliver cutting edge solutions that are cost effective, eco-friendly, and socially beneficial. Their mission is to promote urban social revitalization through environmental restoration. They were also recently featured in a video by Van Jones and the White House Council on Environmental Quality on Earth Day.
http://www.dcgreenworks.org

## DC Master Gardener Program

The D.C. Master Gardener Program is part of the University of the District of Columbia (UDC) Cooperative Extension Service's Environmental and Natural Resources Program. Extension horticulturalists and other local plant science specialists train D.C. residents to integrate gardening interests and horticulture experience with an urban environment. Participants must complete training and 50 internship hours to earn nationally recognized Master Gardener qualifications and a Master Gardener Certificate.
http://www.udc.edu/causes/ces/environment.htm

## DC NATURE

Wildlife abounds within the Beltway of Washington, D.C. Even an urban environment like our nation's capital is home to a rich diversity of plants, animals, and natural places. DC NATURE catalogs and celebrates the impressive range of flora and fauna that exist alongside the human population here in D.C.
http://www.dcnature.com

## DC Schoolyard Greening

The mission of DC Schoolyard Greening is to increase and improve schoolyard green spaces to promote ecological literacy and environmental stewardship among students, teachers, parents and the surrounding community. Through their volunteers they create learning landscapes and curriculum, evaluate the greening process, encourage environmental stewardship, and utilize green design principles.
http://www.dcschoolyardgreening.org

## DC Sustainable Energy Utility (DC SEU)

Designed to help District households, businesses, and institutions save energy and money through energy efficiency and renewable energy programs. Some of the current programs offered by the DC SEU include a Low-Income Multifamily Program, a Single-Family Home Retrofit Program, a Small Business Direct Installation Program, and a Solar PV and Hot Water Program. The DC SEU is partnered with the District Department of the Environment (DDOE) on these programs.
http://www.dcseu.com

## DC Smart Schools

DC Smart Schools is an advocate for a healthy, energy-efficient, environmentally-conscious public school system in D.C. They work to create a mandate for the best high-performance K-12 public school facilities in the nation's capital, coordinated with the development of a K-12 environmental education program for D.C. Public Schools.
http://www.thisoldschool.net

## DC Statehood Green Party

This is the local DC Statehood Green Party Platform for the national Green Party. The DC Statehood Party was founded on the concept that all human beings are entitled to certain rights, that among the rights the right of self-determination in a democratic government is paramount, and that statehood is the best and most necessary means to secure self-determination and other human rights for the citizens of the District of Columbia.

http://www.dcstatehoodgreen.org

## DC Urban Gardeners

DC Urban Gardeners promotes the creation of community and urban gardens that use sustainable gardening practices. In addition, they focus on improving fresh food access and community outreach and education. Their website includes a listing of District community gardens.

http://www.dc-urban-gardeners.com/

## Defenders of Wildlife

Founded in 1947, Defenders of Wildlife is one of the country's leaders in science-based, results-oriented wildlife conservation. They are committed to saving imperiled wildlife and championing the Endangered Species Act, the landmark law that protects them. They work to protect and restore America's native wildlife, safeguard habitat, resolve conflicts, work across international borders and educate and mobilize the public.

http://www.defenders.org

## Downtown DC BID

The Downtown Business Improvement District (BID) is a tax-funded nonprofit that works to revitalize the city's urban core. The District covers a 140-block neighborhood near the U.S. Capitol to the White House where property owners tax themselves to make their community cleaner, safer and more vibrant. The tax is used by the BID to purchase services and capital improvements that supplement those provided by the city. Today, the Downtown BID is enhancing the area by providing vital services such as hospitality, safety, maintenance, public space programming, streetscape, homeless services and transportation improvements, economic development and marketing and communications. The BID promotes Downtown D.C. as a world-class commercial, cultural and residential destination.

http://www.downtowndc.org/programs/greening

## Earth Conservation Corps

The Earth Conservation Corps is a nonprofit organization that engages Anacostia's youth in the restoration of the Anacostia River. As corps members improve their own lives, they rebuild the environmental, social, and economic health of their communities.

http://www.eccl.org

## Earth Force

Earth Force engages young people as active citizens who improve the environment and their communities now and in the future. The local chapter is based in Alexandria, VA.

http://earthforce.org/

## Earth Policy Institute

The Earth Policy Institute was founded by Lester Brown in May 2001 to provide a vision of a sustainable future and a plan for how to get from here to there. As a small organization with a global mission, the Earth Policy Institute has designed a unique information dissemination model, capitalizing on the synergy between a worldwide network of book publishers, the communications media, and the Internet. Through

this distribution network, countless individuals and organizations have become aware of the environmental issues facing the world and many have been inspired to take action.
http://www.earth-policy.org

**Earthbeat Radio**
Since 2003, Earthbeat's co-hosts Daphne Wysham and Mike Tidwell bring you an hour of ground-breaking environmental news and interviews live from the nation's capital. Earthbeat Radio features leading environmental activists and thinkers - the politics and the people behind the efforts to defend the planet. Focusing on a different climate change related theme each week, the hour is devoted to the latest news and views from the front lines of the climate crisis.
http://www.earthbeatradio.org/home

**Earth Day Network**
Earth Day Network's mission is to broaden and diversify the environmental movement worldwide and to mobilize it as the most effective vehicle for promoting a healthy, sustainable environment. They pursue this mission through a combination of education, public policy, and consumer activism campaigns. Campaigns and programs are predicated on the belief that an educated, energized population will take action to secure a healthy future for itself and its children. Earth Day Network has a global reach with a network of more than 17,000 partners and organizations in 174 countries. More than 1 billion people participate in Earth Day activities, making it the largest secular civic event in the world.
http://www.earthday.net

**EarthEcho International**
EarthEcho International's programs are dedicated to the legacy of Philippe Cousteau Sr.; a legacy of devotion to the conservation and restoration of the oceans and one that can be shared by all people. Sadly, the last 50 years has seen the greatest amount of destruction of our Oceans, bringing us to a current state of crisis. However, EarthEcho believes that it is the next 50 years in which we can embrace the new promise of just, healthy, and abundant Oceans. EarthEcho International's programs works to fill these voids in ways that unite the efforts of other prominent organizations to identify and engage the most promising leaders of tomorrow in the struggle for ocean health today.
http://www.earthecho.org

**Earthjustice**
Earthjustice is a public interest law firm dedicated to protecting the magnificent places, natural resources, and wildlife of this earth, and to defending the right of all people to a healthy environment. Far-reaching change is brought about by enforcing and strengthening environmental laws on behalf of hundreds of organizations, coalitions and communities.
http://www.earthjustice.org

**EarthShare**
Earthshare's mission is to engage individuals and organizations in creating a healthy and sustainable environment. They are committed to making support of our environment as easy as possible by giving simple, effective ways to donate to environmental and conservation charities. The EarthShare approach is comprehensive: you don't have to choose between supporting public health or our air, water, land or wildlife.
http://www.earthshare.org

**Earthworks**
Earthworks is dedicated to protecting communities and the environment from the destructive impacts of mineral development, in the U.S. and worldwide. They stand for clean water, healthy communities and

corporate accountability. As such, they are working for solutions that protect the earth's resources and communities.
http://www.earthworksaction.org

## Ecoagriculture Partners

Ecoagriculture Partners (EP) seeks to support the emerging global movement for ecoagriculture. They are centrally committed to food and livelihood security and rural poverty alleviation as key drivers for action; conservation of biodiversity in all its forms; protection of ecosystem services; and supporting agricultural (including pastoral, fisher and forest) communities as primary stewards of our ecosystems and biodiversity.
http://www.ecoagriculture.org

## Ecological Society of America

Ecological Society of American is a nonpartisan organization of scientists founded in 1915. Their goals are to promote ecological science by improving communication among ecologists; raise the public's level of awareness of the importance of ecological science; increase the resources available for the conduct of ecological science; and ensure the appropriate use of ecological science in environmental decision making by enhancing communication between the ecological community and policy-makers.
http://www.esa.org

## EcoStewards Alliance

EcoStewards Alliance (ESA) is a grassroots, membership organization. Guided by heart, spirit, and intellect, it works to heighten awareness of humankind's interrelationship with all life and natural systems. Their mission is to "provide resources for and nourish growing communities of diverse individuals who are making choices that enrich the quality of their lives and restore and protect the local environment." Programs focus on reducing consumption and living more lightly on the Earth. The programs encourage individual choices aligned with personal and environmental balance that enhance our quality of life and support a sustainable future.
http://www.ecostewardsalliance.org

## EcoVentures

EcoVentures International's mission is to inspire, work with, learn from, connect, mentor, and train community members, especially youth, to develop as socially and environmentally committed practitioners, entrepreneurs, and ambassadors of sustainable development. This is achieved through working with community partners to develop and deliver dialogues, trainings, and learning journeys; facilitating and implementing collaborative action projects among diverse stakeholders; establishing networks for development; and developing learning and knowledge sharing to support the ongoing growth and development of the environmental enterprise sector.
http://www.eco-ventures.org

## Endangered Species Coalition

The Endangered Species Coalition is a national network of hundreds of conservation, scientific, education, religious, sporting, outdoor recreation, business and community organizations working to protect our nation's disappearing wildlife and last remaining wild places. Through education, outreach and citizen involvement, they work to protect endangered species and the special places where we live. They specialize in grassroots organizing mobilizing citizens to participate in the democratic political process.
http://www.stopextinction.org

## Energy Programs Consortium

The Energy Programs Consortium is a joint venture of the National Association of State Community Services Programs, representing the state weatherization and community service programs directors; National Association of State Energy Officials, representing the state energy policy directors; National Association of State Regulatory Utility Commissioners, representing the state public service commissioners; and National Energy Assistance Directors' Association, representing the state directors of the Low-Income Home Energy Assistance Program. The purpose of EPC is to foster coordination and cooperation among state and federal agencies in the areas of energy policy and program development.
http://www.energyprograms.org

**Enterprise Community Partners DC**
Enterprise was founded with the ambitious goal of making sure every American lives in a decent, affordable home. It is a national nonprofit with 25 years of experience in the community development and affordable housing field. Central to the mission is Enterprise's fundamental commitment to give people living in poverty an opportunity to move up and out. They believe that these opportunities are best provided in communities with a diverse mix of affordable and market housing options, access to jobs and social supports, and a strong commitment to the environment and civic participation.
http://www.enterprisecommunity.org

**Environment America**
Environment America is a federation of state-based, citizen-funded environmental advocacy organizations. They have a professional staff in 27 states and Washington, D.C., which combines independent research, practical ideas and tough-minded advocacy to overcome the opposition of powerful special interests and win real results for the environment. Environment America draws on 30 years of success in tackling environmental problems.
http://www.environmentamerica.org

**Environment Virginia**
Environment Virginia protects air, water and open space by researching the facts and taking action, in Virginia at the local and state levels, in other state capitals, and in Washington, D.C., as part of Environment America. They work to improve the quality of our environment and our lives. Environment Virginia is a statewide, citizen-based environmental advocacy organization.
http://www.environmentvirginia.org

**Environmental and Energy Study Institute**
The Environmental and Energy Study Institute (EESI) is a non-profit organization established in 1984 by a bipartisan, bicameral group of members of Congress to provide timely information and develop innovative policy solutions that set us on a cleaner, more secure and sustainable energy path. EESI accomplishes these objectives are accomplished through policymaker education, networking and coalition building, and policy development.
http://www.eesi.org

**Environmental Defense Fund**
Environmental Defense Fund is a leading national nonprofit organization representing more than 500,000 members. Since 1967, they have linked science, economics and law to create innovative, equitable and cost-effective solutions to society's most urgent environmental problem. Environmental Defense Fund is dedicated to protecting the environmental rights of all people, including future generations. Among these rights are access to clean air and water, healthy and nourishing food, and flourishing ecosystems. Strong science, innovative markets, corporate partnerships, effective laws, and policy are used to tackle the most serious environmental problems.
http://www.edf.org/home.cfm

## Environmental Information Association
The Environmental Information Association provides the environmental industry with the information needed to remain knowledgeable, responsible, and competitive in the environmental health and safety industry.
http://www.eia-usa.org

## Environmental Justice and Climate Change Initiative
The Environmental Justice and Climate Change Initiative is a diverse coalition of U.S. environmental justice, religious, climate justice, policy, and advocacy networks working for climate justice. The consensus-based coalition develops projects, programs and papers to educate policymakers and connect with thousands of people about the effects of climate change and environmental injustice.
http://ejcc.org

## Environmental Law Institute
The Environmental Law Institutes aims to deliver insightful and impartial analysis to opinion makers, including government officials, environmental and business leaders, academics, members of the environmental bar, and journalists. They publish the Environmental Law Reporter, The Environmental Forum, the National Wetlands Newsletter, and books on environmental law and policy. Capacity building programs are a large part of ELI's agenda and membership program offers seminars. Their work is primarily focused on protecting water resources, land, and biodiversity and improving environmental law and its implementation in the U.S. and internationally.
http://www.eli.org

## Environmental Leadership Program
The Environmental Leadership Program (ELP) nurtures a new generation of environmental leaders characterized by diversity, innovation, collaboration, and effective communications. ELP connects them with peers through regional and national networks. They provide training and other learning opportunities to develop leadership capacity and link them with experienced environmental leaders through substantive interactions and mentoring opportunities. They also offer activity grants and technical support to help them implement innovative projects.
http://www.elpnet.org

## Environmental Resources Trust
ERT is harnessing the power of markets to address the challenges of tempering climate change, securing clean and reliable power, and encouraging environmentally beneficial land use. ERT has developed three focused programs to accomplish its mission. ERT's GHG Registry records validated greenhouse gas ("GHG") emissions profiles with the aim of creating a market that will enable efficient emissions reductions. The EcoPower Program catalyzes the market for clean energy by substantiating and marketing blocks of power that include new renewable sources of energy and have significantly reduced environmental impacts. ERT's EcoLands Program facilitates deals that enable and encourage landowners to make environmentally beneficial land use decisions.
http://www.winrock.org/feature_ert_200802.asp

## Environmental Support Center
Environmental Support Center was created by leaders from the environmental activist, environmental justice and environmental funding communities. Their mission is to help grassroots environmental groups sustain their advocacy over time. Programs have helped over 2,700 organizations from every part of the country. Hundreds of groups have received support several times, particularly though Training and Organizational Assistance (TOA), their flagship program.
http://www.envsc.org

**Environmental Working Group**

Environmental Working Group uses the power of public information to protect public health and the environment. They aim to protect the most vulnerable segments of the human population—children, babies, and infants in the womb—from health problems attributed to a wide array of toxic contaminants. They also work to replace federal policies, including government subsidies that damage the environment and natural resources, with policies that invest in conservation and sustainable development.
http://www.ewg.org

**Fairfax ReLeaf**

Fairfax ReLeaf, Inc. is a volunteer organization who plant and preserve trees, improve community appearance, and restore habitat on public and commons lands in Northern Virginia. The project serves as a practical laboratory for assessing techniques to lessen the impact of development on the environment in one of the most rapidly changing forest/urban interface areas in the country. Their goals are to restore large numbers of native trees on public and commons land where funding for landscaping is lacking and nothing would otherwise be planted and to educate government and the public about the values and benefits of the urban forest.
http://www.fairfaxreleaf.org

**Food & Water Watch**

Food & Water Watch works to ensure clean water and safe food. They challenge the corporate control and abuse of our food and water resources by empowering people to take action and by transforming the public consciousness about what we eat and drink. Food & Water Watch works with grassroots organizations around the world to create an economically and environmentally viable future. Through research, public and policymaker education, media, and lobbying, they advocate policies that guarantee safe, wholesome food produced in a humane and sustainable manner and public, rather than private, control of water resources including oceans, rivers, and groundwater.
http://www.foodandwaterwatch.org

**Forest Stewardship Council**

The Forest Stewardship Council was created to change the dialogue about and the practice of sustainable forestry worldwide. Its purpose is to coordinate the development of forest management standards throughout the different biogeographic regions of the U.S., to provide public information about certification and FSC, and to work with certification organizations to promote FSC certification in the U.S.
http://www.fscus.org

**Forest Trends**

Forest Trends is an international organization that works to expand the value of forests to society. They promote sustainable forest management and conservation by creating and capturing market values for ecosystem services. They also support innovative projects and companies that are developing these new markets. These efforts are aimed at enhancing the livelihoods of local communities living in and around those forests. Program areas include strategic market and policy issues, catalyze connections between forward-looking producers, communities and investors, and develop new financial tools to help markets work for conservation and people.
http://www.forest-trends.org

**Foundation for Environmental Security and Sustainability**

The Foundation for Environmental Security and Sustainability (FESS) is a public policy organization established to advance knowledge and provide effective solutions to key environmental security concerns

around the world. FESS conducts extensive field research in combination with data analysis to produce policy-oriented reports and recommendations that address environmental risks to stability.
http://www.fess-global.org

## FRESHFARM Markets
FRESHFARM Markets builds and strengthens the local food movement in the Chesapeake Bay region. Markets are used to create vibrant urban and community places, to provide economic opportunities for farmers, and showcase the region's agricultural bounty. This creates a sustainable urban-rural partnership that brings healthy, local food to communities and sustains the working landscapes that feed us.
http://www.freshfarmmarket.org

## Friends of Accotink Creek
Friends of Accotink Creek is a volunteer organization restoring Accotink Creek to enhance enjoyment of biking, fishing, jogging, walking and bird watching along a major portion of the Cross County Trail. The Friends of Accotink Creek are committed to protecting, promoting and restoring the water quality, natural habitat, and ecological well-being of the Accotink Creek watershed. They foster environmental awareness, education, and enhance recreational use, reduce storm runoff and its effects; restore habitats, preserve land, and enlist broad-based public and organization participation and support.
http://www.accotink.org

## Friends of Rock Creek's Environment
Friends of Rock Creek's Environment (FORCE) is a nonprofit organization working to promote a healthy and sustainable Rock Creek watershed through conservation, education and restoration. FORCE works in the Rock Creek watershed of Montgomery County, Maryland, and the District of Columbia. Projects include cleanup-up, monitoring, and storm drain marking.
http://www.friendsofrockcreek.org

## Friends of Sligo Creek
Friends of Sligo Creek is committed to restoring to health the water quality, natural habitat, and ecological well-being of the Sligo Creek watershed by bringing neighbors together to build awareness, improve natural habitat, and protect our community's heritage. They put on clean-up and clear-out events in the park, offer indoor programs for learning, and organize guided outdoor explorations. Also, they monitor civic developments and advocate for policies and decisions that will support a healthier Sligo Creek.
http://www.fosc.org/fosc.htm

## Friends of the Earth
Friends of the Earth U.S. is also a part of Friends of the Earth International, the world's largest grassroots environmental network. They fight to protect the rights of all people to live in a safe and healthy environment, both at home or in countries around the world. They believe that the fight for justice and the movement to protect the health of the planet are part of the same struggle. Successes include stopping over 150 destructive dams and water projects worldwide and winning landmark regulations of strip mines and oil tankers. Other topics include bans on international whaling, reforming the World Bank to address environmental and human rights concerns, and eliminating billions in taxpayer subsidies to corporate polluters.
http://www.foe.org

## Friends of the National Arboretum
The Friends of the National Arboretum is an independent, non-profit organization established to enhance, through public and private sector resources, support for the U.S. National Arboretum. This is

accomplished by offering youth programs, providing internships, sponsoring events, working to raise Congressional support, and increasing accessibility to the arboretum.
http://www.fona.org


**Friends of the National Zoo**
Friends of the National Zoo (FONZ) is the dedicated partner of the National Zoological Park, providing exciting and enriching experiences to connect people with wildlife. Together with the zoo, they are building a society committed to restoring an endangered natural world. FONZ has been providing support programs at the National Zoo since 1958. They have become so integral to the Zoo's operations and mission that there are few aspects of the Zoo's work which they do not support in some way.
http://nationalzoo.si.edu/default.cfm

**Geothermal Energy Association**
The Geothermal Energy Association is a trade association composed of U.S. companies who support the expanded use of geothermal energy and are developing geothermal Resources worldwide for electrical power generation and direct-heat uses. Their members have offices or operations in many states and in numerous countries throughout the world. To accomplish this, the GEA advocates for public policies that will promote the development and utilization of geothermal resources, provides a forum for the industry to discuss issues and problems, encourages research and development to improve geothermal technologies, presents industry views to governmental organizations, provides assistance for the export of geothermal goods and services, compiles statistical data about the geothermal industry, and conducts education and outreach projects.
http://www.geo-energy.org

**Global Environmental Options**
Global Environmental Options was created to continue to encourage and implement integrated green design on the building and community scale. Projects have included The Greening of The National Parks, which was launched with the Greening of the Grand Canyon Charrette in 1994, and the first internet-based Green Building Database, now a part of NRDC's on-line green building resources.
http://www.globalenvironmentaloptions.org

**Global Green USA**
Global Green works to address some of the greatest challenges facing humanity. In the United States their work is primarily focused on stemming global climate change by creating green buildings and cities. Internationally, Global Green and its affiliates are working toward eliminating weapons of mass destruction and providing clean, safe drinking water for the 2.4 billion people who lack access to clean water.
http://www.globalgreen.org

**Global Water Challenge**
Global Water Challenge (GWC) is a coalition of 22 leading organizations, who have joined together to catalyze transformational change and create a global movement in the water and sanitation sector. Their goal is universal access to clean water and safe sanitation. GWC focuses on collaborative learning, connecting leaders, and investing in sustainable, scalable, and replicable projects.
http://www.globalwaterchallenge.org

**Goodwill Industries**
Goodwill Industries is one of the largest non -profit organizations providing both jobs and skills training as well as used goods and products for sale. They have many locations in the Washington, D.C. area and

they provide low cost used products and goods, helping keep these items out of our landfills. Goodwill has also recently begun programs to collect items to be recycled such as electronics.
http://www.goodwill.org/page/guest/about

## Greater DC Cares

Greater DC Cares comprehensively mobilizes volunteers and strengthens nonprofits to better impact communities and the key issues in the Greater D.C. Region. They work with a network of more than 500 nonprofits, 12,000 volunteers and a host of corporate and foundation partners working together to positively impact the region.
http://www.dc-cares.org

## Greater Washington Interfaith Power and Light

Greater Washington Interfaith Power and Light (GWIPL) is a non-profit initiative that helps congregations, religious institutions and others in the Washington, D.C. area work for a more just, sustainable and healthier creation by reducing the threat of global warming. GWIPL can help you and your congregation buy clean, renewable energy, cut energy use, and weave energy/justice concerns into your teaching and worship. GWIPL is part of a national movement, with additional Interfaith Power and Light programs currently in 26 states and more information.
http://www.gwipl.org

## Green Building Institute

The Green Building Institute's mission is to foster sustainable building practices through education and example. They offer courses and discussion circles on topics such climate change, energy issues with buildings, and indoor air quality. Memberships, newsletters, and resources are also available.
http://greenbuildinginstitute.org

## Green DMV

Green DMV is non-profit organization seeking to promote sustainability in low-income communities across America as a pathway out of poverty. Their initial focus is our nation's capital and the Washington metropolitan area (Washington, D.C., Maryland and Virginia - DMV) to help influence policy change in the region that will spur sustainable green-collar job growth.
http://www.greendmv.org

## Green Mechanical Council

The Green Mechanical Council's mission is to educate contractors, field technicians, and industry leaders about creating and maintaining environmentally sound residential and commercial mechanical systems. The Green Mechanical Council's goals include providing specialized focus in structural mechanical systems to include plumbing, HVAC, electrical, and related systems, providing recognition of their membership as leaders in energy efficiency materials, technology, design, installation and service, and providing education and training to enable members to maximize the efficiency of existing mechanical systems and specifying high performance replacements.
http://www.greenmech.org

## Green Seal

Founded in 1989, Green Seal provides science-based environmental certification standards that are credible, transparent, and essential in an increasingly educated and competitive marketplace. Their industry knowledge and standards help manufacturers, purchasers, and end users alike make responsible choices that positively impact business behavior and improve quality of life.
http://www.greenseal.org

**Greenspace**

Greenspace promotes green affordable housing and community building as a way of transforming neighborhoods and ensuring that the benefits of sustainable development reach residents at all income levels. They are an active partner on the District Green Building Advisory Council. Greenspace has established itself as a leading expert in green building in the District.
http://www.greenspacencr.org/index.html

**Greenpeace**

Greenpeace opposes environmental destruction in a peaceful, non-violent manner. They use non-violent confrontation to raise the level and quality of public debate. Financial independence from political or commercial interests is ensured. They actively seek solutions for, and promote open, informed debate about society's environmental choices.
http://www.greenpeace.org/usa

**Health and Environmental Funders Network**

The Health and Environmental Funders Network (HEFN) is a network of funders committed to grant making at the nexus of environment and health. By building this cross-cutting philanthropic community, HEFN and its members are supporting an increasingly powerful movement towards healthier people, ecosystems, and communities. They provide information and updates for its members, organize funder events, do outreach in philanthropy, and enable funders to collaborate around shared goals or projects.
http://www.hefn.org

**Healthy Building Network**

Healthy Building Network strives to transform the market for building materials to advance the best environmental, health and social practices. Since 2000, their projects have directly resulted in the introduction of new, healthier building materials into commercial markets, shifting over $4 billion in materials purchases from toxic materials to healthier alternatives that are comparable in both price and performance to the materials they have replaced. They have played a key role in establishing precedent-setting green building guidelines for health care facilities, demonstrating well-built, healthy and green modular homes to the affordable housing market in the Gulf States region and developing the first, on-line evaluation tool for building materials.
http://www.healthybuilding.net

**Humane Society**

The Humane Society of the United States (HSUS) is the nation's largest and most effective animal protection organization—backed by 10 million Americans. Established in 1954, The HSUS seeks a humane and sustainable world for all animals—a world that will also benefit people. They are America's mainstream force against cruelty, exploitation and neglect, as well as the most trusted voice extolling the human-animal bond.
http://www.hsus.org

**Hydropower Reform Coalition**

Originally founded in 1992 as a loose association of conservation and recreation groups, the Hydropower Reform Coalition has grown into a broad consortium of more than 140 national, regional, and local organizations with a combined membership of over one million people. They represent stakeholders from canoeists to conservationists to lake homeowners. Together, their efforts have protected or restored thousands of river miles, thousands of acres of watershed land, and countless opportunities for boating, fishing, and other forms of recreation.
http://www.hydroreform.org

## Institute for Conservation Leadership

The Institute for Conservation Leadership empowers leaders with training and they build volunteer institutions that protect and conserve the Earth's environment. This is done by helping leaders lead better, building connections between groups with similar goals, and supporting groups' progress with fundraising, board development, and other activities.
http://www.icl.org

## Institute for Governance and Sustainable Development

The Institute for Governance and Sustainable Development's mission is to promote just and sustainable societies and to protect the environment by advancing the understanding, development and implementation of effective, accountable and democratic systems of governance for sustainable development. They bring together professionals from around the world who are committed to strengthening environmental law and institutions to promote sustainable development. They work to advance understanding of governance through research and education, effectively implement policies through capacity building, create change on key issues through advice and advocacy, cooperate through networking, and enhance public awareness through film and television.
http://www.igsd.org

## Institute for Local Self-Reliance

The Institute for Local Self-Reliance's (ILSR) mission is to provide innovative strategies, working models and timely information to support environmentally sound and equitable community development. To this end, ILSR works with citizens, activists, policymakers and entrepreneurs to design systems, policies and enterprises that meet local or regional needs; to maximize human, material, natural and financial resources; and to ensure that the benefits of these systems and resources accrue to all local citizens.
http://www.ilsr.org

## Institute for Market Transformation

The mission of the Institute for Market Transformation (IMT) is to promote energy efficiency, green building and environmental protection in the United States and abroad. The organization's activities include technical and market research, educational outreach, and creation and coordination of program initiatives. The term "market transformation" encompasses various strategies for the creation of permanent, self-sustaining success of energy-efficient technologies in the marketplace.
http://www.imt.org

## Institute for Policy Studies – Sustainable Energy and Economy Network

The Sustainable Energy and Economy Network works in partnership with citizens groups nationally and globally on environment, human rights and development issues with a particular focus on energy, climate change, environmental justice, gender equity, and economic issues, particularly as these play out in North-South relations.
http://www.ips-dc.org/seen

## Institute for Sustainable Communities

The Institute for Sustainable Communities' mission is to help communities around the world address environmental, economic, and social challenges to build a better future shaped and shared by all. Their approach is aimed at creating solutions that emerge from within the community, rather than being imposed from the outside. By combining technical expertise and leadership training with strategic investments in local organizations, they spark creative solutions and lasting change.
http://www.iscvt.org

**International Council on Clean Transportation**

The goal of the International Council on Clean Transportation (ICCT) is to dramatically improve environmental performance and efficiency of cars, trucks, buses, and transportation systems in order to protect and improve public health, the environment, and quality of life.
http://www.theicct.org


**International Green Energy Council**

The IGEC is an International non – profit association comprised of individuals and companies that promote "Green" (sustainable) forms of energy production, renewable energy sources, sustainable design practices and advanced thinking in utilizing education and information for the promotion of being better stewards of our environment. The IGEC is comprised of renewable energy companies, developers, builders, material suppliers, subcontractors, consultants, lending institutions, utilities, installers, designers, manufacturers, engineers, inspectors, consultants and others involved in and out of the "green" community.
http://www.greenenergycouncil.com

**International Union for the Conservation of Nature**

The International Union for Conservation of Nature helps find pragmatic solutions to the most pressing environment and development challenges. They support scientific research, manage field projects all over the world, and bring governments, non-government organizations, United Nations agencies, companies and local communities together to develop and implement policy, laws and best practice. IUCN is the world's oldest and largest global environmental network - a democratic membership union with more than 1,000 government and NGO member organizations, and almost 11,000 volunteer scientists in more than 160 countries.
http://www.iucn.org

**Land Trust Alliance**

The Land Trust Alliance unites and champions organizations in local communities working to save natural areas. Conservation program areas include education, conservation defense, public policy, field programs, and the Land Trust Accreditation Commission.
http://www.landtrustalliance.org

**Lead Safe DC**

Lead Safe DC combines a broad family education initiative and a grassroots public policy task force with the goal of ridding the nation's capital of childhood lead poisoning. The program partners with local health centers and maternity wards to provide educational home visits and community center classes on lead. Lead Safe DC also has established the Lead Elimination Task Force, which consists of academics, federal and local officials, nurses and doctors who meet monthly to create strategies, form partnerships and leverage resources to attack the problem of lead poisoning.
http://www.leadsafedc.org

**League of American Bicyclists**

Their mission is to promote bicycling for fun, fitness, and transportation and work through advocacy and education for a bicycle-friendly America. This is done by representing the interests of the nation's 57 million cyclists. With a current membership of 300,000 affiliated cyclists, including 40,000 individuals and 600 affiliated organizations, the League works to bring better bicycling to your community.
http://www.bikeleague.org

**League of Conservation Voters**
To secure the environmental future of our planet, The League of Conservation Voters' (L CV) mission is to advocate for sound environmental policies and to elect pro-environmental candidates who will adopt and implement such policies. Through the National Environmental Scorecard and Presidential Report Card, they inform the public about the most important environmental legislation of the past Congressional session and show them how their own and other representatives voted. They run campaigns to defeat anti-environment candidates, and support those leaders who stand up for a clean, healthy future for America. Additionally, they educate the public, build coalitions, promote grassroots power, and train the next generation of environmental leaders as part of our grassroots efforts.
http://www.lcv.org

**Live Green**
Live Green's mission is to making eco-friendly living and business practices easier and more affordable in D.C. and beyond. They are a membership organization providing support to green businesses and discounts on everyday green products and services for consumers. To this end, they work to find green products and services that are high quality and locally available. Then, they negotiate deals and discounts that ensure their members get good products and prices. They are dedicated to providing their members with simple, straightforward tips on living green, helping new green businesses flourish, and investing in sustainable development projects.
http://www.livegreen.net

**Living Cities**
Living Cities promotes policies on the local, state and national level that have a real impact on urban neighborhoods and their residents, helping them to achieve their human, social and economic potential and to succeed in a global marketplace.
http://www.livingcities.org/

**Living Classrooms of the National Capital Region**
Living Classrooms of the National Capital Region provides hands-on education and job skills training for students from diverse backgrounds, with a special emphasis on serving at-risk youth. The foundation uses maritime settings, community revitalization projects and other challenging learning environments, and a low staff to student ratio. The "learning by doing" education programs emphasize the applied learning of math, science, literacy, history, economics, and ecology. Key objectives of all Living Classrooms programs are career development, community service, elevating self-esteem, and fostering multicultural exchange.
http://www.livingclassroomsdc.org/index.html

**Marine Fish Conservation Network**
The Marine Fish Conservation Network is the largest national coalition solely dedicated to promoting the long-term sustainability of marine fish. With almost 200 members - including environmental organizations, commercial and recreational fishing associations, aquariums, and marine science groups - the network uses its distinct voice and the best available science to educate policymakers, the fishing industry, and the public about the need for sound conservation and better management practices.
http://www.conservefish.org

**Maryland Student Climate Coalition**
The Maryland Student Climate Coalition is a grassroots coalition of students in the University System of Maryland (USM). Their goal is make the USM carbon neutral through energy efficiency, LEED certified buildings, and supplying energy needs using clean power.
http://www.chesapeakeclimate.org/blog/?p=169

**Maryland Master Gardeners**
The Maryland Master Gardener Program is an education-based program that works to train volunteer horticultural educators for University of Maryland Extension. The program also supports the mission of creating a healthier community through environmental stewardship. Participants complete 40 to 50 hours of basic training and proceed to apply their knowledge in their local communities. Master Gardeners teach fellow Maryland residents on sustainable garden cultivation and landscape management skills that result in improved soil and water quality.
http://mastergardener.umd.edu/

**Master Gardeners of Northern Virginia**
Master Gardeners of Northern Virginia (MGNV) is an organization of volunteers who work with the staff of Virginia Cooperative Extension (VCE) to encourage and promote environmentally sound gardening practices. MGNV members must complete over 60 hours of training and 60 hours of volunteer work as interns to become certified by Virginia Tech as Master Gardeners. Additional volunteer work and continuing education are required to maintain certification.
http://www.mgnv.org/

**National Academies, Science and Technology for Sustainability**
The National Academies have established a Science and Technology for Sustainability Program (STS) in the division of Policy and Global Affairs to encourage the use of science and technology to achieve long-term sustainable development - increasing incomes, improving public health, and sustaining critical natural systems. Specific projects under the STS program include the Roundtable on Science and Technology for Sustainability and a workshop series entitled Strengthening Science-Based Decision Making.
http://sustainability.nationalacademies.org

**National Association of Environmental Managers**
NAEM, the premier association for EHS Management, is a non-profit, non-partisan educational association dedicated to advancing the knowledge and practice of Environmental, Health & Safety (EHS) management. NAEM, formerly known as the National Association for Environmental Management, strives to improve awareness and use of efficient, effective leadership methods.
http://www.naem.org

**National Association of Home Builders**
NAHB exists to represent the building industry by serving its members and affiliated state and local builders associations. NAHB strives to create an environment in which all Americans have access to the housing of their choice and the opportunity to realize the American dream of homeownership, builders have the freedom to operate as entrepreneurs in an open and competitive environment, housing and those who provide it are recognized as the strength of the nation. NAHB has developed a green building rating system for residential buildings.
http://www.nahb.org

**National Association of Resource Conservation and Development Council**
The National Association of Resource Conservation and Development Council serves as an advocate for local Councils. They assist them to identify, address, and solve challenges to sustain and improve quality of life in their own communities. It was established in 1988 to represent America's 375 local Resource Conservation and Development Councils. The local councils deliver coordinated resource conservation and rural development assistance throughout rural America.
http://www.rcdnet.org

**National Association of State Energy Officials**
The National Association of State Energy Officials (NASEO) is the only national non-profit organization whose membership includes the governor-designated energy officials from each state and territory. NASEO was formed by the states and through an agreement with the National Governors Association in 1986. The organization was created to improve the effectiveness and quality of state energy programs and policies, provide policy input and analysis, share successes among the states, and to be a repository of information on issues of particular concern to the states and their citizens.
http://www.naseo.org

**National Council for Science and the Environment**
The National Council for Science and the Environment is dedicated to improving the scientific basis for environmental decision-making. They envision a society where environmental decisions by everyone are based on an accurate understanding of the underlying science, its meaning and limitations, and the potential consequences of their action or inaction.
http://ncseonline.org

**National Environmental Education Foundation**
National Environmental Education Foundation partners with professionals in health, education, media, business and public land management to promote daily actions for helping people protect and enjoy the environment. Through their primary programs - Classroom Earth, National Public Lands Day, National Environmental Education Week, Business and Environment, Earth Gauge and Health & Environment - they offer Americans critical knowledge.
http://neefusa.org

**National Hydropower Association**
The National Hydropower Association (NHA) is a nonprofit national association dedicated exclusively to advancing the interests of the hydropower industry. It seeks to secure hydropower's place as a climate-friendly, renewable and reliable energy source that serves national environmental and energy policy objectives. NHA unites the diverse North American hydropower community, providing a powerful advocacy voice among U.S. decision makers, the general public and the international community. Through membership, individuals and organizations gain access to regulatory bodies, influence over energy and environmental policy and a means to exchange valuable information with one's peers.
http://www.hydro.org

**National Jobs Corps Association**
Today, 122 Job Corps centers in 48 states, D.C., and Puerto Rico, train nearly 70,000 students each year. Over 40 years, Job Corps has earned a reputation as the nation's premier workforce training program for disadvantages youth. By consistently being responsive to employers' demands and the nation's workforce needs, Job Corps has succeeded in meeting those needs by offering top-notched vocational training to students. As a testament to these successes, numerous bi-partisan political initiatives have supported Jobs Corps expansion to serve more disadvantaged young Americans with each passing year. With a legacy of success spanning four decades, Jobs Corps is poised to continue delivering results for the nation and the next generation.
http://www.njcaweb.org

**National Marine Sanctuary Foundation**
The National Marine Sanctuary Foundation was created to assist the federally managed National Marine Sanctuary Program with education and outreach programs designed to preserve, protect and promote meaningful opportunities for public interaction with the nation's marine sanctuaries.
http://nmsfocean.org

**National Park Foundation**
For almost forty years, the National Park Foundation–chartered by Congress as the only national charitable partner of America's National Parks–has supported these lands. The mission of the National Park Foundation is to strengthen the connection between the American people and their National Parks by raising private funds, making strategic grants, creating innovative partnerships and increasing public awareness.
http://www.nationalparks.org

**National Park Trust**
The National Park Trust is the nation's only organization dedicated to the completion, and the full appreciation, of the American system of National and State Parks through the identification of key land acquisition needs and opportunities. Their vision is based on the belief that there is a necessity to get people to visit parks, and a particular necessity to get young people to have an American park experience.
http://www.parktrust.org

**National Parks Conservation Association**
The National Parks Conservation Association (NPCA) plays a crucial role in ensuring that the parklands and landmarks are protected in perpetuity. They advocate for the national parks and the National Park Service. They educate decision makers and the public about the importance of preserving the parks and help to convince members of Congress to uphold the laws that protect the parks and to support new legislation to address threats to the parks. Additionally, they fight attempts to weaken these laws in the courts as well as assess the health of the parks and park management to better inform our advocacy work.
http://www.npca.org

**National Recycling Coalition**
The National Recycling Coalition (NRC) is a national advocacy group with members that span all aspects of waste reduction, reuse and recycling in North America. The Coalition represents advocates from every region of the country, in every sector of the waste reduction field. Local recycling coordinators, state and federal regulators, corporate environmental managers, environmental educators and advocates, consumers and waste management professionals are all members of NRC. NRC's objective is to eliminate waste and promote sustainable economies through advancing sound management practices for raw materials in North America.
http://www.nrcrecycles.org/

**National Sustainable Agriculture Coalition**
The National Sustainable Agriculture Coalition (NSAC) is a national alliance of farm, rural development, and conservation groups that organized in 1988 to affect federal agriculture policy. Their member groups advance common positions to support small and mid-size family farms, protect natural resources, promote healthy rural communities, and provide nutritious and healthy food to consumers. By bringing grassroots perspectives to the table normally dominated by big business, NSAC levels the playing field and gives voice to sustainable and organic farmers.
http://sustainableagriculture.net

**National Trust for Historic Preservation**
The National Trust for Historic Preservation believes existing buildings are one of our greatest renewable resources. Through their Sustainability Initiative, the National Trust for Historic Preservation is focusing the nation's attention on the importance of reusing existing buildings and reinvesting in older and historic communities as critical elements in combating climate change. Through its research, the National Trust's Sustainability Initiative is demonstrating that conservation and improvement of our existing built resources are environmentally logical and economically viable elements in combating climate change.
http://www.preservationnation.org/issues/sustainability

**National Wildlife Refuge Association**
The National Wildlife Refuge Association's mission is to conserve America's wildlife heritage for future generations through strategic programs that protect, enhance, and expand the National Wildlife Refuge System and the landscapes beyond its boundaries that secure its ecological integrity. By combining policy, grassroots development, and public education objectives, the National Wildlife Refuge Association works to strengthen the ecological integrity of our national wildlife refuges and thus ensure a diverse spectrum of plants and wildlife well into the future.
http://www.refugenet.org/

**National Wind Coordination Committee**
A consensus-based collaborative formed in 1994, the National Wind Coordinating Collaborative (NWCC) is comprised of representatives from the utility, wind industry, environmental, consumer, regulatory, power marketer, agricultural, tribal, economic development, and state and federal government sectors to support the development of an environmentally, economically, and politically sustainable commercial market for wind power.
http://www.nationalwind.org

**National Whistleblowers Center**
National Whistleblowers Center (NWC) is a non-partisan advocacy organization with a 20-year history of protecting the right of individuals to speak out about wrongdoing in the workplace without fear of retaliation. Since 1988, NWC has supported whistleblowers in the courts and before Congress, achieving victories for environmental protection, nuclear safety, government ethics and corporate accountability. They also sponsors several educational and assistance programs, including an online resource center on whistleblower rights, a speakers bureau of national experts and former whistleblowers, and a national attorney referral service run by the NWC's sister group the National Whistleblower Legal Defense and Education Fund (NWLDEF).
http://www.whistleblowers.org

**Natural Resources Defense Council**
The Natural Resources Defense Council (NRDC) uses law, science and the support of 1.2 million members and online activists to protect the planet's wildlife and wild places and to ensure a safe and healthy environment for all living things. Their purpose is to safeguard the Earth: its people, its plants and animals and the natural systems on which all life depends. To achieve this goal they restore the integrity of the elements that sustain life - air, land and water - and defend endangered natural places. They establish sustainability and good stewardship of the Earth as central ethical imperatives of human society.
http://www.nrdc.org

**NatureServe**
NatureServe's mission is to provide the scientific basis for effective conservation action. NatureServe and its network of natural heritage programs are a leading source for information about rare and endangered species and threatened ecosystems.
http://www.natureserve.org

**Nature's Voice, Our Choice**
Nature's Voice, Our Choice's mission is to preserve, conserve, and restore the world's water resources through education and awareness, ecologically engineered natural waste water treatment systems, and the formation of community stewardship projects that are economically feasible. Projects span issues such as sanitation, depleting water resources, water contamination, land degradation, loss of biodiversity, and poverty resulting from these factors.
http://naturesvoice-ourchoice.org

**NDN**

NDN is a progressive think tank and advocacy organization. NDN's work is organized around a powerful idea – that for progressives to succeed in the 21st century as they did in the 20th, they will have to do three things: offer a new governing agenda that speaks to the challenges of our day; master the new media and technology tools that are changing the way we all communicate and advocate; and understand and speak to the radically new demographic make-up of today's America.
http://www.ndn.org

**Noblis**

Noblis is unique even among nonprofits because when they sit down to solve a problem, there are no strings attached to our thinking. They have no commercial interests to advance, no vendor alliances to protect, and no sponsors to represent. So Noblis is free to focus on what matters most—finding the solution that works best. Noblis offers a variety of services that focus on environmental and energy solutions to existing problems our planet faces.
http://www.noblis.org

**Northern Virginia Clean Water Partners**

The Northern Virginia Clean Water Partners represent nine Northern Virginia local governments, two independent water and sanitary sewer authorities, and one regional commission. The goal is to work collaboratively in an effort to reduce the amount of pollution reaching our individual and shared waterways. Using radio, print, and television advertisements, they maximize the reach of their messages on properly disposing of pet waste and motor oil and proper lawn care practices to over a million residents living, playing, and working in the Northern Virginia region.
http://www.onlyrain.org

**Oceana**

Oceana is led by top advocates, scientists, managers, lawyers and economists with experience in business, entertainment, science, government and the non-profit sector. They bring together some of the most talented and committed marine advocates on the planet. They fight against collapsing fish populations, global contamination, critical habitat under siege, marine life casualties, disappearance of local fishing cultures and jobs.
http://www.oceana.org

**Organization of American States Department of Sustainable Development**

The Department of Sustainable Development (DSD) supports OAS member States in the design and implementation of policies, programs and projects oriented to integrate environmental priorities with poverty alleviation, and socio-economic development goals. Translating sustainable development and environmental protection goals into concrete actions, DSD supports the execution of multiple-country projects in such diverse areas as integrated water management, renewable energy, land-titling, natural hazards-climate change adaptation, biological diversity and environmental law and policy.
http://www.oas.org/dsd

**Our Task**

Our Task is an international network of young adults aged 15-25 who, with help from adult mentors, are developing a Youth Earth Plan for the 21st century. The Our Task members are concerned that young people everywhere will be adversely impacted by many of the decisions being made currently by their parents' and grandparents' generations. They work to initiate a thoughtful, substantive intergenerational dialog on the changes they feel are needed urgently by young people everywhere.
http://www.ourtask.org

**Pew Center on Global Climate Change**
The Pew Center on Global Climate Change was established in 1998 as a non-profit, non-partisan and independent organization. The Center's mission is to provide credible information, straight answers, and innovative solutions in the effort to address global climate change. The Pew Center on Global Climate Change brings together business leaders, policy makers, scientists, and other experts to bring a new approach to a complex and often controversial issue. Their approach is based on sound science, straight talk, and a belief that we can work together to protect the climate while sustaining economic growth.
http://www.pewclimate.org

**Pew Environment Group**
Pew is a major force in educating the public and policy makers about the causes, consequences and solutions to environmental problems. They actively promote strong conservation policies in the United States and internationally. Pew applies a range of tools in pursuit of practical, meaningful solutions - including applied science, public education, sophisticated media and communications, and policy advocacy.
http://www.pewtrusts.org/our_work_category.aspx?id=110

**Partnership for Advancing Technology in Housing**
The Partnership for Advancing Technology in Housing (PATH) is dedicated to accelerating the development and use of technologies that radically improve the quality, durability, energy efficiency, environmental performance, and affordability of America's housing. PATH is a voluntary partnership between leaders of the homebuilding, product manufacturing, insurance, and financial industries and representatives of Federal agencies concerned with housing. Working together, PATH partners improve new and existing homes and strengthen the technology infrastructure of the United States.
http://www.pathnet.org

**Phoenix Bikes**
Phoenix Bikes is a youth program whose mission is to develop youth leaders and social entrepreneurs through hands-on learning experiences and service to the greater D.C. cycling community. Their vision is to provide a fun, safe, and challenging environment for local youth through building and running great community bike shops. They believe this is a unique way for young leaders to learn teamwork, explore social entrepreneurship, develop business and leadership skills, and serve others. The shop also provides affordable bikes and bike repair services to our community.
http://phoenixbikes.org

**Pinchot Institute for Conservation**
The mission of the Pinchot Institute is to advance conservation and sustainable natural resource management by developing innovative, practical, and broadly supported solutions to conservation challenges and opportunities. They accomplish this through nonpartisan research, education and technical assistance on key issues influencing the future of conservation and sustainable natural resource management.
http://www.pinchot.org

**Population Connection**
For forty years, Population Connection (formerly Zero Population Growth) has been educating young people with its award-winning Population Education program and advocating for progressive action to stabilize world population at a level that can be sustained by Earth's resources.
http://www.populationconnection.org

**Potomac Conservancy**
Potomac Conservancy protects the health, beauty, and enjoyment of the Potomac River and its tributaries. The Conservancy's primary focus is protection of water quality through land protection and sound land use practices. Because clean water alone is not enough, the Conservancy also works to preserve and restore the Potomac's scenic landscapes, and to enhance river-based recreational opportunities.
http://www.potomac.org

**Potomac Riverkeeper**
Potomac Riverkeeper, Inc. was established by principals from other environmental organizations, including: the Potomac Conservancy, Piedmont Environmental Council, Audubon Naturalist Society, and Sierra Club. The goal was to create a strong advocate, the Potomac Riverkeeper, and enforce existing federal and state laws governing the Potomac watershed and protecting it from exploitation. Programs cover topics like pollution prevention, fish health, and community awareness and engagement.
http://www.potomacriverkeeper.org

**Public Employees for Environmental Responsibility**
Public Employees for Environmental Responsibility (PEER) is a national alliance of local, state and federal scientists, law enforcement officers, land managers and other professionals dedicated to upholding environmental laws and values. They organize a broad base of support among employees within local, state and federal resource management agencies. To serve as a "watch dog" for the public interest, they monitor natural resource management agencies. They inform the administration, Congress, state officials, media and the public about substantive environmental issues of concern to PEER members and defend and strengthen the legal rights of public employees who speak out about issues concerning natural resource management and environmental protection.
http://www.peer.org

**Rachel's Network**
Rachel's Network encourages women to participate in the political process and promotes women leaders who advocate for a healthy environment. Rachel's Network offers innovative member services that cultivate leadership, instill strategic acuity, provide networking opportunities, and broaden members' understanding of important issues. These signature services allow members to reach their personal and philanthropic goals while connecting with women who share their dedication to strategic philanthropy in conservation, health, and women's empowerment.
http://www.rachelsnetwork.org

**Rails-to-Trails Conservancy**
Rails-to-Trails Conservancy works with communities to preserve unused rail corridors by transforming them into trails, enhancing the health of America's environment, economy, neighborhoods and people. They promote policy at the national and state levels to create the conditions that make trail building possible. They are a leader in the fight to protect the federal Transportation Enhancements program, which is the largest source of funding for trail development. Action is catalyzed at the local level by providing information, technical assistance and training that local trail builders need to succeed.
http://www.railstotrails.org

**Rare Conservation**
Rare Conservation works internationally to help educate people about the value of the natural environment. This is accomplished through the science of behavior change – an arena in which Rare has practiced for more than 35 years. Rare has developed a method for changing attitudes and behaviors called a Pride campaign – so named because it inspires people to take pride in the natural assets that make their communities unique and offers them viable means to protect these assets.
http://rareconservation.org

**Resources for the Future**
Resources for the Future is a nonpartisan organization that conducts independent research – rooted primarily in economics and other social sciences – on environmental, energy, and natural resource issues. Research topics include energy and climate, regulating risks transportation and urban land, the natural world, and human health.
http://www.rff.org

**Restore America's Estuaries**
Restore America's Estuaries' mission is to preserve the nation's network of estuaries by protecting and restoring the lands and waters essential to the richness and diversity of coastal life. To this end, they conduct on-the-ground restoration projects as part of a national campaign to restore one million acres of coastal and estuarine habitat by the year 2010. They unite the national restoration community, key decision makers and local citizens through their biennial national conference and national outreach efforts.
http://www.estuaries.org

**Save America's Forests**
Save America's Forests is nationwide campaign to end clear-cutting and protect and restore our nation's wild and natural forests. They are coalition of thousands of scientists, citizens, and groups throughout America working together to protect local forests. They also work with indigenous people to protect rainforests from development.
http://www.saveamericasforests.org

**Scenic America**
Scenic America is dedicated solely to preserving and enhancing the visual character of America's communities and countryside. They accomplish this mission through national advocacy efforts and technical assistance services, local and national projects, and the support of state affiliates.
http://www.scenic.org

**Seafood Choices Alliance**
Seafood Choices Alliance is an international program that provides leadership and creates opportunities for change across the seafood industry and ocean conservation community. Seafood Choices helps the seafood industry - from fishermen and fish farmers to processors, distributors, retailers, restaurants, and food service providers - to make the seafood marketplace environmentally, economically, and socially sustainable. By building relationships and stimulating dialogue, Seafood Choices is encouraging and challenging all sectors of the seafood industry along the road toward sustainability.
http://www.seafoodchoices.com

**SeaWeb**
SeaWeb is a communications-based organization that uses social marketing techniques to advance ocean conservation. They raise public awareness, advance science-based solutions, and mobilize decision-makers around ocean conservation. SeaWeb's programs combine science, communications and policy expertise to recruit and amplify leading voices for ocean conservation. Their work is grounded in first-rate scientific research and data collection, and they use our strategic communications skills to translate this information into understandable and relevant initiatives. This approach to conditioning the climate for ocean conservation results in both changed behaviors and strong ocean policy.
http://www.seaweb.org

**Securing Americas Future Energy**
Securing America's Future Energy (SAFE) is an action-oriented, nonpartisan organization that aims to reduce America's dependence on oil, addressing business and technology, politics and advocacy, and public education and media.
http://www.secureenergy.org

**Set America Free**
The Set America Free Coalition's mission is to change that, by giving us choice and breaking the oil monopoly. Set America Free strives to educate people about the danger of the U.S. dependence on foreign oil and the need for fuel choice, Increase public demand for and use of flexible fuel vehicles and plug-in hybrids, and support policy solutions that increase fuel choice.
http://www.setamericafree.org/home.html

**Sharing Backyards**
Sharing Backyards links people with unused yard space with those looking for a place to grow food. One of the biggest barriers to growing food in the city is access to land - despite the fact that many yards, lawns, and backyards have plenty of room to spare. If you have a garden and want to share it with someone, or if you are looking for a space to garden, Sharing Backyards is a good resource.
http://www.sharingbackyards.com

**Sierra Club, Washington, D.C. Chapter**
The Sierra Club is the oldest and largest grassroots environmental organization in the nation. The Washington, D.C. Chapter is comprised of more than 3,600 members and supporters and is actively involved in local conservation and politics through events and volunteer opportunities. The chapter maintains a calendar of opportunities to become engaged and informed.
http://www.dc.sierraclub.org

**Smart Growth America**
Smart Growth America is a coalition of national, state and local organizations working to improve the ways we plan and build the towns, cities and metro areas we call home. The coalition includes many of the best-known national organizations advocating on behalf of historic preservation, the environment, farmland and open space preservation, neighborhood revitalization and more.
http://www.smartgrowthamerica.org

**Society for Conservation Biology**
The Society for Conservation Biology is an international professional organization dedicated to promoting the scientific study of the phenomena that affect the maintenance, loss, and restoration of biological diversity. The society's membership comprises a wide range of people interested in the conservation and study of biological diversity: resource managers, educators, government and private conservation workers, and students make up the more than 10,000 members worldwide.
http://www.conbio.org

**Solar Electric Light Fund**
SELF designs and implements sustainable energy solutions for enhancements in health, education, agriculture and economic growth in the developing world. SELF works to deliver solar power and wireless communications to rural villages in Africa, Asia, and Latin America. They facilitate a new generation of "whole village" solar electrification projects to power water pumping and purification, drip irrigation, health clinics (including vaccine refrigeration), schools, household and community lighting, and income-generating micro-enterprises that can be scaled up through the private sector or through public/private partnerships.
http://www.self.org

**Solar Electric Power Association**

The Solar Electric Power Association has more than 500 utility, electric service provider, manufacturer, installer, government, and research members. The mission is to facilitate solutions for the use and integration of solar electric power by utilities, electric service providers, and their customers. To achieve this mission, SEPA: provides products, services, and strategies; fosters business to business networking; shares information on solar electric technologies, applications, programs, and business solutions; and, reports on and evaluates policies, regulations, and legislation
http://www.solarelectricpower.org/

**Solar Energy Industries Association**

The Solar Energy Industries Association (SEIA) is the leading national trade association for the solar energy industry. They work to expand markets, strengthen research and development, remove market barriers and improve education and outreach for solar energy professionals.
http://www.seia.org

**Student Conservation Association**

The Student Conservation Association (SCA) is an American conservation corps. Their members protect and restore national parks, marine sanctuaries, cultural landmarks and community green spaces in all 50 states. SCA's mission is to build the next generation of conservation leaders and inspire lifelong stewardship of our environment and communities by engaging young people in hands-on service to the land.
http://www.thesca.org

**Surface Transportation Policy Partnership**

The Surface Transportation Policy Partnership is a diverse, nationwide coalition working to ensure safer communities and smarter transportation choices that enhance the economy, improve public health, promote social equity, and protect the environment.
http://www.transact.org

**Surfrider Foundation, Washington, D.C. Chapter**

The Surfrider Foundation is a non-profit environmental organization dedicated to the protection and enjoyment of the world's oceans, waves, and beaches for all people, through conservation, activism, research, and education. The core activities and campaigns that the Surfrider Foundation uses to protect oceans, waves, and beaches fall into the categories of clean water, beach access, beach preservation and protecting special places.
http://ww2.surfrider.org/dc/

**Sustainable Business Network of Washington**

The Sustainable Business Network of Washington (SB NOW) works with businesses to help them integrate environmental and social responsibility principles into their operations and strategy. They aim to help improve the quality of life and the environment in the National Capital Region. SB NOW is a community of businesses, non-profits, and individuals dedicated to realizing a common goal: helping Washington, D.C. become a more sustainable place to live and work now and in the future, fully realizing its potential as a world-class capital city.
http://www.sbnow.org

**Sustainable Community Development Group**

Sustainable Community Development Group is a nonprofit that is dedicated to creating sustainable communities, which are inclusive of all individuals and groups. They are frequently speakers at national conferences around issues related to sustainable development. Their expertise includes brownfield

development, sustainability plans and policies, and organizing and facilitating conferences, meetings, and public hearings on sustainability issues. They have worked in many countries around the globe.
http://www.sustainablecommunitydevelopmentgroup.org

**Sustainable Energy Institute**
The Sustainable Energy Institute is committed to improving public awareness and understanding worldwide of future energy supply and demand options and their implications. SEI also facilitates high-level policy dialogue on energy options, focusing particular attention on technological solutions to a cleaner energy future. Led by respected scholars and thinkers in the energy and environmental area, SEI strives to cut through the political rhetoric and promote intelligent debate on sustainable energy solutions. As an independent voice, SEI provides a balanced perspective on energy choices while promoting the development of new energy technologies and working to reduce the impact of the existing options on public health and safety and the environment.
http://www.s-e-i.org

**The Alliance to Save Energy**
The Alliance to Save Energy is a coalition of business, government, environmental and consumer leaders. They support energy efficiency as a cost-effective energy resource under existing market conditions. The alliance advocates for energy-efficiency policies that minimize costs to society and individual consumers, and that lessen greenhouse gas emissions and their impact on the global climate. To carry out its mission, the Alliance to Save Energy undertakes research, educational programs, and policy advocacy, designs and implements energy-efficiency projects, promotes technology development and deployment, and builds public-private partnerships, in the U.S. and other countries.
http://www.ase.org

**The Center for Environmental Leadership in Business**
Companies with a global presence have an opportunity to shift the impact of their activities from environmental harm to ecological stewardship. As business acquires more influence worldwide and public support for conservation grows, companies are discovering new incentives to demonstrate environmental leadership. To catalyze this transformation, Conservation International (CI) and Ford Motor Company established The Center for Environmental Leadership in Business (CELB) to engage the private sector worldwide in creating solutions to critical global environmental problems in which industry plays a defining role. Guided by strategies at the local to the international levels, the Center's programs convene global dialogues to create best practices within key industries worldwide and promote effective policy solutions on issues such as global climate change.
http://www.celb.org/xp/CELB

**The Clean Water Network**
The Clean Water Network is a coalition of more than 1,000 public interest organizations that endorse the National Agenda for Clean Water. The agenda outlines the need for strong clean water safeguards in order to protect public health and the environment. The Clean Water Network includes a wide variety of public interest organizations representing environmentalists, commercial fishermen, recreational anglers, surfers, boaters, farmers, faith communities, environmental justice, labor unions, consumer advocates, and others.
http://www.cleanwaternetwork.org

**The Climate Group**
Over the next five years, The Climate Group's goal is to help government and business set the world economy on the path to a low-carbon, prosperous future. To reach this goal, The Climate Group has created a coalition of governments and the world's most influential businesses – all committed to tackling climate change.

http://www.theclimategroup.org

**The Conservation Fund**
The Conservation Fund is dedicated to advancing America's land and water legacy. With their partners, they conserve land, train leaders and invest in conservation at home. Since 1985, they have helped protect more than 6 million acres, sustaining wild havens, working lands and vibrant communities. Conservation is treated as a business - fulfilling partners' conservation priorities, leveraging charitable donations for maximum impact and forging solutions that work economically and environmentally.
http://www.conservationfund.org

**The Energy Conversation**
The mission of the Energy Conversation is to create a collaborative, networked community of Energy Smart advocates to inform, educate and communicate with the American people on how to successfully build a sustainable energy future. By educating the government and the public about the energy crisis, The Energy Conversation aims to bring people together to understand the technologies, systems, and consequences associated with our actions. There is no one solution to this colossal problem, The Energy Conversation serves to foster and showcase the unprecedented collaboration between government, industry and non profits.
http://www.energyconversation.org

**The H. John Heinz III Center for Science, Economics, and the Environment**
The Heinz Center is a nonprofit, nonpartisan think tank dedicated to improving the scientific and economic foundation for environmental policy. The Center tackles some of the most important environmental issues of our time by convening business, environmental groups, academia and government. Their guiding philosophy is that we must all work together to find lasting solutions to environmental challenges and leave the earth a better place for future generations.
http://www.heinzctr.org

**The Institute for Energy and Environmental Research**
IEER's aim is to provide people with literature which has a quality equal to that in scientific journals, but which doesn't require you to go back to college to get a degree in science to understand it.
http://www.ieer.org

**The International Council on Clean Transportation**
The goal of the International Council on Clean Transportation is to dramatically improve the environmental performance and efficiency of cars, trucks, buses, and transportation systems in order to protect and improve public health, the environment, and quality of life. The council is made up of regulators and experts from leading markets around the world, which participate as individuals based on their experience with air quality and transportation issues.
http://www.theicct.org

**The Joint Global Change Research Institute**
The Joint Global Change Research Institute (JGCRI) houses an interdisciplinary team dedicated to understanding the problems of global climate change and their potential solutions. Joint Institute staff bring decades of experience and expertise to bear in science, technology, economics, and policy. One of the strengths of the Joint Institute is a network of domestic and international collaborators that encourages the development of global and equitable solutions to the climate change problem.
http://www.globalchange.umd.edu

**The Mountain Institute**

The Mountain Institute's (TMI) mission includes economic development and support for traditional cultures, as well as the conservation of natural resources in the world's longest, oldest and highest mountain ranges - the Andes, Appalachians, and Himalayas. They both implement programs directly with communities and work with and through cooperation with a wide variety of development, government, program, academic, and technical partners. TMI's programs now reach more than a quarter of a million people a year, not including the visitors to those national parks we helped to establish.
http://www.mountain.org

**The Nature Conservancy, Maryland/DC Chapter**

The Nature Conservancy is a conservation organization working to preserve the plants, animals and natural communities that represent the diversity of life on Earth by protecting the lands and waters they need to survive.  They use a strategic, science-based planning process, called Conservation by Design, which helps us identify the highest-priority places - landscapes and seascapes that, if conserved, promise to ensure biodiversity over the long term.  Locally, this includes the Potomac Gorge where more than 200 rare species and natural communities live just outside the nation's capital.
http://www.nature.org/wherewework/northamerica/states/maryland

**The National Complete Streets Coalition**

Complete Streets are designed and operated to enable safe access for all users. Instead of fighting for better streets block by block, the National Complete Streets Coalition seeks to fundamentally transform the look, feel and function of the roads and streets in our community, by changing the way most roads are planned, designed, and constructed. Complete street policies direct transportation planners and engineers to consistently design with all users in mind, in line with the 'Elements of Complete Streets Policies' document available at http://www.completestreets.org/policies.html.
http://www.completestreets.org

**The Ocean Conservancy**

Ocean Conservancy promotes healthy and diverse ocean ecosystems and opposes practices that threaten ocean life and human life. Through research, education, and science-based advocacy, Ocean Conservancy informs, inspires, and empowers people to speak and act on behalf of the oceans.
http://www.oceanconservancy.org

**The Recycled Building Network, Inc. (ReBuild)**

Rebuild is a nonprofit formed in May 2008 to acquire a warehouse that can accept used building material donations, sell the products as deeply discounted prices to the public, and use the proceeds to train unemployed and underemployed unskilled workers for "green collar" jobs. Beyond accepting unwanted building materials, equipment, and supplies, they enable builders and homeowners to claim a tax deduction for donating their unwanted material, and establish appropriate training curricula in green collar occupations.  The proceeds are used to provide or subsidize unskilled workers to obtain appropriate industry licenses, certification, on-the-job training, and experience in green collar positions.
http://www.rebuildwarehouse.org

**The Summit Foundation**

The Summit Foundation seeks to promote the health and well-being of the planet - its people and its natural environment.  They work toward achieving a sustainable global population and protecting the earth's biodiversity. The foundation focuses on empowering young people and protecting the Mesoamerican Reef.  Program areas include the conservation of the Mesoamerican Reef, global population and youth leadership, and sustainable design.
http://www.summitfdn.org

## The Trust for Public Land
The Trust for Public Land (TPL) is a national, nonprofit, land conservation organization that conserves land for people to enjoy as parks, community gardens, historic sites, rural lands, and other natural places, ensuring livable communities for generations to come.
http://www.tpl.org

## The Washington Youth Garden at the National Arboretum
Using the garden cycle as a tool, the mission of the Washington Youth Garden at the U.S. National Arboretum is to inspire children and families to engage in self-discovery, explore relationships with food and the natural world, and contribute to the health and well-being of their communities. The goals of the program are to educate youth on food production and systems and nutrition, connect children to the natural world as a learning resource, and develop interpersonal skills, awareness of civic responsibility, and the opportunity for strong family ties.
http://www.washingtonyouthgarden.org

## Transportation for America Coalition
Transportation for America has formed a broad coalition of housing, environmental, public health, urban planning, transportation, equitable development, and other organizations. They help to align our national, state, and local transportation policies with an array of issues like economic opportunity, climate change, energy security, health, housing and community development.
http://t4america.org

## Trout Unlimited
Trout Unlimited is a national organization with more than 150,000 volunteers organized into about 400 chapters from Maine to Montana to Alaska. This grassroots organization is matched by a respected staff of lawyers, policy experts and scientists, who work out of more than 30 offices nationwide. The organization remains committed to applying "the very best information and thinking available" in its conservation work and has developed cutting-edge tools such as the Conservation Success Index (CSI), a sophisticated framework for assessing the health of coldwater fish species throughout their native range.
http://www.tu.org

## Union of Concerned Scientists
The Union of Concerned Scientists is the leading science-based nonprofit working for a healthy environment and a safer world. UCS combines independent scientific research and citizen action to develop innovative, practical solutions and to secure responsible changes in government policy, corporate practices, and consumer choices.
http://www.ucsusa.org

## United States Climate Action Partnership
USCAP is an expanding alliance of major businesses and leading climate and environmental groups that have come together to call on the federal government to enact legislation requiring significant reductions of greenhouse gas emissions.
http://www.us-cap.org

## Urban Land Initiative
ULI initiates research that anticipates emerging land use trends and issues, proposing creative solutions based on that research. ULI's practice program is interdisciplinary and practical, focusing on trends and the basics of many different parts of the industry. ULI documents best practice and publishes books to impart cumulative knowledge to help the development community continuously improve its performance.
http://www.uli.org

## US Green Building Council (USGBC)

The USGBC national headquarters is located in Washington, D.C. The USGBC developed and manages the Leadership in Energy and Environmental Design (LEED) Rating Systems for green building. They have been responsible for much of the green building movement that has happened within the last decade in the country, and they continue to advocate for green building, provided training and education, and develop new guidelines and initiatives to help shape the green building future of our country.
http://www.usgbc.org

## US Green Building Council – National Capital Region Chapter

U.S. Green Building Council - National Capital Region Chapter, a local affiliate of the USGBC, provides locally-based leadership, advocacy, education and resources to create a vibrant and environmentally healthy Metropolitan Washington region. With individual members from every sector of the building industry, they work collaboratively to advance their vision for a responsible, healthy and prosperous environment that improves quality of life. The National Capital Region includes Washington, D.C. and surrounding regions of Virginia and Maryland.
http://www.usgbcncr.org

## Virginia Bicycling Federation

The Virginia Bicycling Federation was formed in the early 1990s by groups of volunteers - individuals, bike clubs, bike-related businesses, and other organizations - coming together to form a unified voice, to promote bicycling throughout Virginia. They work to change public policy and community attitudes, to improve the safety, convenience, and acceptance of bicycling.
http://www.vabike.org

## Virginia Conservation Network

The Virginia Conservation Network is comprised of more than 100 organizations committed to protecting Virginia's natural resources. They work to serve and strengthen our member organizations and advocate for shared environmental priorities.
http://vcnva.org

## Virginia Native Plant Society

The Virginia Native Plant Society (VNPS) was founded in 1982 as The Virginia Wildflower Preservation Society. It is a statewide organization with approximately 2000 members supported primarily by dues and contributions. Membership is open to anyone, amateur or professional. Its purpose is to further appreciation and conservation of Virginia's native plants and habitats. The Society's work and activities are carried out by volunteers. The Society's programs emphasize public education, protection of endangered species, habitat preservation, and encouragement of appropriate landscape use of native plants.
http://www.vnps.org

## Virginia Sustainable Building Network

Virginia Sustainable Building Network (VSBN) is the only statewide organization that brings together representatives from diverse sectors that are interested in building healthy, energy-efficient, environmentally friendly buildings and sustainable communities. VSBN's mission is to promote environmentally sound - or green building - practices for Virginia. These building designs, methods, and materials save energy costs, reduce waste and promote recycling, reduce environmental impacts and exposure to unhealthy substances, strengthen local economies, and contribute to an enhanced quality of life. VSBN frequently organizes events and conferences to bring together green building enthusiasts.
http://www.vsbn.org

**Wallace Global Fund**
The Wallace Global Fund is guided by the vision of the late Henry A. Wallace, former Secretary of Agriculture and Vice-President under Franklin D. Roosevelt. Committed to serving the general welfare, his life exemplified farsightedness, global vision, and receptivity to new ideas. He was keenly interested in scientific innovation as a force to enhance human well-being and had an abiding faith in the individual's spirit and capacity to bring about sound and just social change.
http://www.wgf.org

**Washington Area Bicyclists Association**
The mission of the Washington Area Bicyclist Association is to create a healthy, more livable region. They work towards this by promoting bicycling for fun, fitness, and affordable transportation; advocating for better bicycling conditions and transportation choices for a healthier environment; and educating children, adults, and motorists about safe bicycling. Their goal is a fully integrated transportation system, one that links transit, trails, bicycling, and walking facilities to connect the places you live, work, and play.
http://www.waba.org

**Washington Parks & People**
Washington Parks & People is a capital-area network of community park partnerships. Parks & People is working to revitalize Washington by reconnecting two of its assets: its vast network of public lands and waterways - comprising one of the highest percentages of park land of any city in the world - and its core of dedicated community leaders and organizations. They seek to build a broad, permanent base of organizations, volunteers, resources, funding, and public support for parks.
http://washingtonparks.net

**Wildlife Alliance**
Wildlife Alliance's mission is to protect and preserve wildlife, forests and oceans for future generations. Their field operations train and equip park rangers to fight crimes against nature, and prevent poaching and illegal habitat destruction in Southeast Asia, Latin America, Russia and the Western Pacific through collaboration with governments and communities. They work to improve the management of protected areas, support sustainable development initiatives, and empower countries to enforce transboundary wildlife regulations.
http://wildlifealliance.org

**Wildlife Rescue League**
The Wildlife Rescue League has licensed rehabilitators, located throughout Virginia and suburban Wildlife Rescue League is a non-profit organization providing care for sick, injured and orphaned Maryland, work with animal shelters, humane societies, wildlife groups, nature centers and veterinary hospitals to provide care to creatures in need. WRL operates a wildlife hotline in the Northern Virginia and surrounding areas to assist the public in obtaining information and assistance in locating a wildlife rehabilitator. WRL is also committed to educating the public about the natural history of native wildlife, coexisting with it and preventing the need for wildlife rehabilitation. We can provide brochures, educational material and educational programs to suit your needs.
http://www.wildliferescueleague.org

**Wholeness for Humanity**
Wholeness for Humanity (WFH) is an organization dedicated to increasing accessibility to holistic health, environmental stewardship, social justice, and peace. WFH members are provided with a personal network of experts who offer a wide range of programs and services that contribute not only to one's own health and wellness, but invariably to the wholeness of humanity.
http://www.wholenessforhumanity.com

**Wise Energy for Virginia**
The Wise Energy for Virginia coalition is committed to securing a clean energy future for Virginia. Their mission is to promote clean and affordable energy that will protect our mountains and southwest Virginia communities from mountaintop removal coal mining, invigorate the economy by creating jobs that cannot be exported, and commit the Commonwealth to science-based reductions in global warming pollution.
http://wiseenergyforvirginia.org

**World Business Council for Sustainable Development**
The mission of the World Business Council for Sustainable Development is to provide business leadership as a catalyst for change toward sustainable development, and to support the business license to operate, innovate and grow in a world increasingly shaped by sustainable development issues. The Council provides a platform for companies to explore sustainable development, share knowledge, experiences and best practices, and to advocate business positions on these issues in a variety of forums, working with governments, non-governmental and intergovernmental organizations.
http://www.wbcsd.org

**World Environment Center**
The World Environment Center (WEC) advances sustainable development through the business practices of member companies and in partnership with governments, multi-lateral organizations, non-governmental organizations, universities and other stakeholders. WEC's mission is to promote business and societal value by advancing solutions to sustainable development-related problems; foster leading edge ideas about economic development, environmental protection and social responsibility through roundtables and other forums that engage the leadership of a diverse number of organizations; and recognize performance excellence by companies that advance sustainable development.
http://www.wec.org

**World Resources Institute**
World Resources Institute is an environmental think tank that goes beyond research to find practical ways to protect the earth and improve people's lives. Their mission is to move human society to live in ways that protect Earth's environment and its capacity to provide for the needs and aspirations of current and future generations. Program areas include people and ecosystems, governance, climate protection, and markets and enterprise.
http://www.wri.org

**World Wildlife Fund**
World Wildlife Fund's mission is the conservation of nature. Using the best available scientific knowledge and advancing that knowledge, they work to preserve the diversity and abundance of life on Earth and the health of ecological systems by protecting natural areas and wild populations of plants and animals, including endangered species. They also promote sustainable approaches to the use of renewable natural resources and energy and the maximum reduction of pollution.
http://www.worldwildlife.org

**WorldWatch Institute**
Worldwatch Institute delivers the insights and ideas that empower decision makers to create an environmentally sustainable society that meets human needs. WorldWatch focuses on the 21st century challenges of climate change, resource degradation, population growth, and poverty by developing and disseminating solid data and innovative strategies for achieving a sustainable society.
http://www.worldwatch.org

# Networking

**American Institute of Architects, D.C. Chapter, Committee on the Environment**
The Washington, D.C. chapter brings together area architects and allied professionals creating a sustainable future. Their mission is to promote the awareness and practice of sustainable design and green building with the participation of design firms, organizations, and individuals who support this endeavor. The organization has many programs and initiatives planned this year, such as the Festival of the Building Arts at the National Building Museum and various presentations on sustainable design.
http://www.aiadc.com/01-5%20COTEdc.asp

**Capitol Greenroofs Forum**
A great networking forum that discusses a variety of issues related to green roofs and green building, as well as landscaping and other sustainability issues is one managed by Capitol Greenroofs. Not only is this a forum, but it also has a calendar of events including tours of green roofs, and allows professionals or individuals interested in these topics to connect with one another and share ideas about green issues.
http://capitolgreenroofs.collectivex.com/main/summary

**DC EcoWomen**
DC EcoWomen works to empower women environmentalists by building a community that fosters networking, collaboration, and career building opportunities. By joining DC EcoWomen, members meet many of the movement's most important female leaders.
http://ecowomen.org

**DC Vegan Drinks**
DC Vegan Drinks is a monthly offline social networking event for people interested in sharing veganism and advocating for animal rights. Their mission is to bring together people from all walks of life (lawyers, students, small business owners, etc...) to build a stronger community and promote the sharing of resources.
http://dcvegandrinks.org

**Eco Justice Café**
Eco Justice Café is an event to hang out with friends and network with D.C. Environmental and Social Justice organizations. Events feature music, poetry, open mike, food, and beer and are held at UDC.
http://www.law.udc.edu/events/event_list.asp

**Ecolocity DC**
Ecolocity DC is a social networking site that brings those with interests in intentional community, permaculture, urban farming, local food, clean energy, biotecture, recycling, localization, and green economy.
http://ecolocity.ning.com

**EcoTuesday**
This is an informal networking group for sustainable business leaders that has several groups located around the country. There is a Washington, D.C. group and they meet every fourth Tuesday of each month. Each meeting involves a speaker and then allows for attendees to meet one another and share ideas about sustainable business ideas.
http://www.ecotuesday.com

**Green Drinks**
There is an international network called Green Drinks that serves as an informal social network for individuals and organizations interested in green issues. Often time's people come to the Green Drinks events in search of green job opportunities. If you are new to the Green Drinks scene, try to identify who the organizer of the group is and let them know your interests. They will be more than willing to help introduce you to others at your first meeting. Green Drinks is a great way of catching up with people you know and for making new contacts. Everyone invites someone else along, so there are always new and different people to meet and talk to. Many Green Drinks groups also invite interesting and well-informed guest speakers. Green Drinks has local chapters in Bethesda, Gaithersburg, Washington, D.C., and Northern Virginia.
http://www.greendrinks.org

**Green Drinkz II**
This networking group is a monthly gathering held by the non profit Green DMV that brings individuals together who are involved in the green industry or are just curious about learning more or meeting others with similar interests. Meetings take place at various venues across the D.C. area and the events are designed to be a laid back atmosphere where it is easy to meet other people.
http://www.greendmv.org/green_drinks.html

**Living Green DC/MD/VA**
Living Green DC/MD/VA works to send a message to the community and influence small changes in everyday actions that can have a big impact on our world. As a group, they look for ways to make small changes in the way we live, enjoying the support and friendship of other like-minded people. This meetup grows if members become Assistant Organizers and provide fun and creative ways to socialize, learn, spread the word, volunteer, network, and do fun things.
http://environment.meetup.com/341

**National Academy of the Sciences - Network for Emerging Leaders in Sustainability**
The National Academy of the Sciences has developed a networking group called the Network for Emerging Leaders in Sustainability (NELS), which meets once a month. These meetings typically involve an opening talk or presentation from a well respected leader in sustainability, and then the rest of the time is spent networking and discussing possible partnerships and projects related to sustainability. The group is intended for early-career professionals and professionals who are new to the topic of sustainability.
http://sustainability.nationalacademies.org/NELS.shtml

**Simplicity Matters Earth Institute and Discussion Groups**
The institute is comprised of 30 committed volunteers, located all over the state of Maryland and Washington, D.C. They believe that real change happens within small groups engaging in deep conversations about things that really matter. They are part of the Northwest Earth Institute Sister Network. Organized discussion circles are based on their discussion guides, in addition to their own programs that foster community such as monthly forums, monthly announcements, and online venues.
http://www.simplicity-matters.org

# Local Green Businesses

We are sure that for many of you, the reason that you picked up a copy of this Guide was to identify specific companies and businesses that are green and sustainable in the D.C. metro area, in the hopes of landing a job with one of them. The following list is comprised of the companies and businesses we feel are at the forefront of the green movement in the local area. This list is specifically for-profit businesses, as we have provided a separate list of non-profit organizations in the Guide as well.

As mentioned previously in this guide, there are not many sustainable and green business certifications out there with which to evaluate a company on its green merits and credentials. So in order to filter out the companies we feel are really ahead of the curve, we used a set of simple green criteria. A company did not need to meet all the green criteria, but did need to meet a majority of them. Much of this is very subjective, so opinions may differ on which companies should appear on this list. The green criteria included issues such as:

- Company's mission or goal
- Services and products offered by the company
- The company's operations
- The company's workplace
- Years of experience in the green industry
- Involvement in the local community
- Employees hold green certifications
- Involvement with green conferences, events, associations, and green education
- Personal experiences of Dan and Anca with the company

## Retail Products and Services

### Aquabarrel Rain Barrels
Aquabarrel creates and sells a full line of high quality rain barrels. They carry a wide range of accessories for rain collection systems, such as rain barrel parts, downspout accessories, and mosquito control components. While rain barrels are their specialty, they also offer other gardening products such as composters.
http://www.aquabarrel.com

### Atayne
Atayne aims to make performance apparel that is sustainable and functional. They endeavor to drive positive change in the industry by operate under a model that reduces energy, water, harmful chemicals, emissions, and waste (industrial and consumer); eliminate the use of virgin, synthetic materials; and support efforts to combat climate change and promote environmental preservation.
http://www.atayne.com/

### Earth Presents
Earth Presents produces 100% recycled and recyclable wrapping paper. Their designs are inspired by the artwork of students with special talents and special needs at WVSA, a unique nonprofit organization. A portion of the proceeds from the sale of products benefit WVSA's School for Arts in Learning. Their matching gift tags, ribbon, and bows are also 100% recycled.
http://www.earthpresents.com/

**Eco-Green Living**
Eco-Green Living is a green, organic, and fair trade store in the Washington, D.C. metro area for lifestyle, home remodeling, and personal care. They offer body care, food, green building supplies, and natural lighting products. They specialize in products made from sustainable and renewable materials like bamboo.
http://www.eco-greenliving.com

**FlexEL**
Based in Silver Spring, FlexEl, LLC has developed high capacity and low voltage rechargeable battery chemistry. The FlexEl battery is flexible and film-based with a printable manufacturing process, making it a cost-effective yet high capacity and long lasting battery option. Its unique characteristics make the FlexEl battery particularly useful for powering ultra small electronics such as implantable medical devices and smart cards.
http://www.flexelinc.com/index.html

**Honest Tea**
Honest Tea creates and promotes delicious, healthy, organic beverages. They strive to grow with the same honesty used to craft their products, with sustainability and great taste for all. Their product line includes a wide variety of bottled tea drinks and tea bags.
http://www.honesttea.com

**Pangea**
Pangea is a vegan retail store located in Chevy Chase, Maryland, which offers a large range of products. They only sell goods made in countries where labor laws or unions are in place to protect the workers. They don't sell any products that come from countries that are known for sweatshop labor. Their line of products includes food, clothes, home and office supplies, pet supplies, and cosmetics.
http://www.veganstore.com

**Patagonia**
Patagonia grew out of a small company that made tools for climbers. Alpinism remains at the heart of a worldwide business that still makes clothes for climbing - as well as for skiing, snowboarding, surfing, fly fishing, paddling and trail running. They are innovators of eco-friendly materials and 1% For the Planet. Their store is in Georgetown.
http://www.patagonia.com

**Purple Mountain Organics**
Purple Mountain Organics is committed to offering quality organic garden and growing supplies. Whether it's a backyard garden, community plot, or market farm they can help you grow organically. Their service is to help and do their part in the movement towards a more sustainable future.
http://www.purplemountainorganics.com

**REI**
REI is the largest consumer cooperative in the U.S., selling quality outdoor gear products while promoting a passion for outdoor adventuring and nature. REI donates generously to conservation efforts across the country, ranging from trail building to local habitat restoration. REI also works to reduce its own environmental impact through sustainable and responsible business practices.
http://www.rei.com/

**TranquiliT**
Made from organic, sustainable, luxurious bamboo fabric, eco-luxe TranquiliT is designed with focus on simplicity and versatility for expressing your signature style. Their product line has everything from yoga clothing to bridal gowns.
http://www.tranquilit.com

## Health Care / Personal Care

**Aveda Institute**
Aveda Institute develops artists in the salon and spa industry. Each is committed to delivering the signature Aveda experience that customers expect. They feature organic and environmentally sound practices, so both customers and the planet can see and feel beautiful and healthy effects.
http://www.avedainstitutedc.com

**Circle Yoga**
Circle Yoga is a community-based yoga studio in the District with a mission to bring stress reduction to as many adults, children, and families as possible, and to do so within the context of environmental excellence. All of their employees are 100% dedicated to their environmental efforts. During the renovation of their facility they incorporated many green building elements, and now have a public access Zen garden. Environmental efforts in their business operations include the use of recycled paper and soy inks, using refurbished computers, using environmentally friendly cleaning products, using biodegradable products, using and selling yoga products made from natural and organic materials, reducing energy usage, and striving for zero waste.
http://www.circleyoga.com

**Flow Yoga**
Their philosophy is that a conscious yoga practice can transform individuals both spiritually and physically. The mission of Flow Yoga Center is to be a true reflection of all that yoga is: vibrant, purposeful, meaningful, authentic, conscious, joyful, spiritual and transforming. In doing so, their aim is to serve our community by sharing yoga, encouraging greater physical health, and fulfilled spirits.
http://www.flowyogacenter.com

**Herban Lifestyle**
Herban lifestyle is a place for high-quality, natural, earth-friendly bath and body products. Handcrafted balms, salves, bath salts, and massage oils are all lovingly made with only the finest natural (organic, when available) ingredients. They contain pure oils, essential oils and herbs, the majority of which are either certified organic, pesticide-free/chemical-free and/or ethically wildcrafted. All Herban Lifestyle products come packaged in recyclable containers and labels are printed with soy ink on 100% recycled paper.
http://herbanlifestyle.com/

**InspireNutrition**
InspireNutrition can help you incorporate more whole foods into your daily routine so you can rely less on packaged, processed and artificial foods. They introduce clients to the importance of locally grown and produced foods by teaching how to find locally grown and produced foods during our grocery store tours. Those who attend cooking classes are educated about the importance of purchasing organic foods as much as possible. They also educate clients about the health and environmental sustainability benefits of eating less meat and supporting wind power.
http://balancingurlife.com/Home_Page.php

**Natural Spa**

With locations in D.C, Maryland, and Virginia, this spa and shoppe offers both health care products as well as natural body services such as massage, facials, and body therapy. Natural Spa uses environmentally friendly products that are derived from natural plants, and are free of preservatives and chemicals. The company has also made a commitment to sustainability through its efforts to green their facilities through recycling, energy conservation, purchasing renewable energy, and water conservation. The D.C. location anticipates achieving LEED Certification.
http://www.naturalbody.com

**Nusta Spa**

Located in downtown Washington, D.C, Nusta Spa offers a full range of customized spa services for women and men. Nusta Spa is the first urban day spa of its kind designed with high performance "green" interiors that are healthier, more efficient, and environmentally responsible. Nusta Spa is the first and only Washington, D.C. spa to achieve the Gold level of certification under any of the USGBC's LEED rating systems. From the treatments they offer to the products they use, from the music selection to the color of the lighting in the treatment rooms, their service philosophy is based on creating a unique spa experience for each guest, customized to his or her individual needs and preferences.
http://www.nustaspa.com

## Restaurants and Cafes

**Bread and Brew**

Bread and Brew features artisan pizzas, organic espresso and coffee, sandwiches, soups, and more made with fresh, natural ingredients from lots of local purveyors. Bread & Brew used environmentally friendly practices through-out. This includes biodegradable to-go containers and catering packaging.
http://breadandbrew.com

**Coppi's Organic Restaurant**

Coppi's Organic opened in 1993, with the intent to bring the freshest food inspired by the Ligurian Riviera in Northern Italy to Washington, D.C. Through the years, they have developed relationships with organic farmers and food cooperatives throughout the region. Their commitment is fulfilled by using sustainably sourced fish, seasonal local organic produce, grass fed/free range meats/poultry, a wood burning oven, wind power electricity, and low wattage light bulbs.
http://www.coppisorganic.com

**Java Green**

Java Green uses only organic ingredients in their food and drinks and strongly believes in supporting small farmers by buying "Fair Trade" products, such as coffee, tea, sugar, bananas, cocoa powder and syrups. Java Green purchases 100% of wind power. They also use real chinaware to reduce the use of disposable containers and offer clients biodegradable serving ware and carry-out bags. Their fusion menu items are vegetarian or vegan.
http://www.javagreencafe.com

**Founding Farmers**

Founding Farmers is the first restaurant in the District of Columbia to receive LEED certification, and the first full-service, upscale-casual restaurant in the entire United States to carry this honor. The restaurant understands the journey of their products from seed to harvest, and from Farm-to-Table. Owned by a collective of American family farmers, Founding Farmers exists to promote the products and services of family farms, ranches, and fisheries.
http://www.wearefoundingfarmers.com

## Hook

Hook Restaurant's eco-friendly practices are a reflection of a deeper ideology: the two things than link every human on the planet are food and environment and we cannot live without either. The menu changes daily to reflect whatever sustainable fish are in season and available. They also use locally grown produce, and humane meat and dairy products.
http://www.hookdc.com

## Occasions Caterers

Occasions Caterers is committed to creating environmentally sustainable events that contribute to a greener future. With Occasions, you can have exceptional, ecologically responsible events without sacrificing style. Implementing new sustainable practices in accordance with this organization has allowed them to become a Certified Green Restaurant Caterer. They work daily with suppliers, vendors, and employees to achieve their sustainability goals in the following practices: certification, local organic sustainable food, recycling composting and eco disposables, and printing.
http://www.occasionscaterers.com/oc2003_www/home.html

## Poste Moderne Brasserie

Poste Moderne Brasserie has been deeply committed to environmental and sustainable practices for several years. They have their own chef-led eco program which has helped them to implement standards which reduce waste, source organic ingredients, buy locally as often as possible, offer a wide selection of biodynamic and organic wines, and maintain a highly-functioning organic herb and vegetable garden. They have converted portions of their outdoor patio space into a sustainable and organic vegetable and herb garden. Other efforts include the use of 100% recyclable paper and soy inks for menus and other printing needs, energy-saving bulbs in all lighting, a recycling program, composting of all food scraps and converting cooking oil into diesel fuel, using only environmentally friendly cleaning products, and the use of bio-degradable corn-based straws, utensils, and packaging.
http://www.postebrasserie.com

## Restaurant Nora

In 1999, Restaurant Nora became America's first certified organic restaurant. This means that 95% or more of everything that you eat at the restaurant has been produced by certified organic growers and farmers all who share in Nora's commitment to sustainable agriculture. Nora always offers seasonal, fresh organic food, prepared in a healthy, balanced way. Grass-fed beef, free-range chickens, creamy hand-made goat cheeses, juicy heirloom tomatoes, fresh picked wild mushrooms, and local applewood smoked trout are some of the ingredients they prepare daily when in season.
http://www.noras.com

## Sonoma Restaurant and Wine Bar

Sonoma's mission is to highlight the Mid-Atlantic's best naturally-raised and local ingredients and pair the creations with the best American and Italian wines. They strive to integrate sustainable practices in all their restaurants: from sourcing local ingredients, to their use of renewable energy sources.
http://www.sonomadc.com

## Sweetgreen

Sweetgreen offers customers delicious, all-natural, salads, and refreshing frozen yogurts. With award winning décor and operational simplicity, Sweetgreen creates a chic atmosphere and a unique dining experience. They try to implement eco-friendly methods into every aspect of the restaurant from the design to the operation as indicated by being a Green Certified Restaurant by the Green Restaurant Association and purchasing 100% wind energy offsets.
http://www.sweetgreen.com/

### The Big Bear Cafe

The Big Bear Cafe is a small cafe located at 1st St NW and R St NW that is thoroughly committed to business practices that promote sustainability. From the food and drinks they serve, to the way they operate their facility; they have made great efforts to be as sustainable as they can. The cafe sources locally and sustainably grown produce whenever possible, sources coffee from companies with sustainable and fair trade practices, and provides educational and training opportunities for customers and the community about sustainable agriculture practices. At their cafe they have started recycling and composting, use products that are biodegradable and reusable, implemented energy savings strategies, and improved the storm water management on their site in a sustainable manner.
http://www.bigbearcafe-dc.com

### Vegetate

Vegetate is located in the Historic Shaw neighborhood in northwest Washington, D.C. They believe in using the best possible ingredients from local and regional farms, purveyors and businesses. They also work with small, family and independently-owned businesses, which ensure that they know the origin of their food and drink. They have a seasonal menu and full bar featuring seasonal cocktails, micro brewed beers and a boutique wine list.
www.vegetatedc.com

## Hospitality and Lodging

### Gaylord National

As the newest member of the Gaylord Hotels family, Gaylord National was built with energy and conservation in mind, incorporating lessons learned from sister properties. This luxurious Washington, D.C.-area resort was built with water-conserving fixtures, "comfort management," and room-occupancy sensors in every one of its 2,000 guest rooms, ensuring water and energy conservation occurs across all rooms. Energy-saving initiatives also are implemented throughout the resorts numerous restaurants, on-site spa, and large back-of-house area. The waste management and recycling that happens back-of-the-house at Gaylord National translates into literally tons of paper, cardboard, plastic and other items being averted from landfills. Additionally, the outdoor irrigation systems utilize rain sensors.
http://www.gaylordhotels.com/gaylord-national/green-lodging.html?intcmp=gn-snav-green

### Guest Services

Guest Services is a hospitality management company that has been located in the Washington, D.C. area for almost 100 years and has built a great reputation for providing its clients with great services. Guest Services has been committed to environmental practices and has developed its own environmental management program called "Our Planet". A major part of this program means that all facilities must be built and operated in compliance with these environmental management guidelines. Some of their major initiatives include recycling programs, the use of green cleaning products, using renewable energy, and composting.
http://www.guestservices.com

### Hostelling International – Washington, D.C.

Located near the city's most famous attractions, Hostelling International-Washington, D.C. (HI-DC) offers a friendly and inexpensive lodging experience for travelers. They provide both private rooms and dormitory style accommodations. Most of our private rooms have shared bathrooms. They are Energy Star Certified and the only hostel in the D.C. area to be designated an Eco-Friendly hostel by Hostel World. They have a variety of environmentally friendly practices, and are currently renovating all

guestrooms using low VOC paint and carpet that is low VOC, made from recycled materials, and is itself 100% recyclable.
http://www.hiwashingtondc.org

**Kimpton Hotels (Topaz, George, Madera, Helix, Monaco, Palomar, Rouge)**
Kimpton's mission is to be a leader in the hospitality industry in supporting a sustainable world, while continuing to deliver a premium guest experience with non-intrusive, high quality, eco-friendly products and services. Kimpton owns and operates a variety of hotels in the Washington, D.C. metro area including Topaz Hotel, Hotel George, Hotel Madera, Hotel Helix, Hotel Monaco, Hotel Palomar, and Hotel Rouge. Through the pioneering Kimpton Hotels' EarthCare program, their green hotels deliver a refreshing, healthy hotel atmosphere while promoting a sustainable planet.
http://www.kimptonhotels.com

**Phoenix Park Hotel**
Already a hallmark for genuine Irish hospitality, this luxurious Washington, D.C. green hotel extends this commitment not only to their guests, but also to maintaining precious resources by being caring stewards of the environment. Crestline Hotels & Resorts, Phoenix Park's management company, recently introduced EarthPact, an extensive sustainability initiative that includes an Energy Management Plan that sets comprehensive guidelines for sustainable business practices. Phoenix Park hotel has adopted new programs and procedures to reduce their impact on the environment, from utilizing energy-efficient light bulbs, equipment and appliances to recycling and using recycled materials whenever possible.
http://www.phoenixparkhotel.com/specialty/going_green.html

**Residence Inn Washington, D.C./Capitol**
This hotel features a smoke-free policy, full "home touch" buffet breakfast served daily and evening dinner socials. Their location is within walking distance to the Smithsonian Museums, National Monuments, and US Capitol building. Through green initiatives, the hotel purchases 50% of its electricity from renewable wind power.
http://www.marriott.com/hotels/travel/wascp-residence-inn-washington-dc-capitol

**The Beacon Hotel & Corporate Quarters and The St. Gregory Luxury Hotel**
Capital Hotels & Suites takes protecting the environment as a priority. They have developed a comprehensive policy to promote business practices that help preserve the environment. Their goals are to "Reduce - Reuse - Recycle" as much as possible. Both The Beacon Hotel & Corporate Quarters and The St. Gregory Luxury Hotel take part in the "Green Program - Conserve to Preserve." By asking guests when they would like their sheets and towels changed, they hope to contribute to saving thousands of fresh water a month while also reducing waste water and the use of chemicals and energy resources.
http://www.capitalhotelswdc.com/environment.friendly.green.program.policy.htm

**The Fairmont Washington, D.C.**
Located in Washington's fashionable West End and adjacent to historic Georgetown, The Fairmont Washington, D.C. hotel welcomes guests in capital style. Known for its engaging service and stylish surroundings, the Washington, D.C. hotel offers 415 spacious guest rooms and suites that provide guests with a welcome retreat. A relaxing visit to the hotel's fitness center, indoor pool and serene courtyard garden also provide guests with an array of rejuvenating experiences. Fairmont Hotels have signed on to the WWF's Climate Savers Program that includes a pledge to reduce $CO_2$ emissions from its facilities, and Fairmont also has green initiatives to implement a green procurement policy, update facilities to LEED standards, and providing education around green issues to suppliers, employees, and customers.
http://www.fairmont.com/Washington

## Finance / Economics / Banking

### Calvert Group
More than 400,000 investors have approximately $12.5 billion in assets with Calvert. They offer one of the largest families of responsible mutual funds whose holdings are screened across seven key areas: Governance and Ethics, Workplace, Environment, Product Safety and Impact, International Operations and Human Rights, Indigenous Peoples' Rights, and Community Relations.
http://www.calvert.com

### New Energy Finance
New Energy Finance is a leading provider of industry information and analysis to investors, corporations and governments in clean energy, low carbon technologies and the carbon markets. Their global network of 125 analysts, based across 10 offices in Europe, the Americas, Asia, and Africa, are continuously monitoring market changes, deal flow, and financial activity allowing instantaneous transparency into the clean energy and carbon markets. Through New Carbon Finance they provide market-leading analysis and research for the global carbon markets. This includes analysis, price forecasting, consultancy, and risk management.
http://www.newenergyfinance.com

### Reznick Group
Reznick Group is a national leader in accounting, tax and business advisory services. Ranked among the top 20 public accounting firms in the United States, Reznick Group maintains 10 offices nationwide, with its headquarters located in Bethesda, Md. Industry groups served include renewable energy.
http://www.reznickgroup.com/index.php

## Green Building

### Abrams Design Build
Abrams Design Build has been involved with green building for many, many years, and have set themselves apart as one of the most knowledgeable contractors in the D.C. area when it comes to green building and sustainable design. They offer both design and construction services and focus mainly on residential projects. They have received many awards over the years for their projects.
http://www.abramsdesignbuild.com

### Amicus Green Building Center
The Amicus Green Building Center is a source of genuine green products, resources, and expert support to help you create a healthy, environmentally friendly, stylish, energy smart and sustainable building. They have in-house architects, integrated project design consulting, energy analysis, research reports, coaching and engagement, and sustainable building advisory services for developers and project funders.
http://www.amicusgreen.com

### Ardently Green
Ardently Green is committed to providing homeowners in the Washington, D.C. metro area with the solution to reduce energy costs and improve air quality and comfort. They offer a systematic, research-based process and practical solutions for reducing residential energy use and improving environmental health within the home and greater community. The process begins with a whole-house energy audit. The resulting recommendations will result in noticeable decreases in homeowners' energy costs and immediate improvements in personal comfort including breathing healthier air in the home.
http://ArdentlyGreen.com

**Clark Construction**

Founded in 1906, Clark Construction Group is today one of the nation's most experienced and respected providers of construction services, with over $4 billion in annual revenue and major projects throughout the United States. Their LEED Accredited Professionals collaborate with owners, designers, subcontractors, and manufacturers to ensure maximum economic and environmental rewards. Clark has a long history of working with owners and architects to implement green and sustainable elements into all manner of construction projects. They have built some of the most notable green and LEED certified structures in the country, including the first project to ever achieve LEED Platinum certification.
http://www.clarkconstruction.com

**DPR Construction Inc.**

To assist customers with developing and implementing the best strategy to meet environmental and business goals, DPR combines experienced people, a collaborative methodology and custom tools to achieve sustainable success. DPR offers a wide variety of high-performance green building services tailored to fit the specific needs of clients. Whether you would like a training seminar on green practices and LEED certification or you want DPR's "Green Team" to facilitate a charrette to enhance the performance of your next project, they are prepared to deliver the most innovative services to move your business forward.
http://www.dprinc.com

**Ecoipso**

Ecoipso is based in the North Capital Region and provides green building and sustainable design consulting for businesses, government, pre-K-12 schools and educational institutions. They provide sustainable design and LEED consulting, public speaking on green building topics, green school and daycare makeovers, sustainable design reviews, and high performance design guidelines. They also provide green building and LEED training, development of green building standards and tools, consulting on green building legislation, and green coaching and go green workshops.
http://www.ecoipso.com

**EMSI**

EMSI is an international leader in green building consulting. They work in the US, as well as many other countries around the world, with many projects in China. Their mission is to foster a sustainable built environment by helping our clients create buildings and community developments that provide attractive returns-on-investment, reduce carbon emissions and other environmental impacts, create comfortable and healthy places to live and work, and increase employee job satisfaction and productivity. Their clients have included Fortune 500 companies and their services include LEED consulting, Energy Modeling and Energy Auditing, and helping schools identify capital funding for green improvements and construction.
http://www.emsi-green.com

**Everyday Green**

Everyday Green is a newer company, but that doesn't mean that haven't already accomplished a lot in the green building industry. They specialize in helping clients with LEED for Homes certification, as well as Energy Star support, strategic planning, and green product recommendations. Everyday Green helped to certify the first LEED for Homes project in Washington, D.C. on a home in Mt. Pleasant that achieved Platinum certification.
http://www.everydaygreendc.com

**Forrester Construction**

They provide general contracting, pre-construction, construction management, design-build, and sustainable construction services. Sustainable Construction is an ongoing key Forrester strategic initiative and has been integrated into the corporate values of the company. Forrester's current LEED initiative

includes a fully dedicated Director of Sustainable Programs, who is a LEED Accredited Professional. In addition, all Forrester Operations Team Members are required to complete the LEED™ certification program. Team Members also receive professional training in environmental compliance through Forrester's own internal curriculum and through programs sponsored by agencies such as the Maryland Department of the Environment's Water Management Administration.
http://www.forresterconstruction.com

## GreenShape
GreenShape guides remarkable, economical and sustainable building through offering a variety of green building consulting services. They help building developers, architects, engineers and construction teams identify and implement achievable strategies for improved building performance. GreenShape has developed quite the reputation for being one of the firms people go to when they have green building questions.
http://www.greenshape.com

## GreenSpur
GreenSpur is a green design build firm in the Washington, D.C. metro area. Its mission is carbon neutrality through energy efficiency. GreenSpur takes the time to plan the most sustainable way to build each project based on the clients' needs, the building site, and its past experiences on other projects. They are always striving to push the green envelope and they also do a great job of providing green building educational materials to their clients and the general public.
http://www.greenspur.net

## Group Goetz Architects
The approach of GGA Architecture and GGA Interiors is to use design as a tool to improve our quality of life, balancing human needs with the business goals and objectives of their clients. Since their founding in 1978, GGA has been dedicated to enhancing the built environment through its design excellence approach using innovation, building system integration, sustainability, and economic sensitivity in its approach to architecture and interior design.
http://www.gga.com

## Healthy Buildings International
Healthy Buildings International strives to create buildings that people want to spend time in and that have healthy indoor environments. They provide services such as indoor air quality, green building, and environmental consulting to the commercial real estate industry. Their expertise in indoor air quality testing, design, and guidelines has set them apart from other firms.
http://www.healthybuildings.com/

## Helicon Works
Helicon Works is a virtual collaborative, practicing architecture with a holistic complement of team members: architects, landscape architect, renewable energy and energy-efficiency consultants, green specifications consultants, lighting designer specializing in low-energy solutions, feng shui consultants, and a structural engineer. Each project is a unique exploration, seeking (with the team's broad expertise) the most effective ecologically conscious response to the client and place.
http://www.heliconworks.com

## HITT Contracting
To provide their clients with the resources needed for these unique construction projects, HITT has developed the in-house expertise to assist project teams with proper interpretation and implementation of LEED requirements. The Director of Sustainable Construction is responsible for developing solutions

that meet the challenges of sustainability on the jobsite while adding value to their clients. This is accomplished by seamlessly incorporation sustainability into the construction process without compromising project profitability. Key projects include the first building within the District of Columbia to receive LEED Certification and the first LEED Platinum K-12 school in the world.
http://www.hitt-gc.com

## HOK

HOK is a global provider of planning, design and delivery solutions for the built environment. They employ more than 2,000 professionals linked across a global network of 24 offices on four continents. Industry surveys consistently rank HOK among the leading firms in numerous building types, specialties and regions, and they have earned many awards and honors for their projects, people and practice. HOK is committed to building a better world and leading clients toward a sustainable future. In addition to writing a book on sustainable design, they are advancing green innovations for every building type, region and budget. Given the urgency of global climate change, HOK understands the importance of creating a carbon neutral design future.
http://www.hok.com

## Indigo Engineering Group

Indigo Engineering Group is a full service engineering, architecture and construction management firm specializing in green and sustainable designs. They offer clients a variety of services including: green-focused mechanical, electrical, and plumbing engineering, architecture, structural engineering, geotechnical engineering; environmental engineering; construction services, and land development support. They have provided energy modeling, energy audits, LEED consulting, Green Communities consulting, and Sustainability Action Plans for clients.
http://www.indigoengineering.com

## KTA Group

KTA Group was founded in 1989 as an engineering design and consulting firm with an emphasis on healthcare design. They expanded their client base with the design of telecommunications space, mission critical space, commercial interiors, government and schools. The firm, with over 100 associates strives to provide the highest level of responsiveness and quality engineering design services to clients. KTA is current with the latest developments in the industry to provide quality, healthy buildings, which are environmentally and fiscally responsible. KTA is a member of the U.S. Green Building Council and has several LEED accredited professionals on staff.
http://www.ktagroup.com

## LAND Engineering

LAND Engineering provides solutions to a wide range of civil engineering and land development projects. Their regional knowledge and experience ensures the most appropriate design solution for the communities being served. Key relationships with jurisdictional officials help to ensure the most expedient permitting process. Services include site design and construction documents, LEED project administration, lot grading, storm water management design, erosion and sediment control, floodplain analysis, roadway design, water and sewer system design, design-build, and site/civil construction specification.
http://www.landengineeringplc.com

## Landis Construction

Landis Construction has been in business for 17 years specializing in residential remodeling, design & build projects. They are remodel contractors that focus on Washington, D.C. and the surrounding metro area including suburban Maryland and Virginia. They keep current on the trends in DC design and the complex zoning regulations for DC, Maryland, and Virginia construction. They encourage all their

clients to explore different options, such as contemporary space planning and remodeling green, which includes energy efficient construction, sustainable construction materials, and methods and healthy building materials, finishes, and systems to promote indoor air quality and environmentally sensitive construction.
http://www.landisconstruction.com

## LEEDAdvisors

LEEDAdvisors is a sustainability consulting firm located in the Washington, D.C. metro area. They work with building owners, tenants, and managers to reduce carbon emissions by implementing LEED Sustainable Business Practices. The LEEDAdvisors team is well versed in all LEED rating systems and can provide the preliminary analysis, sustainability planning, and documentation guidance necessary to support and expedite the work of the facility team.
http://www.leedadvisors.com

## Marion Construction

While implementing more conventional construction projects gave the company its start, Marion is dedicated to the development of a flourishing green building movement throughout the Washington, D.C. Metropolitan Area and the entire state of Virginia. To this end, the two main principals in the firm have been actively involved for more than 10 years with the US Green Building Council and the Virginia Sustainable Building network. They are uniformly recognized as leaders in the field of Green Building through direct job responsibilities as well as volunteer efforts as employees and active members of various Boards of Directors. Marion Construction seeks to actively integrate sustainable green practices into all that it does.
http://www.marionconstructioninc.com

## Peabody Architects

Peabody Architects' projects include new houses, alterations, and additions in the metropolitan Washington, D.C. region, with an increasing amount of work in other states. They are committed to practicing sustainable design by making homes with a smaller carbon footprint. These homes consume a fraction of the energy used by "standard" homes, and are filled with non-toxic, recycled materials and are durable. They work with a team of engineers, interior designers, materials suppliers, energy consultants, and green builders towards this common goal.
http://www.greenhaus.org

## Quinn Evans

Quinn Evans is a full service architectural firm founded in 1984 in Ann Arbor, Michigan and Washington, D.C. The firm is committed to the adaptive use of historic structures and the traditional design of new buildings, through projects that revitalize neighborhoods and commercial centers, and through preservation of cultural landscapes and important community icons. Preservation and sustainable design have a shared vision: conserving natural and cultural resources for future generations. Sustainable design is integrated throughout the design methodology from beginning to end. At every step, there are opportunities for sustainable design – not only in the recycling of buildings, but also by incorporating innovative systems, materials, and design principles that promote the conservation of precious resources.
http://www.quinnevans.com

## Sebesta Blomberg

Sebesta Blomberg provides engineering, construction support, commissioning, facility support, energy management, and environmental services to private and public sector markets. Sebesta Blomberg provides sustainable technical and business solutions that improve operational efficiency, enhance the quality of the work environment, and reduce the cost of facility operation. They provide an array of services including engineering design, construction support, commissioning, facility support, energy

management, environmental services, sustainability services, and central plant and renewable energy services aimed at enhancing facility performance.
http://www.sebesta.com

**Sergio Martinez Architect**
Sergio Martinez's mission is to create beautiful authentic works of integrity and substance, from environmentally responsible materials, that allows human beings to be green and poetically dwell. Sergio works with the utmost care and reverie for the materials selected: wood, metal, glass, and concrete. The wood used for his work is recycled, reclaimed, scrap or FSC certified. Being green, Sergio uses environmentally friendly products and materials that promote sustainability while maintaining biodiversity and healthy ecosystems for the long term preservation of the forests.
http://www.sergiomartinezarchitect.com/index.html

**Steven Winter Associates**
Steven Winter Associates, Inc. is a 36-year-old architectural/engineering research and consulting firm, with specialized expertise in green technologies and procedures that improve the safety, performance, and cost effectiveness of buildings. SWA's staff that encompasses over 65 architects, engineers, and building scientists works to make buildings safer, more energy efficient, durable, affordable, accessible, and overall, more sustainable. They take a "whole building" approach to incorporating energy and resource efficiency measures into residential, commercial, educational, institutional and community building projects. The range of services they offer reflects this approach - whether its accessibility issues, challenges specific to multifamily buildings, or building homes that use zero net energy.
http://www.swinter.com

**Sustainability By Design**
Sustainability By Design was founded to assist the real estate community, architects, and engineers in obtaining LEED Certification, Energy Star Benchmarking, guidance in alternative energy, and investigation of all federal, state, and local tax and other incentives. By combining the many facets that affect the design, development and financing of large commercial projects, Sustainability By Design is able to provide comprehensive assistance to guide owners, architects, engineers, and contractors through the required processes.
http://www.sustainabilitybydesign.com

**Sustainable Design Consulting**
Drawing from their advanced experience in the field of sustainable design, they help developers, architects, and builders create more environmentally-sensitive structure and settings. They provide assessments, consultations, reviews, and a range of LEED services.
http://www.sustaindesign.net

**Sustainable Design Group**
Their mission since 1973 has been to design and build buildings that were in complete harmony and balance with nature and self sufficient in energy, water, waste and food production. They make use of technology to harness the solar, wind and biological cycles to provide a complete life support system for people through integrated design that mimics nature. By working with the forces of nature and the resources of the place, they provide all the basic life support functions of the home including: healthy shelter, clean water, waste processing, hot water, cooking, heating, cooling and electricity.
http://www.sustainabledesign.com

**Turner Construction Company**
Turner is committed to the success and increased adoption of sustainable construction practices throughout the industry. As part of this effort, they train all new hires in the theory and practice of green

building, emphasizing the LEED rating system. Turner has extensive experience across a wide variety of sustainable construction projects, enabling them to create a detailed databank of cost-effective green materials, processes, and suppliers to assist their clients. They have completed 80 LEED Certified projects and completed or are currently working on more than 120 additional projects that are registered with the U. S. Green Building Council.
http://www.turnerconstruction.com

### Wiencek & Associates
Wiencek & Associates Architects and Planners is an AIA-award winning architectural design firm that designs socially responsible, sustainable solutions to create, improve, or revitalize the D.C. Metro Community. For more than 20 years we have served great clients by master planning and designing important projects that have helped transform the local areas. Success has helped them grow into the 30+ professional firm they are today.
http://www.wiencek-associates.com

## Energy and Climate Issues

### Access Green
A leading provider of energy efficiency and conservation solutions - from residential to commercial, and from the private sector to work with governments. Access Green is also firmly committed to lifting up underserved communities through workforce development programs. Access Green has worked with the Green Pathway DC program to help train several hundred DC residents in green building, weatherization, and smart meter installations.
http://www.accessgreenonline.com/index.html

### Alternative Energy Matters
Alternative Energy Matters specializes in solar energy and sustainable roofing solutions. They can provide assistance throughout the entire process of financing, designing, and implementing solar thermal and photo-voltaic systems. They also can provide LEED certification support services and advice on current solar tax credits and incentives.
http://www.alternativeenergymatters.com

### Clean Currents
Clean Currents is a clean energy broker/aggregator licensed by the Maryland Public Service Commission and the District of Columbia Public Service Commission, operating in Maryland, D.C., Chicago, Texas, and other areas where there is a competitive electricity market. They believe that businesses have a responsibility to protect and hopefully improve our natural environment while conducting their operations. As an environmentally responsible business, their commitment to sustainability runs through all facets of their business operations.
http://www.cleancurrents.com

### Continuum Energy Solutions
For over 19 years, the goal of Continuum Energy Solutions is to benefit the world through the installation of residential solar energy systems, reducing carbon emissions using free energy from the sun. At CES, they focus more on the environmental benefits and impacts of their actions and not just earnings and growth. Education about the benefits of installing a system and energy audits complement their energy reduction goals. CES combines the latest in technology to show customers how viable and cost efficient their systems are, like solar monitoring which can show on the internet live results of energy production and carbon reduction from your system. Site survey requests include a full site assessment and picture from Google Earth to assist in system design.
http://www.ces-va.com

**Earth Sun Energy Systems**

Earth Sun Energy Systems seeks to build bridges to a sustainable future by assisting in the transition to sustainable housing and buildings. Towards this end, they do energy audits, install solar systems (PV and solar thermal), and consult with architects, builders, and homeowners on energy issues. They are a licensed contractor in D.C., MD, and WV, and are NABCEP and HERS certified.
http://www.earthsunenergy.com

**Ecobeco**

A one-stop shop for eco-friendly solutions for your home. The mission of the company is to help save energy, money, and the environment. Ecobeco specializes in residential energy audits for single family as well as multi-family buildings. They also sell products that can improve your home energy efficiency on their website. Ecobeco has an experienced staff that will help any homeowner make informed decisions about the best energy efficiency improvements to make to their home.
http://www.ecobeco.com

**Elysian Energy**

Elysian Energy focuses on assessing energy consumption and recommending cost-effective improvements. Their mission is determining which improvements will lower your bills and increase comfort. They are known for their personal attention and willingness to discuss energy efficiency, renewable energy technologies as well as carbon impact mitigation. Elysian Energy has been providing Energy Audits to residential customers and helping them save energy as well as money. For each Energy Audit they supply a detailed Energy Report Card that shows the current energy use, and provides recommendations on how to make improvements.
http://www.elysianenergy.com

**EMO Energy Solutions**

EMO Energy Solutions is a leading expert in energy solutions for residential and commercial buildings. They offer many different services that help their clients identify ways to reduce energy usage, reduce consumption of natural resources, and provide the best life cycle performance of buildings. Among the services they offer are Energy Audits and Energy Modeling. EMO has presented at many green building conferences around the country.
http://www.emoenergy.com

**Energy Efficiency Experts**

Energy Efficiency Experts is an energy audit firm that specializes in saving clients money on utility bills while helping to protect our environment. With a passion for the environment and your financial well-being, Energy Efficiency Experts helps you reduce your carbon footprint as well as save about $2,000 a year. Through a thorough evaluation, experts identify cost effective solutions to your energy problems. They also install measures such as weather-stripping on all doors as well as sealants to your attic and basement, at no extra charge. Energy audits can be performed for residences and small businesses.
http://www.energyefficiencyexperts.com/

**Electric Advisors**

Electric Advisors (EA) is an energy consulting firm that provides customized energy solutions to commercial businesses. EA enables businesses to purchase retail electricity in the emerging deregulated electricity market place at a lower rate than currently offered through your local utility's 'Standard Offer Plan'. EA understands that each business has unique energy consumption patterns and has the experience

and relationships to match your energy needs with the appropriate supplier. EA specializes in clients with single and multiple locations throughout the Mid - Atlantic States.
http://www.electricadvisors.com

## First Climate
First Climate is a carbon sales and trading company that helps its clients offset its emissions or identify opportunities to invest in the carbon market. First Climate was formed in 2008 when 3C - The Carbon Credit Company and Factor Consulting + Management AG merged. Among the services that First Climate offers are Carbon Asset Development, Carbon Investment Advisory, Sales and Trading, Project Finance, and Climate Neutral services.
http://www.firstclimate.com

## Geothermal Options
Geothermal Options serves as a consultant on geothermal system selection and design, as well as other energy efficiency technologies. They have the knowledge and expertise to help you choose the right geothermal system for your home or business as part of an integrated approach to energy and cost savings. Geothermal Options is also the exclusive distributor of EarthLinked(TM) Direct Exchange (DX) geothermal heat pump systems in Washington, D.C., Maryland, and Northern Virginia.
http://www.geothermaloptions.com/GTO/Welcome.html

## Go Green 360°
Go Green 360° is an online information bank for reducing your personal environmental impact. The website provides lists of links to green products, green cities, youth organizations, pro-environment politicians, and green money-saving tips.
http://www.gogreen360.com/default.aspx

## Got Green Energy
Got Green Energy's team will help you calculate and manage your carbon footprint, implement cost promoting energy efficiencies, and optimize your return on investment with carbon offsets.  Their experience includes a global reach, working with both national and international corporations, calculating and managing companywide carbon footprint inventories. Their verification and validation projects also span the globe.  They have experience working with a number of clients on top tier carbon offset projects.
http://www.gotgreenenergy.com

## GreeNEWit
GreeNEWit is dedicated to providing customers with energy-efficient and low cost energy solutions for residential, commercial, and government operations in Baltimore and Washington, D.C. GreeNEWit uses the most up-to-date technology to identify inefficiencies in building infrastructure and offers sustainable and economical methods for improvement.
http://www.greenewit.com/

## Green Power Living
Green Power Living is an energy efficiency and renewable energy consulting firm. They offer a range of services including home energy audits, HERS ratings, ENERGY STAR New Homes certification, LEED for Homes consulting, and solar site assessments. Green Power Living also offers various green products that can help you make your home greener and save energy, water, and other resources.
http://www.greenpowerliving.com

**Reluminati**
Reluminati is a company that helps their clients by providing services to help them get tied in with the renewable energy industry. They are mainly a marketing and communications firm, but they also can help with project development as well as project financing. Reluminati staff includes experts in engineering, solar power, wind energy, fuel cells, batteries, telecommunications, law, policy, utility and energy regulation, marketing, communications, sales, distribution and other disciplines. In a diverse set of circumstances Reluminati brings the tailored skill-set needed to provide better, cleaner, energy solutions.
http://www.reluminati.com

**SOLgenics**
SOLgenics supports and promotes construction using renewable materials and innovative construction methods. They construct residential, commercial and industrial buildings. They design and build net-zero energy buildings that have solar power at the center of design. The flagship product is the C.L.E.A.N.™ Home, America's first production, Net-Zero Energy CarbonLessEnergy® Home that establishes the highest standards for new home construction by integrating ultra-efficient designs, on-site power generation and superior building practices. Some of the specific services that SOLgenics offers are solar thermal and solar phototvoltaic systems, energy audits, and supplying a variety of green construction materials including insulation, lighting, and solar energy systems.
http://www.solgenics.com

**Standard Solar**
Standard Solar is a full service, turnkey solar system developer and integrator. Their mission is to provide solar solutions to residential, commercial and government customers by safely delivering the most efficiently engineered and designed solar PV systems that are constructed of the highest quality, most cost effective materials, on schedule and within budget for every project they install. Their team of dedicated professionals, installers, electricians and managers offer simple and dependable solar energy solutions to both homeowners and businesses.
http://www.standardsolar.com

**SunEdison**
SunEdison provides solar energy services that deliver renewable electricity to complement your existing electricity. They offer comprehensive services for commercial, government and utility customers. Their mission is to make solar services a viable and rewarding alternative to traditional energy sources. SunEdison owns and operates more solar power plants and deliver more megawatt hours than any other solar energy services provider in North America, as well as have now expanded their services to other countries such as Spain and Canada.
http://www.sunedison.com

**Sustainable Building Partners**
SBP offers building professionals and end-users precise energy efficiency and sustainable solutions for new and existing assets. SBP will draw from extensive project experience to provide cost effective and timely investment grade solutions tailored to meet the needs of each individual project and client. SBP ultimate goal is to provide full circle solutions addressing maintenance, reliability, durability, life cycle, and sustained energy performance while enhancing comfort and experience. Services include energy modeling, energy auditing, and commissioning.
http://www.sustainbldgs.com/

**TerraLogos**
TerraLogos is one of the longest standing home energy audit providers in Maryland. Their team of energy experts will provide residential customers with specifics on how they can make their homes more energy

efficient. They have performed hundreds of full scale energy audits in Maryland to date, and their staff holds many certifications such as HERS and LEED AP. TerraLogos also offers other services with a sustainability and green building focus including consulting and design services. They have also made a company commitment to green practices, which is illustrated by initiatives such as being powered by wind energy purchased through green tags. They often give presentations on energy related issues for homes. http://www.terralogosghs.com

## The Stella Group
The Stella Group is a strategic marketing and policy firm facilitating distributed energy generation which leverages key partners, financing and unique customer relationships for applications utilizing advanced batteries, concentrated solar energy, fuel cells, microgenerators, modular biomass, photovoltaics, small wind and "smart" interconnection. Their website offers articles, broadcasts, databases of renewable energy installation projects, and other resources for learning more about sustainable energy sources. http://www.thestellagroupltd.com

## ThinkBox Group
ThinkBox Group is a proven team that develops, finances and operates sustainable energy and water projects. They partner with end-users that need to make significant capital investments in energy and water infrastructure, but lack the in-house capabilities to evaluate complex projects and / or the necessary financial resources execute them. ThinkBox is also a recognized leader in sustainable energy, water, and economic development research. Their specialties include Water and Wastewater, Bio-energy (Transportation Biofuels, Biochemicals, and Renewable Power), and Energy Efficient Infrastructure. http://www.thinkboxgroup.com

## Think Energy
Think Energy is a full-service renewable energy company that works both in the United States and internationally to accelerate the transition to clean energy markets and economies. The team at Think Energy helps users and generators of clean energy and those that would like to join the clean energy marketplace. They provide expertise in mechanical, chemical and civil engineering; architecture; economic and financial analysis; project management for renewable energy installations and purchases; comprehensive corporate and organizational strategy; and policy assessment. http://www.thinkenergy.net

## Verdeo Group
Verdeo Group works with businesses to identify, develop and monetize emission reduction opportunities. Their customers include leading industrial companies and investor groups that believe adopting a proactive plan to understand and manage their emissions will lead to improved financial performance, energy savings, and competitive advantage. http://www.verdeogroup.com

## World Energy Solutions
World Energy Solutions operates leading online exchanges for energy and environmental commodities. They have to online exchange platforms that are the World Energy Exchange, which transacts electricity, natural gas, fuels, and green power, and the World Green Exchange, which transacts renewable energy certificates and greenhouse gas emissions credits. The only publicly traded company in the sector, and by far the leader in processed transaction volume, World Energy is becoming the energy marketplace of choice for retail, wholesale and green energy market participants. http://www.worldenergy.com

## Food and Agriculture

### Food and Earth Systems

Food and Earth Systems International is an independent private consultancy company, specializing in organic and sustainable agriculture. Food and Earth Systems International consultants provide a package of services for primary production, processing, and marketing, world-wide. To Food and Earth Systems International, developing organic agriculture means stimulating an environment friendly and economically sound agricultural system that produces healthy food and pays better prices to producers. Food and Earth Systems International stimulates the integration of organic production and fair trade.
http://www.foodandearth.com

### My Organic Market

My Organic Market (MOM's) stocks an overall higher percentage of organic items than any other major grocery chain, and sell only 100% USDA Certified Organic Produce. They buy local whenever possible to reduce fuel usage, supports small businesses, and boosts our local economy. They use a variety of green business practices for their operations, particularly in energy and waste, and have a full-time Environmental Coordinator that ensures policies and procedures are executed and enforced in daily operations.
http://www.myorganicmarket.com

### Urban Sustainable

Since opening in 2010, the Urban Sustainable storefront in Adams Morgan has been supplying the District with its selection of seeds, organic nutrients, hydroponic systems, and other home-growing products. Urban Sustainable aims to provide D.C. residents with the tools they need to farm and garden sustainably in limited space, indoors or outdoors. It also looks to raise awareness about food deserts in the city and emphasize the importance of local, community-based agriculture.
http://www.urbansustainable.org/

## Natural Resources / Environmental

### Global Environmental Resources

Global Environmental Resources has a great deal of experience in international environmental consulting. They offer a comprehensive program of research, analysis, training, education and liaison designed to enhance the effectiveness of their clients while maintaining the integrity of the environment and contributing to sustainable communities. They are committed to helping clients develop sustainable goals, policies and programs by taking into account the causes and effects of business and public policy decisions that affect growth and development, environmental and health factors.
http://www.gerinc.com

### Imhotep Consulting

Imhotep Consulting is a full service environmental, health and safety scientist and consulting firm. They provide audit, safety, policy, inspection, compliance, assessment, sustainability, environmental, commissioning, indoor air quality, and occupational health consulting services. Their sustainability consulting services include selecting sustainable and recycled materials, life cycle assessment, land and sustainable landscapes, advanced building systems, technologies, and interactions between environment and building occupants, including: environmental site analysis; energy efficiency and conservation; water conservation and wastewater management.
http://imhotepconsulting.com

**New Forests**
New Forests is an international forestry investment management and advisory business. New Forests specializes in institutional and private equity investments that generate returns from sustainably managed plantation forests and from environmental assets, such as carbon, biodiversity and water. With every project, they carefully investigate the best solutions that include the most sustainable forest practices as well as the best economic benefits to their clients.
http://www.newforests-us.com

**Renew and Sustain**
Renew and Sustain is a sustainability consulting firm whose mission is environmental sustainability. To achieve these goals, they work with their clients to provide the following services: consultation on energy alternatives, sustainable design solutions, how to renovate in a sustainable & practical approach, recommendation & selection criteria for vendor's & other sustainable products, consultation on eco-tourism, unique solutions to growing conservation challenges, and seminars & project management.
http://www.renewandsustain.com

**Wetlands Studies and Solutions (WSSI)**
WSSI is the leading natural and cultural resources consultant in Northern Virginia. Their staff of wetland scientists, engineers, regulatory specialists, and archeologists assists developers and public works agencies with the permitting process and create innovative solutions to water quality issues affecting the Chesapeake Bay region. They have years of experience working on projects that involve wetland and stream restorations.
http://www.wetlandstudies.com

**World Resources Company**
World Resources Company (WRC) is an environmental risk management company serving the technology sector by providing environmental compliance and innovative and cost effective recycling of non-renewable metal and mineral resources. Environmental services are available to support clients' environmental performance, sustainability goals and energy security. For more than 30 years, WRC has been engineering management recycling technology solutions, conserving energy, and supporting sustainability by reducing the energy consumption required to produce metals and minerals that are returned to the mainstream of commerce. WRC has an internal Energy Conservation and Sustainability Policy that it strictly adheres to in all of its activities and actions.
www.worldresourcescompany.com

## Recycling/Composting

**Community Forklift**
At Community Forklift's large warehouse, you can donate new and used building materials to receive a tax deduction, or you can purchase materials at prices that are 40% - 80% below retail. Located in greater Hyattsville, Maryland, it is a project of Sustainable Community Initiatives, a nonprofit organization. It aims to revitalize communities, reduce construction industry waste, promote environmentally-friendly building materials and methods, and develop career opportunities for nearby residents.
http://www.communityforklift.com

**DeConstruction Services, LLC**
DeConstruction Services has been helping residential and commercial buildings salvage, recycle, and reuse building materials for years. The company's mission is to maximize the amount of used building materials recycled or salvaged for use in order to save dwindling landfill space, natural resources, embodied energy, and the creation of additional greenhouse gases. Regardless of whether you need an

entire building deconstructed, or only part of a building, DeConstruction Services can help you be more sustainable in your operations.
http://www.deconstructionservices.com

## EnviRelation

EnviRelation, LLC is the hospitality industry's answer for services that improve environmental sustainability. They offer their clients services in food composting, emissions quantification, and sustainability reporting. Any food related business can have EnviRelation come by on a daily or every other day basis and take their food waste to local composting facilities.
http://www.envirelation.com

## Green Earth Consulting

Green Earth Consulting is a solid waste management and recycling outsourcing solution to the residential and commercial market. Green Earth performs various tasks for clients to increase efficiencies in the waste management and recycling area of the business, while controlling costs. Green Earth performs tasks such as designing office recycling programs for building tenants, solving vendor/client agreement issues, and realigning current services to better affect the goals of the property manager.
http://www.greenearth-consulting.com

## Junk in the Trunk

Junk in the Trunk Removal Services has been serving residential and business clients in the Washington, D.C. metro area since 2003. Their junk removal service can eliminate almost anything, including: appliances, furniture, donation items, construction material, and landscaping debris. The Ecovery Box allows them to recycle or donate items safely and efficiently, which helps keep excess junk out of landfills. They will also send receipts for any items donated.
http://www.jitt.com

## Transportation

## EnviroCab

EnviroCab believes that taxicab users should have the alternative to ride in an environmentally sustainable taxicab. An EnviroCab is estimated to produce 60% less emissions than standard cabs now operating in Arlington. Besides just reducing emissions they also offset remaining emissions by buying offset credits. In order to actually be carbon negative, they offset the pollution of two 16 mpg standard taxi cabs currently operating in Arlington County, for each taxi cab that EnviroCab puts in operation.
http://www.envirotaxicab.com

## National PediCab

National Pedicabs seeks to start a revolution in D.C. transportation. Cabs are faster than walking, can maneuver through heavy traffic, are environmentally friendlier than busses or trains, and are fun and entertaining. They maintain a fleet of 115 state-of-the-art, 21-speed pedicabs all along the East Coast. All the bikes are equipped with lights, reflectors, shock-absorbed seating, bells and hydraulic breaks. Depending on conditions, their cabs have all-weather full-cabin coveralls and warm fleece blankets.
http://www.nationalpedicabs.com/pages/about.html

## Capital Bikeshare

Previously known as SmartBike D.C., Capital Bikeshare is an alternative transportation network that uses the latest technologies to facilitate user access and is structured to enhance the city's public transportation system. Backed by corporate partners such as the District Department of the Environment (DDOE), the U.S. Green Building Council, and the World Bank, the Capital Bikeshare fleet consists of 1,100 bicycles

across the D.C. Metro area. Those interested can sign up online to access the Bikeshare for one day, five days, a month, or a year.
http://www.capitalbikeshare.com/

## Zipcar

Zipcar's mission is to enable simple and responsible urban living. They envision a future where car-sharing members outnumber car owners in major cities around the globe. Most residents of these cities will live within a five-to-ten-minute walk of a self-service Zipcar. They hope to be an integral part of these vibrant communities of well-informed, connected people who enjoy urban life and transportation options.
http://www.zipcar.com

## Car2Go

A relatively new entrant to the car sharing market in Washington DC, Car2Go was first introduced in Austin, Texas in 2009 and has Smart Cars for rent. The idea has been called point-to-point car sharing. Register online with a one-time membership fee.
http://www.car2go.com/washingtondc

## Cleaning Services

### Clean City

Founded in 1993, Clean City serves the D.C. Metro area with professional and residential cleaning services. Clean City specializes in implementing customized maintenance solutions for sustainability-minded building and facility managers. Clean City's Green Cleaning program includes the reporting process required for LEED points, and promotes environmental stewardship through their use of green cleaning products.
http://cleancityllc.com/

### Eco-Harmony

Eco-Harmony offers eco-friendly residential cleaning services. They have expanded their services to include window washing, lawn cleanup, landscape design, interior painting, concierge service, green home evaluations and coaching, and retail sales of household items. All services and products are provided as non-toxic and eco-friendly alternatives. They are currently researching and planning to expand their services to also include handyman service, lawn maintenance, laundry service, general contracting, HVAC duct cleaning, carpet cleaning, and any other service that can help their clients have a lighter impact on the environment.
http://www.ecoharmonyservices.com

### Green and Clean

Green and Clean provides cleaning services to both residential and commercial building customers. Green and Clean uses the most advanced natural products available, combined with healthy doses of "elbow grease" to produce healthful environments for their clients. Green and Clean offers the most eco-friendly cleaning products and services at competitive prices.
http://greenandcleandc.com

### The Green Mop

The Green Mop is a small eco-friendly cleaning company that has been serving the Metropolitan Washington, D.C. area since 2007. They emphasize the affordability of green cleaning, the positive health effects of not using harsh chemicals, and the environmentally friendly nature of their service.
http://www.thegreenmop.net

## Landscaping / Gardening

### American Plant Food

American Plant Food is a gardening center that is known for its commitment to organic gardening, sustainable practices, and providing quality gardening supplies and merchandise. American Plant Food educates its customers and staff about alternative gardening techniques, and subscribes to the EarthWise gardening method, which means they use natural methods and no chemicals. The company has also committed to greening its operations and its facility.

http://www.americanplant.net

### Bradley Site Design

Bradley Site Design is a woman-owned business providing landscape architectural and planning services for municipal, institutional, commercial, and residential clients. Their designs are characterized by their sensitivity to the historic and physical attributes of the site, to the local community, and to the people who will experience the spaces we create. The goal is to create environments that are, "biologically wholesome, socially just, and spiritually rewarding."

http://www.bradleysitedesign.com

### Capitol Greenroofs

Capitol Greenroofs has quickly made a name for itself as one of the leading green roof companies in the D.C. area. They offer a full line of services that includes green roof design, installation, and maintenance. Capitol Greenroofs has been involved with a large amount of the green roofs that have been installed in the area, and they offer a variety of different green roof systems that incorporate the latest technologies. They also use plants and vegetation from local sources and maintain a networking forum on their website for those interested in the latest news and developments in the green roof industry.

http://www.capitolgreenroofs.com

### Jordan Honeyman Landscape Architecture

Jordan Honeyman Landscape Architecture aims at designing beautiful and purposeful landscapes through innovative, site-specific landscape architecture. With backgrounds in landscape architecture, environmental planning, biology, horticulture, floriculture, and architecture, they possess a holistic, sustainable attitude towards the landscape. They use indigenous building materials, plantings and other resources where possible to recapture the relationship of the site to its context and help clients feel more connected to their environment.

http://www.jordanhoneyman.com

### Lee + Papa and Associates

Their approach to landscape architecture focuses on the successful integration of natural systems and the built environment. They strive to combine innovative technology with environmentally sensitive design while taking into consideration both scheduling and budget. Lee + Papa and Associates is experienced in organizing and managing cross-disciplinary planning teams that incorporate the talents of architects, urban designers, economic development planners, transportation planners, cultural resource planners, and infrastructure planners. They are also experienced in citizen engagement and consensus building. Additionally, cultural resources are among their specialized services.

http://www.leeandassociatesinc.com

### Natural Resources Design

Natural Resource Design offers a variety of services including consultations on design, plantings, natural habitats, and drainage issues. Design/Site Analysis services include a thorough site analysis of existing

conditions including vegetation, slopes, sun/shade patterns, wet/dry conditions, micro-ecosystems, human access, and usage. They also create master plans for residential, commercial, and community projects. Other services include project management, presentations, and lectures.
http://www.naturalresourcesdesign.com


### Sustainable Life Designs

Sustainable Life Designs provides innovative planning and design services – creating healthy communities, buildings, and landscapes for their clients. Services include planning, design and construction services for every aspect of a project - from initial conception and project feasibility to inspection and delivery of completed work. Specific expertise in urban and environmental planning and design studies, sustainability indicator development and management, and architectural and landscape design, construction and installation.
http://www.sustainablelifedesigns.com

### Washington Gardener

Washington Gardener magazine is a the gardening publication published specifically for the local metro area - zones 6-7 - Washington, D.C. and its suburbs. The content of the magazine gives real examples that you can use immediately in your own garden. It will save you time and show you how to stretch your garden resources. It will inspire you with new ideas and new ways of looking at things.
http://www.washingtongardener.com

## Green Business Consulting

### BCV Solutions

The management team of BCV Solutions brings over 20 years of expertise in partnering with government, commercial and educational customers to deliver premier management consulting solutions. They specialize in delivering exceptional management consulting and technology services in administrative and management support, workforce development, technical support and green solutions. Organizational sustainability and green solutions services include coop planning, energy efficiency and fleet management, and sustainable design.
http://www.bcvsolutions.com

### Eco-Coach, Inc.

Eco-Coach's services are centered on providing clients with the knowledge and tools to incorporate sustainability into their business operations and daily lives. They do this by meeting their clients wherever they are in the process – whether they have just started on the path and need to identify how to incorporate sustainability intro their strategy, daily operations and employee education, or have been doing this for some time and need additional support and guidance or to quantify their environmental impact. Business services include green business assessments, strategic planning and benchmarking, training and educational workshops, and LEED certification and consultation. Residential services include workshops, webinars and in-home eco-audits.
http://www.eco-coach.com

### Green Living Consulting

Green Living Consulting (GLC) believes in a holistic approach to helping your business or household achieve realistic and cost effective green goals. The GLC process of "getting green" will help you seamlessly adopt sustainable practices and technologies while creating a culture of green in your daily life. GLC will develop a green plan that: incorporates your goals and objectives; maps realistic actions within your budget and timeframe; guides implementation; and tracks, measures, and reports results.
http://www.greenlivingconsulting.com

## Greentrack Strategies

Greentrack Strategies provides their clients with strategic environmental management services. They can provide comprehensive planning and management strategy for businesses that are interested in ensuring that they are committed to sustainability and realize the economic and environmental benefits of doing so. Greentrack Strategies has been involved with several conferences on sustainability practices and also has publications on sustainability issues.
http://greentrack.com/wordpress

## Strategic Sustainability Consulting

Strategic Sustainability Consulting provides organizations with the tools and expertise they need to actively manage their social and environmental impacts. They specialize in helping under-resourced organizations implement sustainable solutions usually reserved for large, multinational companies. Their products and services help to identify core social and environmental impacts; create a sustainability plan that aligns your "triple bottom line"; calculate your carbon footprint and find ways to go "carbon neutral"; develop a communications strategy that speaks credibly about your commitment; and manage your supply chain according to your values and vision.
http://www.sustainabilityconsulting.com

## SustainAbility

SustainAbility is a consulting firm that helps clients identify opportunities and risks related to social responsibility and sustainable development. They have been in business for over 20 years, and they have continued to work towards a just and sustainable world for present and future generations. SustainAbility has worked on projects all over the globe and has built a strong network of professionals that offer sustainability consulting to their clients.
http://www.sustainability.com/about/washington.asp

## Sustainable Products Corporation

With the mission of meeting and increasing the demand for sustainable products, Sustainable Products Corporation is helping businesses across the country identify which products are sustainable, and why it is important to care. SPC offers training programs as well as a manual on procurement of sustainable products with a focus on the life cycle of products and a set of criteria that SPC has developed.
http://www.sustainableproducts.com

## Legal Services

### Arent Fox

With nearly 350 lawyers in offices in Washington, D.C., New York, and Los Angeles, Arent Fox has 29 practice groups and emphasizes real estate, life sciences and intellectual property law. Arent Fox provides legal services to energy-related sectors, including wind energy, biomass, coal, geothermal energy, hydroelectric power, natural gas and transportation and many others. They provide counsel on broad spectrum of environmental questions, ranging from traditional regulatory and litigation areas of hazardous and solid waste management and cleanup, air and water pollution, workplace safety and health, insurance coverage, dangerous goods transportation and toxic torts, to emerging areas such as brownfields redevelopment, environmental justice, global environmental protection and biotechnology and agro-sciences regulation.
http://www.arentfox.com

**Bradley Arant Boult Cummings**
With more than 360 attorneys, they maintain seven offices strategically located in Alabama, Mississippi, North Carolina, Tennessee, and the District of Columbia. Industries served includes accounting, automotive, banking and finance, biotechnology, construction, education, emerging business, energy, equipment leasing, forest products, health care, insurance, manufacturing, materials and aggregate production, media and communications, mining, municipal and public finance, oil and gas, pharmaceuticals and medical devices, public utilities, real estate, retail, steel, technology, telecommunications, textiles, transportation, and venture capital. Bradley Arant has addressed the increasingly complex area of environmental law with attorneys who have broad experience in the interpretation and application of the vast array of federal, state, and local environmental laws and regulations.
http://www.babc.com/

**Holland & Knight**
Holland & Knight has more than 1,100 attorneys in the US and abroad to address client interests spread across the scope of the United States and international marketplace. Holland & Knight's Environmental Team has kept pace with this critical and evolving national imperative. Their comprehensive experience includes such issues as brownfield redevelopment, clean air, coastal issues, compliance auditing and corporate governance, endangered species, litigation including superfund and toxic torts, environmental issues in corporate and real estate transactions, environmental health and safety, Indian law, environmental permit approvals in major project development, NEPA and state equivalents, solid and hazardous waste, water pollution, and wetlands and natural resources. Holland & Knight's energy law lawyers are experienced in the wide array of legal issues involved in renewable and alternative energy.
http://www.hklaw.com

**L.A.D Reporting**
Specializing in complex litigation, L.A.D. Reporting & Digital Videography is the leader in real-time and general court reporting services. With state-of-the-art technology and excellent service, they provide an end to end solution throughout the litigation lifecycle. They feature green initiatives to reduce the environmental impact of their operations including recycling and buying supplies made from recycled materials.
http://www.ladreporting.com

**Nixon Peabody**
Nixon Peabody has launched a "legally green" initiative to help their clients achieve their business goals and join with them in promoting environmental responsibility. Their services include negotiating and structuring involving acquisition of an equity interest in wind, geothermal, or solar facilities; developing a sustainable real estate project; financing a project with renewable energy tax credits; protecting the intellectual property associated with innovative cleantech technology; advising on siting and permitting of proposed energy facilities; forming a green investment fund; and navigating the emerging legislative and regulatory proposals involving climate change.
http://www.nixonpeabody.com

**O'Malley, Miles, Nylen & Gilmore**
Since the 1950s, attorneys of O'Malley, Miles, Nylen & Gilmore and its predecessor firms have counseled and represented clients throughout Suburban Maryland and the District of Columbia. Their attorneys practice in the trial and appellate courts of Maryland, Virginia and the District of Columbia as well as the United States District Courts for Maryland, Virginia and the District of Columbia and the United States Circuit Court of Appeals for the Fourth Circuit. They also represent clients in administrative law and

governmental relations matters at the municipal, county and state levels in Maryland. OMNG has several LEED AP's on staff that can provide assistance with green building projects.
http://www.omng.com

## Seyfarth Shaw

Founded in 1945, Seyfarth Shaw is a full-service law firm serving clients throughout the globe. The Environmental, Safety & Toxic Torts Group regularly assists clients in navigating environmental and safety laws to find practical business solutions to environmental problems. They are able to take an environmental problem from the formulation of an initial compliance strategy to any form of dispute resolution, including mediation, arbitration, jury trial and appeal.
http://www.seyfarth.com

## Venable

Venable is one of America's top 100 law firms, with offices all over the country. They have a local office in the D.C. area, and offer expertise in a wide spectrum of law services. Venable has LEED AP's on staff, and is frequently involved with green conferences related to green and sustainability issues and how lawyers can help. Venable has maintained a high level of involvement in the communities where they work and often provide their services pro bono.
http://www.venable.com

## Watt, Tieder, Hoffar & Fitzgerald

Watt, Tieder, Hoffar & Fitzgerald (WTHF) is one of the largest construction and surety law firms in the world, with a practice that encompasses all aspects of construction contracting and public procurement. Since its inception over 30 years ago, WTHF has been involved in major development and construction projects, including highways, airports and seaports, rail and subway systems, military bases, industrial plants, petrochemical facilities, electric-generating plants, communication systems, and commercial and public facilities of all types in the United States and around the globe. WTHF has provided advice and publications on green building law for several years.
http://www.wthf.com

## Whiteford Taylor Preston

With over 155 attorneys in six offices in the mid-Atlantic region, Whiteford, Taylor & Preston serves clients across the nation and around the globe. They advise individuals, public and private companies, emerging businesses, educational institutions, nonprofit organizations, and governments as well as professional services firms on complex business, litigation, and bankruptcy matters. Whiteford, Taylor & Preston's Green Building and Sustainability attorneys are a multidisciplinary team of attorneys from their corporate, intellectual property, litigation, construction and surety, real estate development and leasing, and community association practices. The Green Industry Group seamlessly integrates in-depth understanding of sustainable development with the firm's existing practices. They are one of only a few law firms with two LEED Accredited Professional attorneys.
http://www.wtplaw.com

## Publishing and Printing

### Contribucheck

Contribucheck is a certified MBE company that specializes in providing customized business forms, fine paper products and office shredders to non-profits, businesses, and the government. They also offer a unique Affinity Check program for organizations looking for non-dues income. They use unique quality control factors like recycled check stock options and Soy-based inks to ensure that their company follows socially responsible business practices.

http://www.contribucheck.com

**Design Byline**
Design Byline was founded with a mission to add to the body of knowledge of architecture, business management, design technology, and sustainable design, through research, writing and publishing. Their articles are published in AIArchitect, Bethesda magazine, CE News for the business of civil engineering, Home & Design - Washington, Maryland, Virginia, New Old House, Washingtonian, and Waterfront Home & Design.
http://www.design-byline.com

**Ecoprint**
Ecoprint is involved in environmentally responsible printing process. Their eco-ink product takes ink to a new level of environmental sensitivity and their printing process is 100% carbon neutral. They offer integrated services along with printing, including conceptualization and design, data work, storage, project management and mailing services
http://www.ecoprint.com

## IT / Electronic Services

**Community IT Innovators**
Community IT Innovators (CITI) is an employee-owned company committed to helping social mission organizations effectively use technology. As a sustainable, triple bottom line business, they also serve their community and seek to lower their impact on the environment and encourage their clients to do the same. Since 1993, they have served over 800 organizations. Services consist of infrastructure support, business IT consulting, online strategy, web development, custom development, design, and holistic technology assessment.
http://www.citidc.com/template/index.cfm

**Innovate**
Innovate is a small, green, woman-owned business providing geospatial solutions, software engineering, IT security services, management consulting and transformation consulting services. Primary clients are the EPA, USGS, USDA, and many state, tribal and US territory environmental departments. Their focus is to drive efficiencies and business results through innovative consulting techniques IT solutions. They specialize in helping public sector agencies transform themselves into business-based, customer-focused organizations.
http://innovateteam.com

**ITF Consulting**
ITF Consulting (ITF) is a professional services firm founded in 1996 that is focused on the non-profit community and the for-profit sustainable business community. Although they provide a wide range of services including event planning, foundation management, and training, their primary business is setting up and supporting users of CitySoft's Community Enterprise web platform. They are an official CitySoft partner agency.
http://www.itfconsulting.com

**LimeLeap Solutions**
LimeLeap was recognized by AlwaysOn.com as one of the top 100 green companies. Creating new business opportunities in green technology, LimeLeap provides its clients with IT services and software solutions that allow them to stay at the forefront of sustainability. As a company LimeLeap has made a strong commitment to maintaining its status as a green business leader.
http://www.limeleap.com

## Real Estate

### Akridge

Akridge is a full-service commercial real estate firm in the Washington, D.C. area. Their projects total over 12 million square feet of office, industrial/flex, residential, retail, and entertainment space at a value of over $2.0 billion. They are involved in every aspect of commercial real estate development, construction, leasing, and management. In cooperation with the Washington, D.C. recycling law, Akridge is committed to providing all necessary information needed to implement and maintain an efficient recycling program. Akridge manages 11 properties that are Energy Star Labeled; the firm has been awarded the 'Energy Star Leader' recognition and a 'Top Performer' honor. To lead Akridge's efforts in sustainability for business operations and development and operating properties, the firm has a designated 'Green Team' and a staff member dedicated to the Energy Star benchmarking and implementation process.
http://www.akridge.com

### AtSite

AtSite, a sustainable buildings company, offers clients an innovative, performance-based approach to the design and construction process by diligently managing building projects from concept to completion. Built on years of experience and fundamental knowledge, sustainability is an integral element of AtSite's forward thinking approach to design and construction management. AtSite is a founding member of the Sustainable Buildings Alliance, a group of leading AEC firms assisting building owners in establishing sustainable platforms for their existing buildings through the implementation of innovative, smart solutions. They are also a participating member of numerous organizations supporting modern design and construction approaches as well as the implementation of creative sustainable solutions.
http://www.atsiteres.com

### Bennett Group

Bennett Group has two decades of experience in development, construction, and property management. They use an innovative multidisciplinary approach with responsive personalized service. As a LSDBE and LEED accredited business, they offer holistic solutions that efficiently deliver the best possible product, conserving time, energy and money without cutting corners.
http://www.bennettgroupdc.com

### CB Richard Ellis

CB Richard Ellis (CBRE) is a full-service real estate services company with a strong position in support of environmental sustainability. As the world's largest real estate services firm, they directly manage more than 1.7 billion square feet of property and corporate facilities, and advise the owners and occupiers of billions more square feet.
http://www.cbre.com

### CoStar

CoStar Group is a leading provider of information services to commercial real estate professionals in the United States and the United Kingdom. Their suite of services offers customers online access to a comprehensive database of commercial real estate information: space available for lease, comparable sales information, tenant information, properties for sale, property information for clients' web sites, industry professional directory, analytic information, data integration, property advertising and industry news. CoStar has been selected by the U.S. Environmental Protection Agency (EPA) to receive the 2009 Excellence in Energy Star Promotion Award. CoStar continues to provide valuable reports and

information to the construction and real estate industries through its work on green building and energy efficiency in the commercial building sector.
http://www.costar.com

## Evolution Partners

Evolution Partners is a boutique real estate investment advisory and private equity firm specializing in financing high-performance, environmentally responsible real estate projects. Their clients are real estate developers, investors, and tenants who demonstrate commitment to creating and preserving long-term asset value by developing and/or occupying cutting-edge projects that meet or exceed the US Green Building Council's LEED and/or EPA Energy Star standards of excellence. They specialize in developing flexible and innovative structured finance solutions for green projects of all sizes and types across North America, securing the capital necessary to bring a project to life, and sustain it financially for the long term.
http://www.evolutionpartners.com

## Forest City Washington

Forest City Enterprises creates lively, mixed-use environments at complex urban sites. Forest City's Washington office, a core regional office, focuses on residential, retail, office, and mixed-use components. Among Forest City's strengths is its ability to transform underutilized urban sites into vibrant, revitalized urban destinations blending new construction with adaptive reuse and historic preservation of existing structures. Sustainable growth and operation components are also cornerstones of Forest City's values.
http://www.fcwashington.com

## GreenDC Realty

GreenDC Realty was developed to bridge the divide between traditional real estate and the green buildings market. Aside from the services offered through Keller Williams Capital Properties, the GreenDC Realty team has also established relationships with core affiliates across the renewable energy sector, bio-based building services, green building suppliers and a dedicated team of lending and settlement services. The Green DC Realty Marketing Advantage Guarantee is a specifically designed plan they developed to market homes as higher performing properties.
http://greendcrealty.com

## JBG Companies

Since 1960, the JBG Companies has been an active investor, owner and developer in the Washington metropolitan area's real estate market. Their diverse portfolio encompasses millions of square feet of office, residential, hotel and retail projects, and includes many of the region's most distinguished properties. They are committed to a corporate philosophy of "Building Smart, Thinking Green." Smart, transit-oriented growth in urban areas is an established development philosophy they focus on. By redeveloping and using already existing infrastructure, their business practice is inherently green.
http://www.jbg.com

## Louis Dreyfus

Louis Dreyfus conducts its real estate activities through Louis Dreyfus Property Group, which was organized in 1971 to own, develop, manage and operate properties in North America and Europe. It has acquired and developed in excess of 8 million square feet and has in development an additional 2.5 million square feet. Louis Dreyfus's portfolio consists primarily of high quality, central business district and suburban office buildings with the majority of the properties characterized as Class A office assets in major urban locations. Office buildings and development sites, some of which are held in joint ventures with other parties, are located in Washington, D.C., suburban New York, and Paris. Louis Dreyfus has

been at the leading edge of green building in the D.C. area by achieving LEED certification on many of its projects.
http://www.louisdreyfus.com

## PN Hoffman

Since 1993, PN Hoffman has been developing upscale condominium residences and mixed-use properties in the Washington, D.C. area. PN Hoffman strives to find innovative ways to give their residents the ultimate "Fine Urban Living" experience. As part of this mission, PN Hoffman embraces the U.S. Green Building Council's LEED green building rating system. It is this environmentally conscious mindset that drives PN Hoffman's goal of "Healthy Living through Healthy Design."
http://www.pnhoffman.com

## Studley

Studley's multidisciplinary specialists provide a variety of strategic brokerage and consulting services that enable their clients to achieve their business and financial goals. Studley's Sustainable Real Estate Practice includes LEED Accredited Professionals nationwide who understand how businesses can create eco-friendly work environments that improve the quality of life for their employees and the community at large. They are also experienced at identifying environmentally responsible processes that need to be included in lease or purchase negotiations.
http://www.studley.com

## The Tower Companies

The Tower Companies strive to develop eco-progressive real estate that transcends traditional approaches to the built environment, teach people how to engage with their surroundings, promote the balance of body and mind, optimize human achievement and treat the planet with respect. Currently, The Tower Companies is the only real estate developer in America to buy renewable energy to meet 100 percent of their energy needs. As an EPA Climate Leader, Energy Star Partner, and Green Power Partner, The Tower Companies are committed to reducing their impact on the global environment by completing a corporate-wide inventory of their greenhouse gas emissions, setting long-term reduction goals, and annually reporting progress to the EPA and to their stakeholders through the Tower Footprint, their annual sustainability report.
http://www.towercompanies.com

## William C. Smith + Co.

William C. Smith + Co. has been a multidisciplinary real estate firm in D.C. for four decades. In complement to its development, construction, sales and financial divisions, the firm owns and/or manages a portfolio in excess of 12,000 units of residential real estate. With a group of subsidiary service companies under the William C. Smith + Co. umbrella, the firm is able to offer exemplary service to its clients. William C. Smith + Co. has been dedicated to giving back to the community and is very involved with educating about green issues as well as partnering with other green organizations to make a difference in the D.C. area.
http://www.williamcsmith.com

## Communications / Media

### BetterWorld Telecom

BetterWorld Telecom is the only nationwide, full-service voice and data telecommunications carrier solely focused on serving businesses and organizations that support social justice and sustainability. They work to help cut costs for their clients as well as provide sustainable communications solutions. They have become carbon neutral, greened their office operations, and partner with several other sustainability focused organizations to help have a greater global impact on integrated sustainability and business.

**Ecofusion**
Based in the heart of Washington, D.C., Ecofusion is a business communications consulting and media company dedicated to the world's leading change makers in the fields of sustainability, social enterprise, and green business. Ecofusion provides the following services to their clients: communications planning, public relations, new media, branding, packaging, design, and interactive media tools. Ecofusion believes that achieving sustainable and healthy communities depends on everyone working toward the same goal. They have also purchased Green Tags to help offset their carbon emissions from operations.
http://www.ecofusion.com

**emPivot**
emPivot.com is the first online network to bring together the wide range of user generated and premium video content related to the environment. They are a pivot point to empower users to share video content, connect with each other to share media and utilize the strong video search engine to find the most relevant green-related video content from emPivot.com and the rest of the web. emPivot.com also is dedicated to being a sustainable company by greening its operations as well as giving back to the community.
http://blog.empivot.com

**Free Range Studios**
Free Range is a full-service firm with 23 full-time staff members and offices in Washington, D.C. and Berkeley, CA. Free Range is known for *The Meatrix* and *Grocery Store Wars*. Those projects are the most public face of a portfolio that includes print, web and strategy materials non-profits, political campaigns, and socially responsible businesses. They work with smaller groups as well to achieve their mission of helping the sustainability movement.
http://www.freerangestudios.com

**Grand Junction Design**
Grand Junction Design (GJD) is a small design and development studio that works exclusively with nonprofits, foundations, and organizations committed to environmental sustainability. GJD focuses on assisting and empowering progressive nonprofit groups. They have remained small by design, so that they can limit their work to select groups whose missions they support personally, and continue to provide their clients with the highest quality service. Web services include content management, design and development, and online communication strategy. Print services include brochures and flyers, newsletters, annual reports, and other publications, and identity, letterhead and business cards.
http://www.grandjunctiondesign.com

**Ideal Design**
Ideal Design was founded to address the unique needs and principles of non-profits and socially conscious businesses. Ideal design provides graphic design and communications services with the aim of creating positive change. They conceive, design, and produce a variety of print materials. With partners, they offer consulting/art direction, print management, photography and illustration, and web sites. Since they serve non-profits and socially conscious businesses, they are committed t to minimal overhead and conservative project management.
http://www.idealdesignco.com

**Productions 1000**
A media and production company creating positive communications and content for energy, environment, and sustainability initiatives. Services include strategy and planning, design and branding, film and video production, marketing and event planning, and media and communications. Productions 1000 strives to achieve clients' marketing and communications goals.

http://www.productions1000.com

## Local Green Business Listings

We are also providing you with a list of websites where you can find green business listings for particular industries. While we wanted to create a list of our own, which is above, to include a variety of different industries, we also realize that there are websites that list green companies. So we figured it would be good to inform you of these websites as well, since they are another great resource for finding green businesses.

**US Green Building Council National Regional Capitol Member Listings**
The U.S. Green Building Council - National Capital Region Chapter (includes surrounding regions of Virginia and Maryland), a local affiliate of the USGBC, provides locally-based leadership, advocacy, education and resources to create a vibrant and environmentally healthy Metropolitan Washington region. The listing provides individual members from every sector of the building industry in order to work collaboratively to advance their vision for a responsible, healthy and prosperous environment that improves quality of life.
http://www.usgbcncr.org/_dir/member

**SB NOW Member List**
The Sustainable Business Network of Washington (SB NOW) works with companies to help them integrate environmental and social responsibility principles into their operations and strategy. We do this to help improve the quality of life and the environment in the National Capital Region. The list contains members that have joined in SB NOW's network and efforts.
http://www.sbnow.org/members/index.cfm

**Live Green Member Listings**
Live Green makes eco-friendly living and business practices easier and more affordable in D.C. and beyond. Live Green's membership organization provides support to green businesses and discounts on everyday green products and services for consumers.
http://www.livegreen.net

**Think Local First DC**
Think Local First DC is a network of local business owners, non-profit leaders, and community members who are committed to building a sustainable local economy and preserving the vibrant character that makes Washington, D.C. a unique place to live and visit. The site provides various resources on locally related environmental issues in the D.C. area.
http://www.thinklocalfirstdc.com/

**Green Builders Council DC**
In the spirit of cooperation and partnership, the Green Builders Council of DC offers their services, advice, and counsel to the District of Columbia as the city strives to build a robust Green Economy. The site provides sources for green building design, projects, and certification, in addition to modules for green job training.
http://www.builditgreendc.org

**Washington Gardener Regional Community Gardens Listing**
The Washington Gardner specifically targets Washington, D.C. area gardening enthusiasts. The source is in the process of expanding a list of all local community gardens for the DC region.
www.washingtongardener.com/index_files/CommunityGardens.htm

**Eco-Partners Directory**
Eco-Partners businesses are recognized as delivering the very best in products, services and value in the above listed areas. The directory provides a listing of active member of Eco-Partners.
http://www.ecopartnersdc.org

**Green Building Institute Supporters**
The Green Building Institute seeks to foster sustainable building practices through education and example. This link provides an avenue of resources to its supporters and education.
http://www.greenbuildinginstitute.org

**DC Energy Office Listing of Solar Contractors**
This listing from the DC Energy Office providers a list of the solar contractors in the Washington, D.C. metro area that can help residents and businesses switch to alternative energy and take advantage of grants and tax incentives and credits. These companies might also be able to help you educate yourself about solar energy.
http://green.dc.gov/green/lib/green/2009.03.05_REIP_Contractors_and_Installers.pdf

**DC Department of Small and Local Business Development (DSLBD) Green/Sustainability Resources**
The Department works to stimulate and expand the local tax base of the District of Columbia, to increase the number of viable employment opportunities for District residents, and to extend the city's economic prosperity to local business owners, their employees, and the communities they serve. DC DSLBD provides links of several green companies in the area as well as tips on how to green small businesses.
http://dslbd.dc.gov/DC/DSLBD/Business+Resources/Green-Sustainability+Business+Resources

**Arlingtonians For a Clean Environment – Green Home Building and Remodeling Directory**
Arlingtonians For a Clean Environment (ACE) is a resource for public education about the local environment and for volunteer involvement in environmental improvement efforts. The directory is intended for homeowners, residents, designers, or builders to make projects more sustainable, and environmentally friendly. The directory features suppliers and installers for a variety of green products, as well as identifies a number of firms with expertise and consulting in the design and construction of green buildings. The listing also provides a variety of government agencies, non-profit organizations, and other entities with useful information and resources on green home building and management.
http://www.arlingtonenvironment.org/greenchallenge/green_directory.pdf

**Green (formerly Coop) America National Green Pages**
The National Green Pages is a directory listing nearly 3,000 businesses that have made a firm commitment to sustainable, socially just principles, including the support of sweatshop-free labor, organic farms, fair trade, and cruelty-free products. The National Green Pages lists baby care products, organic, fair trade, flavored teas, and fuel-efficient cars for rent among the thousands of products.
http://www.coopamerica.org/pubs/greenpages/index.cfm

**Sustain Lane DC Listings**
Sustainability Lane is a people powered sustainability guide. The site provides comprehensive sources to greening one's life.
http://www.sustainlane.com/search.do

# Local Green Government Websites

While there has been much talk about the federal government getting more involved in green initiatives, there are many local government agencies that have been creating green programs and initiatives for several years now. Below you will find a list of some of these agencies and you can use the information provided to track the latest developments around green initiatives and jobs by visiting their websites. A lot of times, these local government agencies will hold public hearings or have events that are open to the public, so consider trying to attend some of these events. It is a great way to get the inside scoop on what the major issues and initiatives are, and it also gives you another avenue for networking and providing your thoughts to local government officials and employees.

## Washington, D.C.

### DC Department of the Environment
This site is a comprehensive resource on environmental issues, consisting of information about current programs, policies, services, events, and issues. It has climate change resources about DC's initiatives and information for public awareness. There are links for information about the integration of sustainable building operations and natural resource protection. Resources for sustainable development address green building, rain gardens, and land use. Waste and hazards information includes recycling reports and disposal directions. There is a section of eco-tips: practical steps individuals can take for sustainability.
http://green.dc.gov/

### DC Office of Planning
The District's planning agency is involved in several sustainability initiatives. Capital Space is a coalition that works to coordinate management of the district's parks and open space, and also to create plans for enhancement. The Green Collar Jobs Initiative is a partnership with other government, for-profit entities, non-profit organizations, and academic institutions to help prepare District residents and businesses to take advantage of the growing green sector of the economy. Healthy by Design are programs to create a healthier, more livable and walkable D.C.
http://planning.dc.gov/DC/Planning

### DC Department of Public Works
The Department of Public Works operates programs to dispose of environmentally harmful waste. They provide services for hazardous household waste, recycling of electronics, general recycling, and leaf pickup. They also sponsor neighborhood cleanup and enforce illegal dumping laws.
http://dpw.dc.gov/DC/DPW/

### DC Urban Forestry Administration
Located within the Department of Transportation, UFA's goal is to establish healthy trees along streets in a safe manner. They provide tree services and information about urban forestry. They also partner with non-profits to support these programs.
http://ufa.ddot.dc.gov/ufa/site/default.asp

### DC Water and Sewer Authority
Besides supplying water and sewer services, the agency has many initiatives to improve the environmental quality of the city. They do so by upgrading sewer infrastructure, treating biosolids and using them for agricultural fertilizer, reducing nitrogen runoff into waterways, and cleaning waterways of debris. They sponsor community events and offer information on water conservation and watersheds.
http://www.dcwasa.com/

---

### National Capital Planning Commission

The NCPC is the federal government's planning agency for federal land and buildings in D.C. They are involved in the Capital Space partnership. The coalition works to coordinate management of the district's parks and open space, and also to create plans for enhancement.
http://www.ncpc.gov/

### DC Department of Small and Local Business Development

The DSLBD is currently involved in several green initiatives to help provide assistance and education to small and local businesses in D.C. on green issues. They recently launched a Green Restaurant Certification program to offer technical assistance through workshops and consultations to help restaurants achieve green certification and make their everyday business practiced more sustainable. The DSLBD often holds events for small and local businesses that include presentations on green business issues and economic opportunities, as well as networking opportunities.
http://dslbd.dc.gov/DC/DSLBD

## Montgomery County

### Montgomery County Green Economic Development Initiative

This is a partnership between the Department of Environmental Protection and the Department of Economic Development that was created to lay the foundation for Montgomery County to become a national leader in building a green economy. The County Executive has also appointed a Green Economy Task Force to work closely with the Departments of Economic Development and Environmental Protection in implementing Green Economic Development Initiative.
http://www.montgomerycountymd.gov/mcgtmpl.asp?url=/content/ded/green_intro.asp

### Montgomery County, MD Department of Environmental Protection

This department's goals of conservation and restoration are met through a variety of programs. Principle among them are air and water management, the Montgomery County Climate Action Initiative, Cool Counties program and other climate and energy related programs, conservation and protection, storm water management, and watershed restoration. For residents, they provide trash and recycling services and information on property care. These include grasscycling, composting, and noise control.
http://www.montgomerycountymd.gov/deatmpl.asp?url=/content/dep/dephome/index.asp

### Montgomery Soil and Water Conservation District

The soil and water conservation district assists and educates landowners in implementing soil and water conservation techniques. They have a cost-share program for implementation plans, an academic contest for young adults, and programs for urban storm water management and best management practices.
http://www.montgomeryswcd.org/

### Montgomery County Planning Department

The planning department is responsible for creating the county's master plan, evaluating proposed development, and creating public information. They have programs for conservation of forests, legacy spaces, and Special Protection Areas such as streams or wetlands. A green infrastructure plan is being developed to make the most of the environmental services offered by the county's ecosystems. Water and sewer regulations and the water resources plan protect water quality. They are also conducting an environmental review on the Intercounty Connector (ICC).
http://www.montgomeryplanning.org/

**Montgomery County Department of Parks**
Beyond recreation programs and park maintenance, the department has Park Development and Park Planning & Stewardship divisions. Stewardship subdivisions address natural resource issues. Programs include pollution control, review of development proposals, creation of natural resource management plans, vegetation management, and wildlife management.
http://mcparkandplanning.org/parks/

## Prince George's County

### Prince George's County, MD Department of Planning
The Environmental Planning Section is responsible for programs related to the protection of the natural environment as well as human health and welfare issues. The section evaluates the impact of land use plans and development proposals on air quality, noise, landscape features and habitat. It also identifies appropriate mitigation measures and future waste treatment and disposal needs.
http://www.mncppc.org/pgco/

### Prince George's County Department of Parks and Recreation
The department maintains nature centers and the Old Maryland Farm, along with the management of conservation areas and natural parks. They also offer nature and outdoor recreation programs.
http://www.pgparks.com/

### Prince George's County Department of Environmental Resources
The department is responsible for animal management, environmental services, and waste management. Animal management includes pet and wild animal services. Environmental services include air, flood, and water management, community outreach, and pollution prevention. Waste management operates the landfill and recycling program.
http://www.princegeorgescountymd.gov/Government/AgencyIndex/DER/index.asp

### Prince George's County Green Building Steering Committee
The committee has created green building goals for PG County. They work to obtain a LEED Silver rating or better for all new county buildings. They are creating incentives for private construction to obtain the same rating. Establishing education and outreach programs and ensuring that LEED accredited staff are available are also goals.
http://www.princegeorgescountymd.gov/Government/AgencyIndex/GoingGreen/

## Fairfax County

### Fairfax County, VA Department of Public Works and the Environment
This agency provides a long list of environmental services to residents. Their programs include solid waste management, hazardous waste, sewers, storm water management, and noise. Other natural resource programs include walkways and trails, information on tree planting and care, and watershed management. They have also signed onto the Cool Counties program to reduce greenhouse gas emissions and created an Environmental Improvement Program.
http://www.fairfaxcounty.gov/dpwes/

### Fairfax County Northern Virginia Water and Soil Conservation District
To achieve the goal of promoting clean streams and protection of natural resources, the agency provides conservation information, technical assistance, educational programs, and volunteer opportunities. They

provide technical information and services for drainage and soil erosion, pond management, stream restoration/stabilization, and suburban horse farm management. Stewardship and education opportunities include workshops, academic programs for young adults, and volunteer monitoring. They also publish materials on a variety of topics, such as tips for homeowners on watershed-friendly landscaping.
http://www.fairfaxcounty.gov/nvswcd/

**Fairfax County Park Authority**
The Park Authority maintains gardens, lakefront parks, campgrounds, nature centers, and farmers markets. The Resources Management Division is responsible for natural resources management. Current projects include invasive management, creation of an arboretum, and riparian buffer restoration. The division also participates in park and strategic planning, resource management, technical support, land acquisition, development review, and education and outreach.
http://www.fairfaxcounty.gov/parks/

**Fairfax County Department of Planning and Zoning**
The planning department is actively involved in several important environmental issues. Their activities include air quality monitoring, Chesapeake Bay preservation ordinance amendments, an easements program, the Environmental Quality Advisory Council, noise issues and resources, the Occoquan watershed, and wetlands permits.
http://www.fairfaxcounty.gov/dpz/

**Fairfax County Planning Commission**
The planning commission has an environment committee that addresses water quality, storm water and floodplain management, stream protection and restoration, sidewalks and trails, and tree preservation. Additionally, they make recommendations to the comprehensive plan.
http://www.fairfaxcounty.gov/planning/

## Arlington County

**Arlington, VA Environmental Programs**
Arlington provides a variety of environmental services concerning air quality, energy, recreation, green buildings and homes, plants and trees, solid waste management, and water issues. Among them is the Green Home Choice Program, which provides incentives for green building. The Arlington Beautification Committee encourages the landscaping of public areas. The Arlington Initiative to Reduce Emissions has retrofitted government facilities, greened their vehicle fleet, and encouraged green building in private construction. The county also boasts a community garden program, in which residents pay a small fee for a garden plot in one of their eight sites.
http://www.arlingtonva.us/Portals/Topics/TopicsEnvironment.aspx

## D.C. Metro Area

**Metropolitan Washington Council of Governments**
A regional organization of Washington area local governments, it has a Department of the Environment which addresses regional environmental problems. Water resources are a major issue encompassing the restoration of the Anacostia Watershed, regional water quality monitoring, water supply coordination, and policy analysis for the Chesapeake Bay. For another major issue, climate change, they have developed partnerships, goals, and carbon reduction programs. Related initiatives include energy resource management programs, a green building group, a green infrastructure forum, and streetlights program. They are also involved in air quality monitoring, airport noise abatement, and urban forestry.
http://www.mwcog.org/environment/

**Washington Suburban Sanitary Commission**
The WSSC provides water and sewer services to Montgomery and Prince Georges counties. As such, they have several environmental initiatives. Their FOG program provides permitting, inspection, enforcement, and public education about eliminating the presence of fats, oils, and grease in the sewer system. A partnership with area non-profit groups works to fix sewage overflows. They also have conservation and recreation programs for their properties.
http://www.wssc.dst.md.us/

**The Maryland-National Capital Park and Planning Commission**
The commission is a state entity that manages the public park system and land use planning surrounding D.C. in Montgomery and Prince Georges counties. They operate each county's park and planning departments.
http://www.mncppc.org

**Northern Virginia Regional Park Authority**
The Northern Virginia Regional Park Authority represents three counties and three cities - Arlington County, Fairfax County, Loudoun County, the City of Alexandria, the City of Falls Church and the City of Fairfax. Regional Park Authority staff, volunteer board members appointed from each jurisdiction, and many friends of the regional parks working together have preserved more than 10,000 acres of the rolling and wooded Virginia countryside for you and created a priceless legacy for future generations.
http://www.nvrpa.org

# Federal Green Government Websites

As you may have heard, there is a lot of excitement and progress being made by the federal government to create a greener economy and green jobs. The following list will provide you with information about some of the departments and agencies of the federal government that are involved with various aspects of the green movement.

**Energy Information Administration**
The Energy Information Administration provides policy-neutral data, forecasts, and analyses to promote sound policy making, efficient markets, and public understanding regarding energy and its interaction with the economy and the environment.
http://www.eia.doe.gov

**Federal Energy Regulatory Commission**
The Federal Energy Regulatory Commission regulates and oversees energy industries in the economic, environmental, and safety interests of the American public.
http://www.ferc.gov

**National Renewable Energy Laboratory**
NREL's mission and strategy are focused on advancing the U.S. Department of Energy's and our nation's energy goals. The laboratory's scientists and researchers support critical market objectives to accelerate research from scientific innovations to market-viable alternative energy solutions.
http://www.nrel.gov

**National Fish and Wildlife Foundation**
The National Fish and Wildlife Foundation (NFWF) preserves and restores the nation's native wildlife species and habitats. Created by Congress in 1984, NFWF directs public conservation dollars to the most pressing environmental needs and matches those investments with private funds. The Foundation's method is to work with a full complement of individuals, foundations, government agencies, nonprofits, and corporations to identify and fund the nation's most intractable conservation challenges.
http://www.nfwf.org

**National Oceanic and Atmospheric Administration**
NOAA's aim is to create an informed society that uses a comprehensive understanding of the role of the oceans, coasts, and atmosphere in the global ecosystem to make the best social and economic decisions. To this end, they strive to understand and predict changes in the Earth's environment and conserve and manage coastal and marine resources to meet our Nation's economic, social, and environmental needs.
http://www.noaa.gov

**U.S. Centers for Disease Control and Prevention**
The Centers for Disease Control and Prevention serve as the national focus for developing and applying disease prevention and control, environmental health, and health promotion and health education activities designed to improve the health of the people of the United States. They also operate the National Center for Environmental Health.
http://www.cdc.gov

## U.S. Department of Agriculture
The Department of Agriculture deals with issues such as agriculture, food and nutrition, natural resources and the environment. The recently passes American Recovery and Reinvestment Act of 2009 provides funding for the following programs within the USDA: increasing the nutrition assistance to Americans, developing water and waste facilities, and protecting and conserving the nation's forests and farm land.
http://www.usda.gov

## U.S. Department of Energy
The Department of Energy's overarching mission is to advance the national, economic, and energy security of the United States; to promote scientific and technological innovation in support of that mission; and to ensure the environmental cleanup of the national nuclear weapons complex. The Department's strategic goals to achieve the mission are designed to deliver results along five strategic themes: Energy Security, Nuclear Security, Scientific Discovery and Innovation, Environmental Responsibility, and Management Excellence.
http://www.energy.gov

## U.S. Department of the Interior
The Department of the Interior (DOI) is the nation's principal conservation agency. Their mission is to protect America's treasures for future generations, provide access to our nation's natural and cultural heritage, offer recreation opportunities, honor their trust responsibilities to American Indians and Alaska Natives and their responsibilities to island communities, conduct scientific research, provide wise stewardship of energy and mineral resources, foster sound use of land and water resources, and conserve and protect fish and wildlife.
http://www.doi.gov

## U.S. Department of Labor, Employment and Training Administration (ETA)
## "Green Jobs Initiative"
ETA is working to leverage its knowledge base to support and expand Green Jobs in our economy. ETA is positioned to provide labor market intelligence and work with core-constituencies of labor, industry, and education to identify relevant Green Jobs skills and develop competency models leading to meaningful career ladders. Through its strategic partnerships, ETA can foster the development of Green Jobs by providing career information and guidance; developing education and training models in concert with apprenticeship programs and community colleges; and by aligning its own programs.
http://www.doleta.gov/brg/GreenJobs

## U.S. Environmental Protection Agency
Since 1970, EPA has been working for a cleaner, healthier environment for the American people. EPA leads the nation's environmental science, research, education and assessment efforts. The mission of the Environmental Protection Agency is to protect human health and the environment.
http://www.epa.gov

## The U.S. Fish and Wildlife Service
The U.S. Fish and Wildlife Service will receive $290 million under the recently passed American Recovery and Reinvestment Act of 2009 - an investment that will create local jobs, address critical conservation needs and help strengthen the agency's infrastructure for the 21st century. The Act provides funding for deferred maintenance, construction, and capital improvement projects on National Wildlife Refuges and National Fish Hatcheries and for high priority habitat restoration projects. It also provides funding for construction, reconstruction, and repair of roads, bridges, property, and facilities and for energy efficient retrofits of existing facilities.
http://www.fws.gov

**U.S. Forest Service (agency of the U.S. Department of Agriculture) "Economic Recovery Plan"**
Many of the communities most affected by the economic downturn are located near national forests. Using funding from The American Recovery and Reinvestment Act, the Forest Service will create and maintain private sector jobs for communities by funding projects to remove hazardous biomass, restore watersheds, repair trails, bridges and roads, and make fish passage improvements. We will also update facilities to increase their efficiency in the use of energy and water. The Plan is expected to create almost 30,000 new private sector jobs over the next two years, which will be concentrated in the Wildland Fire Management and Capital Improvement and Maintenance projects.
http://www.fs.fed.us/

**U.S. House of Representatives Green the Capitol Initiative**
In 2007, the Speaker and the Majority Leader directed the Chief Administrative Officer of the House to develop a "Green the Capitol Initiative" that would demonstrate leadership to the nation by providing an environmentally responsible and healthy working environment for employees. Their goals are to operate the House in a carbon-neutral manner by the end of the 110th Congress; reduce the carbon footprint of the House by cutting energy consumption by 50% in 10 years; and make House operations a model of sustainability.
http://cao.house.gov/greenthecapitol

**U.S. National Park Service**
The National Park Service preserves unimpaired the natural and cultural resources and values of the national park system for the enjoyment, education, and inspiration of this and future generations. The Park Service cooperates with partners to extend the benefits of natural and cultural resource conservation and outdoor recreation throughout this country and the world.
http://www.nps.gov

# Local Green Blogs

Within the last few years, a new trend on the internet, blogging, has become extremely popular. There are thousands of blogs that are based on local issues and topics. Many of these blogs specialize in green and sustainable topics. These websites can be good resources to find out about events that are coming up, as well as learn specific skills that might help you out in your attempts to become more knowledgeable about the green scene in the D.C. area.

**Calendula and Concrete Blog**
Calendula and Concrete is a blog about different experiences with organic gardening on the edge of Washington, D.C.
http://cc-calendula.blogspot.com

**City Renewed Blog**
The City Renewed blog is meant to be part of a comprehensive green resource guide for living in the metropolitan D.C. area.
http://www.cityrenewed.com

**DC Blogs**
This website provides a list of hundreds of different blogs with content specific to the D.C. area.
http://www.dcblogs.com/index.php?page_id=590

**Eco-Coach Blog**
The purpose of the Eco-Coach blog is to provide information, news and tidbits about healthy and natural living, and related topics.
http://www.eco-coach.com/blog

**Green Building Law Update**
A blog written by a local lawyer that focuses on issues related to green building law.
http://www.greenbuildinglawupdate.com

**Going Green DC**
Blogs about green culture, shopping, festivals, etc. in D.C.
http://goinggreendc.wordpress.com

**Green DC Girl Blog**
A blog that provides information on anything green happening in the D.C. area from policies to events.
http://greendcgirl.wordpress.com

**Green Muslims in the District**
A network of Muslims in the District of Columbia (and surrounding areas) working proactively to help their communities understand and implement sustainable and eco-conscious ways of living while relating it to their faith and a holistic world-view.
http://dcgreenmuslims.blogspot.com

**Herban Lifestyle Blog**
Here you will find information and ideas on herbal self-care, as well as upcoming events.
http://herbanlifestyle.wordpress.com

**Neighborhood Farm Initiative Blog**
The Neighborhood Farm Initiative provides D.C. with fresh, community-based, locally grown food while bringing youth and adults together to learn about urban agriculture. At the blog, you can get updates regarding ongoing NFI projects, see photos and videos of NFI projects in action, get healthy recipes, and access the NFI calendar of upcoming events.
http://neighborhoodfarm.blogspot.com/

**Righteous Restyle Blog**
The blog is to help in efforts to live a stylish, sustainable life in the Nation's Capital, while fending off a Target habit. It's also about things, people and places that might help you live a more stylish, sustainable life, too.
http://www.righteousrestyle.com

**Strategic Sustainability Consulting Blog**
Strategic Sustainability Consulting provides organizations with the tools and expertise they need to actively manage their social and environmental impacts. We specialize in helping under-resourced organizations implement sustainable solutions usually reserved for large, multinational companies.
http://sustainabilityconsulting.wordpress.com

**Sustainable Business Network of Washington (SB NOW) Blog**
The SB NOW is a blog about leveraging the power of business for the positive change in the 'Capital of Capitalism.'
http://sustainnow.blogspot.com

**Sustainable Gardening Blog**
This is one of the better blogs out there if you are interested in the topic of sustainable gardening. It is written by a long time expert gardener.
http://www.sustainablegardeningblog.com

**The Daily Ground Blog**
One D.C.'s resident's adventure in eating locally and seasonally.
http://dailyground.blogspot.com

**The Green Miles Blog**
This blog covers a wide variety of green and sustainability topics in the D.C. metro area.
http://thegreenmiles.blogspot.com

**The Slow Cook Blog**
Notable D.C. Gardener Ed Bruske chronicles his efforts to grow food in local gardens.
http://www.theslowcook.com

**Washington Gardener Magazine Blog**
This blog is written by the folks at Washington Gardener Magazine.
http://www.washingtongardener.blogspot.com

**Washington Youth Garden Blog**
The Washington Youth Garden is an educational garden located at the U.S. National Arboretum that is used to teach D.C. schools children about gardening and growing their own food. This blog provides updates on the program and has lots of pictures of the children working at the garden.
http://www.washingtonyouthgarden.blogspot.com

# National Green Jobs Websites

**Apollo Alliance**
The Apollo Alliance is a coalition of labor, business, environmental, and community leaders working to catalyze a clean energy revolution that will put millions of Americans to work in a new generation of high-quality, green-collar jobs to position the country to thrive in the 21$^{st}$ century. Inspired by the Apollo space program, Apollo Alliance promotes investments in energy efficiency, clean power, mass transit, next-generation vehicles, and emerging technology, as well as in education and training.
http://apolloalliance.org

**Clinton Climate Initiative**
President Clinton launched the Clinton Climate Initiative (CCI) in August 2006 to make a difference in the fight against climate change in practical, measurable and significant ways. In its first phase, CCI is serving as the exclusive implementing partner of the C40 Large Cities Climate Leadership Group, an association of large cities around the world that have pledged to accelerate their efforts to reduce greenhouse gas emissions. In May 2007, CCI launched its Energy Efficiency Building Retrofit Program which brings together many of the world's largest cities, real estate firms, energy service companies and financial institutions in a landmark effort to reduce energy consumption in existing buildings across the public and private sectors. Expanding upon its work with the C40, CCI has extended the benefits of its building retrofit program to additional cities, building owners and institutions.
www.clintonfoundation.org

**Energy Action Coalition**
The Energy Action coalition unites a diversity of organizations in an alliance that supports and strengthens the student and youth clean energy movement in North America. The partners of Energy Action work together to leverage their collective power and create change for a clean, efficient, just, and renewable energy future. The work of Energy Action is focused on four strategic areas: campuses, communities, corporate practices, and politics.
http://energyactioncoalition.org

**Go Green Initiative**
The Go Green Initiative is a simple, comprehensive program designed to create a culture of environmental responsibility on school campuses across the nation. Founded in 2002, the Go Green Initiative unites parents, students, teachers and school administrators in an effort to make real and lasting changes in their campus communities that will protect children and the environment for years to come.
http://gogreeninitiative.org/

**Green Business Blog**
This blog has articles related to green business and is written by Glenn Croston who wrote the book "75 Green Businesses You Can Start to Make Money and Make a Difference." If you are interested in starting your own green business and being green entrepreneur, there is some valuable information both on this blog and in Glenn's book.
http://www.75greenbusinesses.com/blog

**Green Career Central**
The Green Career Central website is one of the best around if you want a one stop resource for everything and anything related to Green Jobs and Green Careers. The website provides resources for green jobs, information on emerging green industries, information on green job fairs, a wealth of articles on green

career advice, and some feedback on green policies. There is also a job posting feature as well as a blog on this website.
http://www.greencareercentral.com

### Green Collar Blog
This is a great website that includes much more than just a blog. The entire website is devoted to green collar jobs, and there is information on job openings, upcoming green job career fairs and events, and listings of green collar jobs reports and organizations that work to provide green collar jobs training and education.
http://www.greencollarblog.org

### Green For All
The primary objectives of Green For All is to research and connect green collar jobs, employers and workforce development/job training to begin development of a green jobs model similar to existing East and West Coast Initiatives. The initiative explores and identifies employment and job training that will prepare workers for emerging green jobs related to sustainability, natural resource conservation and environmental related technology.
http://www.greenforall.org

### Green Schools Alliance
The mission of the GSA is to galvanize pre-K to grade 12 schools' individual concerns about climate change and the environment into collective action to protect our shared future.
http://www.greenschoolsalliance.org/

### Jim Cassio
Jim Cassio is one of the nation's leading experts on green jobs, and his website offers resources that can be very helpful for individuals seeking green jobs. He offers a free e-book on green careers, and also has a blog where he discusses recent developments in green jobs industries.
http://www.cassio.com/

### Joel Makower's Blog
Joel Makower is nationally renowned as a leading voice on green business and green jobs. He maintains a website that is tied to his recent book which also has a blog on it. The blog is one of the most informative and thoughtful websites around as far as taking on challenging topics related to green business and green jobs. He usually offers a new post every couple of days, which are very detailed and interesting to read.
http://makower.typepad.com/joel_makower

### Grist Magazine
Grist has been dishing out environmental news and commentary with a wry twist since 1999 and their website that is full of green jobs information. One of their writers, Kevin Doyle is an expert on the green economy and he often writes articles that provide green jobs advice. Grist also has a great green jobs board and frequently provides commentary on green jobs.
http://www.grist.org

### Power Shift Blog
The Power Shift blog provides information on events related to rebuilding the nation's economy and reclaiming the future through bold climate and clean energy policy.
http://www.wearepowershift.org/blogs

**Rocky Mountain Institute**

The Rocky Mountain Institute (RMI) is an independent, entrepreneurial, nonprofit organization. They foster the efficient and restorative use of resources to make the world secure, just, prosperous, and life sustaining. RMI has been one of the leading voices in the green and sustainability realm for several decades.

http://www.rmi.org

**SmartPower**

SmartPower uncovers consumer barriers that the American people face when considering a clean energy or energy efficiency purchase. SmartPower uses innovative research approaches that help pinpoint the most effective messages to customers; build partnerships with stakeholders, utility companies, state agencies and clean energy funds to develop ground level approaches that connect interested consumers and prospective customers with their message; provide marketing tool kits for local use that deliver the clean energy message in a compelling, breakthrough way; spread the renewable energy message through the latest traditional and new media approaches to help build a strong voluntary market.

http://www.smartpower.org/

**Southface Energy Institute**

Southface is a 501(c)(3) nonprofit corporation with a longstanding reputation for providing sound environmental education and outreach programs.

http://www.southface.org

**Veterans Green Jobs**

This organization was formed to empower our country's vets to restore our environment, economy, and communities. Veterans Green Jobs provides several career track training programs that teach veterans specific skills they can use in green job industries. The website also offers resources for veterans seeking green jobs.

http://veteransgreenjobs.org

# About the Authors and Collaborators

## Dan Triman, CSBA, LEED AP+, EIT

Dan Triman is a sustainability consultant, green building contractor and consultant, and an environmental educator in Washington, D.C.. Dan currently provides consulting and contractor services for several different companies in the Washington, D.C. area. They include Eco-Coach, Indigo Engineering Group, Sustainable Design Consulting, Shinberg.Levinas Architectural Design, and DC Greenworks. He assists clients on greening construction projects, sustainable operations and maintenance of facilities, improving sustainable business practices, and installing and maintaining green roofs. He also provides environmental education services for non profit organizations such as DC Greenworks, Audubon Naturalist Society, and Saturday Environmental Academy. He recently has started volunteering for the Resource department of the Association for the Advancement of Sustainability in Higher Education (AASHE). He is a LEED (Leadership in Energy and Environmental Design) Accredited Professional and is also a CSBA (Certified Sustainable Building Advisor). Prior to coming to Washington, D.C., he spent some time living in Portland, Oregon immersing himself in the green scene there and helped to co-author the *Portland 2008 Green Guide to Networking and Jobs.*

Before switching to a green career, Dan worked at several engineering firms and construction companies where he gained experience in carpentry, materials testing, engineering design, and project management. Several years ago, Dan decided to change career tracks to follow his passion for helping individuals and companies operate sustainably, as well as educating about environmentally friendly construction practices. Since the switch to a green career Dan has tried his hand at solar panel installations, energy audit report writing, natural building construction, creating art sculptures out of construction waste, environmental education, green roof installation and maintenance, and LEED consulting, among other jobs. Dan is very involved in the community and spends time volunteering at various conferences, events, and helping out on local green building projects. He loves to spread the word about green and sustainability issues and help others find their own green career path. Dan is well versed in the green job searching process as he has gone through it several times himself, and he has a knack for connecting people to one another and to valuable resources.

Dan has a Bachelor of Science degree in Civil Engineering from the University of Maryland at College Park.

## Anca Novacovici, LEED AP, MBA

Anca Novacovici is the founder and president of Eco-Coach, Inc., a Washington, D.C. based sustainability consulting company that provides services for businesses and individuals to become more environmentally friendly, energy-efficient, and healthy. Clients include Fortune 500 companies as well as smaller businesses and individuals. Anca is a LEED (Leadership in Energy and Environmental Design) Accredited Professional and is on the Board of the Green Building Institute. She is the co-author of this book as well as a book to help businesses get started on the path to sustainability, entitled 'Sustainability 101: A Toolkit for your Business'. She is also an Adjunct Professor at Montgomery College, in Montgomery County, Maryland, speaks frequently on various aspects of sustainability, and is a blogger with the Huffington Post.

Her passion for, and involvement with, environmental issues led to her to start Eco-Coach in 2006, which combines her management consulting expertise with her interest in green, healthy businesses and buildings. Prior to founding Eco-Coach, Inc., Anca was a management consultant, first with Davies Consulting Inc., and then with her own company, Axis Business Consulting Inc. She has over ten years of experience with strategic planning, change management, business process redesign, benchmarking, training and communications. She has worked with companies in the energy, health care, utility, and telecommunications sectors, and with international lending institutions.

Anca obtained her Masters of Business Administration in International Management from Thunderbird, the American Graduate School of International Management, and her Bachelor of Science degree in Foreign Service from Georgetown University.


## Gail Nicholson, MA, LPC

Gail Nicholson provides a blend of career and personal counseling in her private practice in Portland, Oregon. Gail takes a holistic approach to help her clients develop meaningful careers. Along with Vicki Lind, Gail provides workshops on Jobs in Sustainability and has written the *Portland Green Guide to Networking and Jobs.* Gail holds an MA in Counseling from Antioch University and is a Licensed Professional Counselor.


## Vicki Lind, MS, NCC

Vicki Lind is a career counselor and marketing coach with a private practice in Portland, Oregon. Vicki works with individuals in person and virtually to help them find a career direction or carry out a robust job search in this competitive economy. Along with Gail Nicholson, Vicki provides workshops on Jobs in Sustainability and has written the *Portland Green Guide to Networking and Jobs.* Vicki holds an MS in Counseling Psychology from the University of Oregon and a certificate in Human Resource Management.


## Jim Cassio

Jim Cassio is a career information and workforce development consultant who has been commissioned to conduct hundreds of labor market studies and has published numerous occupational resource books. Jim specializes in green workforce issues, as well as industry, occupation, and skills research, analysis, and resource product development. Jim's recent publications include: *Career Pathways Handbook; Green Careers Resource Guide; Clean Energy and Green Building Careers in Silicon Valley;* and *Green Careers: Choosing Work for a Sustainable Future (with co-author Alice Rush).*

www.ingramcontent.com/pod-product-compliance
Lightning Source LLC
Chambersburg PA
CBHW080328270326
41927CB00014B/3135